Borrowed
Identities

# Intersections in Communications and Culture

Global Approaches and Transdisciplinary Perspectives

Cameron McCarthy and Angharad N. Valdivia
*General Editors*

Vol. 5

PETER LANG
New York • Washington, D.C./Baltimore • Bern
Frankfurt am Main • Berlin • Brussels • Vienna • Oxford

Jennifer Kelly

# Borrowed Identities

PETER LANG
New York • Washington, D.C./Baltimore • Bern
Frankfurt am Main • Berlin • Brussels • Vienna • Oxford

Library of Congress Cataloging-in-Publication Data

Kelly, Jennifer.
Borrowed identities / Jennifer Kelly.
p. cm. — (Intersections in communications and culture; vol. 5)
Includes bibliographical references and index.
1. Group identity—Canada. 2. Adolescence—Canada. 3. High school students,
Black—Canada—Social conditions. 4. High school students, Black—Canada—
Attitudes. 5. Youth, Black—Canada—Race identity. 6. Mass media and youth—
Canada. 7. African diaspora. I. Title. II. Series.
HM753.K45 2003   305.235'089'96071—dc22   2002154660
ISBN 0-8204-6127-X
ISSN 1528-610X


Bibliographic information published by **Die Deutsche Bibliothek**.
**Die Deutsche Bibliothek** lists this publication in the "Deutsche
Nationalbibliografie"; detailed bibliographic data is available
on the Internet at http://dnb.ddb.de/.

Cover art by Clara Spencer
Cover design by Lisa Barfield


The paper in this book meets the guidelines for permanence and durability
of the Committee on Production Guidelines for Book Longevity
of the Council of Library Resources.

Printed in the United States of America

# Contents

# Acknowledgments

In writing this book I have drawn on the help and support of a number of people including Ann Marie Decore, Ray Morrow, Jerrold Kachur, and Chinelo Nwankwo who read and commented on earlier drafts. I would also like to acknowledge the support of Cameron McCarthy, who has encouraged me through the various stages of the manuscript.

A very big thank you goes to the students who participated in the research; without their time and patience this book would not have been possible. Thanks also to all the teachers in various parts of the education system who talked willingly and openly and who were able to open the "gates" to enable me to undertake this research. I would like to especially acknowledge the help and support of Helen Thompson, Rosalind Smith, Malcolm Azania, Patrick Powell, and Kathie and Percy Zalasky.

Thanks also to my children Rosa, Clara, and Leon for their patience with my past absences. And to my partner Bruce, who is trying to teach me that weekends exist.

# Preface

**B**orrowed Identities discusses how youths receive, interpret, and make use of media and youth culture in their everyday lives. In particular, the students' narratives in this book illustrate the ways in which proliferation of media images (music, magazines, films, and television) from the United States affect the formation of youth identities in general and African-Canadian youth identities in particular. The book highlights the intersection of the local and the global—how media is proliferated across national borders and comes to produce a United States–driven dominant black youth culture in Canada.

This specific historical period of the early twenty-first century has produced a huge increase in the ability of youths to access media technology and simulation, all of which have meant an expansion of the "language" that is available for use in social interaction. The students' narratives highlight the ways in which technological changes in the late twentieth century and early twenty-first have enabled access to the social spaces previously bounded by time and geographic borders, a process identified by Thompson (1990) as "mediazation"—a flow of images across time and space.

Consequently, this blurring of the boundaries between the local and the global has led to the reconceptualization of social experiences, knowledge, and identity. Of import, though not always explicit, is the way in which this process of mediazation is concomitant with a change in how we come to redefine and give meaning to everyday lives. For many of the African-Canadian students interviewed, this world of changing representations of culture and media that extend beyond geographic boundaries has important symbolic carriers for discourses of identity and "reality." Within these practices of consumption the students draw on media culture in order to represent and give meaning to everyday experiences and their identities. As Herman Gray (1995) indicates, "what characterizes youth culture in the 1990s and therefore warrants careful attention is the central role of the commercial cultural industry and mass media in this process" (p. 53). In analyzing these links between local identity and global formations Appadurai (1990) identifies not only a tension between homogenization and heterogenization but also argues that:

> because of the disjunctive and unstable interplay of commerce, media, national policies and consumer fantasies, ethnicity, once a genie in the bottle of some sort of locality (however large) has now become a global force, forever slipping in and through the cracks between states and borders. (p. 306)

In terms of the conceptualization and understanding of black identities, culture, and media, the work of Gilroy (1993; 2000), Hall (1991), hooks (1992), Omi & Winant (1993), McCarthy (1997), Walcott (1995), Alexis (1995), and Bannerji (2000) on social formation and media representation of "race" and identity in Britain, North America, and Canada have proved useful texts. Such texts enable theorizing to move from a biologically essentialist standpoint of viewing "race" and identity as fixed entities towards a position that recognizes race and identity as socially constructed and not necessarily homogenous in terms of constituents. Recognition of such fluidity problematizes the concept of black identity and community—the idea that black students have an automatic affinity with each other. Yet, within the study, there is also recognition of what Paul Gilroy describes as "the changing same," in other words, that historical memory also plays a role in the formation of culture and meanings that students give to various everyday activities. Exploration of identity and race as social constructs also allows for the consequent recognition "that there is not one 'culture' in 'society' but that any 'society' consists of a plurality of historically specific cultures structured in relations of dominance and subordination to each other" (Stratton & Ang, 1996, p. 377).

This recognition of fluidity of identity enables exploration of the way African-Canadian students individually and collectively manage incoherent and conflictual racialized meanings and identities in their lives. In conjunction with the latter, the viability of a hybrid racial identity that does not require total adoption or rejection of a dominant culture is analyzed (Bhabha, 1990; Hall, 1990). Investigation of this hybrid identity indicates how some students who are defined as "mixed" come to position themselves in relation to a black identity. The definition of identity that underscores Borrowed Identities is congruent with Stuart Hall's postulation that identity is "a narrative of the self; it is the story that we tell about the self in order to know who we are" (Hall, 1991, p. 16).

Further, this study explores the stories that African-Canadian students tell about themselves; a story often mediated by youth culture. Analyses of such media culture reveals a site for the students to invest cultural objects with meaning and to access a venue within which these meanings are remade and argued over in a range of everyday encounters. In some ways, the study attempts to take up Angela McRobbie's

(1991) challenge for cultural studies to return to ethnographic cultural analysis which takes as its object of study "[t]he lived experience which breathes life into [the] . . . inanimate objects [of popular culture]" (pp. 3–4).

As part of that taking up of an ethnographic cultural analysis it is important to not only examine the students in terms of their consumption and production of identities but to also indicate the other dimensions to their identity production.

## Outline of the Book

The argument presented in this book is that black identity formation is a complex cultural process refracted through raced, classed, gendered, sexualized, and religious selves. There is a movement away from a singular essentialist viewpoint of regarding black identity as fixed and automatic. Black identity is socially constructed, achieved through social interaction, and mediated through popular culture. It is more about borrowing than biology, more about resources than origins.

Chapter 1 presents an overall description of the ways in which the research was conducted as well as my placement within the research project. More specifically, the chapter also indicates the ways in which the youths have been chosen for the study and the reasons for selecting specific aspects of their narratives. Although 14 students are discussed in the study, not all of their narratives are presented. Instead I have chosen to use thematic coding in order to highlight commonalities across the narratives. The chapter also provides an economic and historical context through which *Borrowed Identities* as a whole can be read. This introductory chapter poses the main question that drives the book, namely, how do U.S. popular culture and the growing processes of mediazation and economic globalization mediate black youth identity formation?

Chapter 2 highlights how the students position themselves in relation to the diaspora and what Gilroy (1997) identifies as "dynamics of remembrance and commemoration"—a positioning that can lead to a sense of consciousness not dependent on the nation state. Having seen (in Chapter 1) the ways in which the students view African-Canadian identity as problematic, this chapter allows us to look again at the narratives and examine the ways in which a sense of blackness as "sameness" gets played out in their everyday culture. In other words, on what basis do the students construct a site for common identification—a commonness that moves beyond phenotype yet still allows them to refer to themselves as black? In examining this concept of "identification" more closely, we can note Kathryn Woodward's (1997) postulation that it is a "process of identifying with others, either through lack of awareness of difference or separation or as a result of perceived similarities" (p. 14). Further, examination of processes of identification allows for recognition of the ways in which culture operates within a political framework.

As well, Chapters 3, 4, and 5, examine directly the media in terms of reception of music and films and the production of style, and identify how representation works intertextually to contour meaning via regimes of representation. Such representations offer students a potential source for identification as well as for the production and reproduction of cultural forms. Within these chapters, questions of receptivity are posed as to how the students receive youth cultural forms and how these forms intersect gender, economic status, sexuality, and parental authority. Language is the means of communication highlighted in this study. It is via language that these students come to construct and know the world. This coming to "know the world"—how we recognize it as having a reality external to the self—becomes an important mediating force in terms of how the students place themselves in relation to media texts that highlight blackness. Through analysis of the narratives and discourse of the students, I am able to explore media culture and the cultural representations of blackness that such youth cultures provoke in the everyday lives of the students. In order to ascertain the meanings that the students give to the youth culture that they encounter, one has to analyze the interactional process and the subject positions that are produced. Denzin (1989) argues that as such:

> meaning is biographical, emotional, and felt in the streams of experience of the person. Locating meaning in the interaction involves uncovering how a person emotionally and biographically fits an experience into their emerging, unfolding definitions of self. It is assumed that this is done through the production of personal experience and self-stories. Meaning is anchored in the stories persons tell about themselves. (p. 62)

However, it is more than language per se that is under examination here. Also implicated are discourses; discourses as a system of representation, discourses as a social formation.

Chapter 6 identifies quite clearly how media are "resources to think with." Further, it illustrates how the students use style as a signifier to connote meanings in other areas of their lives. As well, what is evident in the narratives are the ways in which discourses struggle with each other to produce "truth effects." This production of truth does not refer to a truth in the absolute sense but rather a discursive formation sustaining a truth (Jensen, 2002). Such issues of truth production become intertwined with power relations, especially through the three main themes highlighted: a racialized urban legend related to style; division of urban space based on style; and the ways in which black identity, through style, becomes at times identified as "acting."

Both Chapters 7 and 8 present an analysis of the students' discourses and attempt to locate them intersubjectively in a larger social and economic framework that accounts for intersections of class, gender, sexuality, geographic region, religion, age, and racialized discourses. In particular, Chapter 7 draws on the theme of "borrowed identities" to interpret/reinterpret earlier students' narratives (presented in Chapters 2 to 6) in relation to black identification and cultural formations. The metaphor of borrowing illustrates the ways in which African-Canadian youth take on identities that are constructed in another location (the United States) and reproduce meanings within their own locale. In Chapter 8 a similar form of analysis is undertaken. In listening to and reading the narratives, it becomes clear that hip-hop/youth culture uses a specific language as part of the hip-hop discourse and that the ability of the students to use this language allows them to present themselves within or in relation to specific subject positions. As part of accessing a style, communication, via argot, enables the formation of a group identity and the creation of boundaries between "them" and "us." Also illustrated in this chapter is the way in which the distinction between the public and private sphere is highly contested. Such distinctions between the public and the private sphere are being contested through a process that Norman Fairclough refers to as "conversationalizing discourses." It can be argued that such contestation is evident not only in media but also in other areas of life where public and private space overlap.

Chapter 8 draws on Gilroy's (2000) concept of stylish solidarity to illustrate the ways in which black youth culture has become identified with the body and style. A sense of collectivity is based on style rather than on a more direct, politicized understanding. A section on knowledge and experience indicates the intertextual nature of the way in which meaning gets translated from one social situation to another. Also highlighted are the ways in which youth culture as a communicative resource is accessed through the use of slang and slurs to develop an argot, a common culture that is produced/reproduced in a public sphere.

The final chapter, 9, attempts to bring some closure to the topic under discussion while also opening up new pathways to understand the issues raised throughout the study. In particular, the chapter examines the school as a site for the production of meaning through style and indicates ways in which a cultural studies framework might help to develop pathways to work with and through some of the data in the study. Thus Stuart Hall's concept "politics of representation" is explored as a means to developing a complex understanding of students' experiences as well as knowledge production. As Toby Daspit argues, "[r]ather than contest the fact, as teachers are apt to, that students' experiences are profoundly influenced by music, television, films, comic books, video games, etc., educators must 'discover' relevant points of appropriation that facilitate empowerment" (1999, p. 67).

# CHAPTER 1

# Mapping the Terrain

*There can be no true and authentic account, . . . lives and identities*
*being chronicled are necessarily partial, fluid, performed and constituted*
*in the context of that particular ethnographic moment.*
MCROBBIE, 1999, p. 89

## Introduction

Throughout the twentieth century critical cultural theorists have tried to account for the effect of mass communication on the production of subjectivity and group culture (Adorno, 1991; Bell, 1976; Marcuse, 1964; McLuhan, 1964; Thompson, 1990; Jameson, 1991). Overall, this question of the effect of media on the audience has provided fertile and often contentious grounds for theorization. This book attempts to link the meanings that students make from and through media to the material world of their everyday lives. Thus it avoids a binary positioning reminiscent of the argument between cultural populism and political economy (Murdock, 1997). Analysis is undertaken on the empirical and the theoretical level in order to examine the lived experiences of youth. In particular, this study examines the consumption by African-Canadian youth of these media products in the globalized market place and attempts to understand how youth produce subjectivities through this consumption.

In terms of dominant theoretical discourses, postmodernism and globalization have provided much thought and many academic papers in an attempt to make sense of what are perceived as unsettling times. Both these frameworks affect the ways in which the experiences of the students in the study are analyzed. As well, caution needs to be taken in any wholesale adoption of a specific theoretical framework since frameworks of analysis produce discourses that then become part of a wider academic contestation and production of truth effects (Foucault, 1980). For some theorists, such as Baudrillard (1983), the social effects of present-day mass communication and its production can be explained as a break with modernism, a new postmodern cultural epoch wherein, to quote Marshall Berman, "all that's solid melts into air." This shift and expansion in media technology is viewed as removing the sense of reality and space from our everyday understandings. However, for other cultural theorists such as Stuart Hall, this increase in the ability of the media to reach out, digitally, to wider geographic areas and to break down barriers between time and space is a stage of capitalism. Further, Hall's analysis does not identify this breaking down of barriers with a profound shift and disjuncture in the way society is organized. Instead, Hall argues that analysis of this specific historical juncture suggests continuities and "the accentuation of certain important tendencies in the culture of the overdeveloped 'west' which, if we understand the complex histories of modernism properly, have been in play in an uneven way since modernism emerged" (Grossberg, 1996, p. 133). Although theorists might contest the social effects of mass communication, there is some agreement that these important tendencies characterize "a transnational and global capital that valorizes difference, multiplicity, eclecticism, populism, and intensified consumerism in a new information /entertainment society" (Kellner, 1995, p. 5).

Theoretically, this books draws on newer formulations of critical cultural studies that move beyond a class analysis to offer a framework for investigating the complex way racialized/political identities such as "black" overlap and intertwine with class, gender, ethnicity, power, and popular culture to give meaning to social divisions and everyday life (Hartley, 1994, p. 71). Critical cultural studies, is a prime area within which to study the crossover areas (mediazation, youth culture, nationalism, and political/racialized identities) highlighted within this study. In particular, such cross disciplinarity allows for recognition of the fluidity in social relations that is indicated by postmodernisms while being able to ground the production of student discourses within a specific economic and cultural formation.

Within cultural studies there is a distinction between *critical* British cultural studies and the more textually based North American variant. In particular, I draw on critical cultural studies theorists attempt to analyse the cultural formations that develop in relation to movements of populations across and between state boundaries, between margin and periphery (CCCS, 1982). This movement is exemplified through an emphasis on the African diaspora and the scattering of population to North America, the Caribbean, and beyond. More specifically, the book draws on black cultural studies theorists whose work indicates a paradigm shift from race-relations sociology to a more cultural studies orientation (Mercer, 1994; Gilroy, 1987; Hall, 1989; Diawara, 1996; hooks, 1994; 1996; Carby, 1994).

As well, the multi-disciplinary framework of cultural studies is useful, because the study deals with the complexity of the experiences of high school students whose lives (like most lives) do not follow the logic and coherence of an abstract one-dimensional theoretical model. This acknowledgment of the changing nature of lived experiences also gestures to poststructuralist literature in terms of its ability to recognize change and, at times, fragmentation within identity formation while also trying to deal with situations where continuity seems to be more evident. Further, within the trajectory of black British cultural studies, there has been extensive scrutiny of the ways in which social and cultural identities are formed in relation to "others" within postcolonial societies. In linking these two areas of popular culture and identity formation, Gilroy (1995) argues that:

> black popular culture does not determine the formation of social and cultural identities in any mechanistic way, but it supplies a variety of symbolic, linguistic, textual, gestural, and, above all, musical resources that are used by people to shape their identities, truths, and models of community. (p. 25)

Categorization as "youths," rather than adults, provides an important intersection in the social matrix, comprising of race, class, gender, religion, sexuality, and ethnicity. Relations of domination operate through this matrix. Within present-day social formations, youth are regarded as immature in the classic Kantian sense in that they are perceived as unable to use reasoning without the direction of another. At times the link between the growth of cultural studies and theorization of youth culture and media culture seems symbiotic.[1] As Todd Gitlin intimates:

> the ascendancy of cultural studies is mediated by the boom in the scale of popular culture, and its significance in the lives of individuals in Western societies. With the success of Keynesian policies, high employment, and collective bargaining came a boom in disposable income among the young in more privileged countries. . . . It is not simply that the market in popular culture grew enormously in scale after World War II but that from the 1960s on, the young have come to define themselves by their taste, specially their taste in popular music. (Gitlin, 1997, p. 26)

The significance of Gitlin's comment for this study lies in his highlighting how youth have come to define themselves through consumption. Thus, cultural studies has consistently identified that youth relate not only *to* the music that they listen to, but relate also *through* the music in such a way that they develop a sense of cultural membership and orientation to morality. So, it is that:

> cultural studies has a long-standing tradition of mapping the contours of media culture and the ways in which it educates youth to think, feel, desire, and act. Youth in this perspective is less an element to be controlled than a complex formation to be analysed, interpreted, and engaged within largely representative apparatuses of youth socialisation. (Giroux, 1996, p. 15)

As part of this recognition of youth as a complex formation, it should be noted that popular culture and media act as "institutions to think with," resources to use in the formation and production of identities.

For other cultural theorists, such as John Thompson (1990),[2] it is not just that through media "individuals remould the boundaries of experience and reuse their understanding of the world and themselves"(p.10). The social and cultural effects of the breaking down of time-space barriers between geographic regions—a process whereby social interaction is no longer based upon face-to-face interaction within the same physical locale—are a concern as well. Thus, the breaking down of economic barriers via the growth in information and media technology affects social relations within society. This breaking down of geographic barriers has been described both as a "shrinking of time" (Harvey, 1989) and a "time-space distanciation" that implies a stretching of time and place (Giddens, 1990). While these theorists might not agree on whether space is shrinking or time is stretching, they would concur that this increased broadcasting of media to an extended audience can not only "create new and unpredictable forms of connection, identification and cultural affinity, but also dislocation and disjuncture between people, places and cultures" (Gillespie, 1995, p. 7).

It is the latter identification of the ways in which communication technologies create new and unpredictable forms of connection that is pertinent to this study: the students are able to access "outer national" media sources for identification. In particular, popular culture has been one area in which mainstream white culture has been able to provide an ideological framework of symbols, concepts and images through which we understand, interpret, and represent "racial differences" (Omi, 1989). Thus, the ability of the United States to dissipate its cultural forms around the globe via digital pulses has an effect on the formation of black identity in Canada as well as the social construction of racialized understandings and identities among all social groups. These shared racialized understandings are not individual responses but are constructed intersubjectively—shared to a degree by all members of a culture or subculture (Fiske, 1994, p. 157).

## Branding

Racialized youth identities and media are linked not only through intersubjectivity and meaning making that take place but also through the economic discourses of globalization. A United Nations Educational, Scientific, and Cultural Organization (UNESCO) report showed that the world trade in goods with cultural content almost tripled between 1980 and 1991—from $67 billion to $200 billion. Much of this cultural growth was in relation to the entertainment industry that has been dominated by U.S. products. The importance of the expansion of cultural goods has been exacerbated by organizations such as the World Trade Organization (WTO), which prioritizes the "free market" over national borders. For example, in Canada "the WTO has already deemed both Canadian magazine legislation, promoted as a defence of Canadian culture and the Auto Pact to be contrary to WTO provisions" (McBride, 2001, p. 130).

That media play such an important role in identity formation among youth should not be a surprise since the political and economic imperatives of globalization are at a stage of acute proliferation. Naomi Klein's book *No Logo* (2000) illustrates quite clearly this relationship between youth culture commodification and branding. Her book offers a parallel analysis within the economic realm as to how the process of commodification has grown in the past twenty years and how the bodies of black males, in particular, have become commodified as "hyper masculine" through the media. In examining these trends, Klein has been able to periodize how these pioneers of branding took opportunity of trade liberalization and labor law reforms in order to expand their manufacturing overseas and to increase an emphasis on style. As Klein argues, "what these companies produced primarily were not things, they said, but *images* of their brands. Their real work lay not in manufacturing but in marketing" (Klein, 2000, p. 4). If one follows the narratives of the students it is evident how these specific economic configurations affect their everyday reality. The world that they attempt to think through, to make sense of, is one that is formed through economics. Although *Borrowed Identities* foregrounds their meaning making and, in some sense, the micro-level of analysis, there is an evident link to the macroeconomic framework against which their purchases are made and identities are formed. It is interesting to note not only how school youth are willing to pay an exorbitant amount for a "brand" item of clothing but also to specifically identify ways in which access to such branded goods can be used as "surplus value" to contour and produce subjectivity. Certainly times have changed from earlier generations when concern was expressed about the place of production as well as the brand for sale. Not only have times changed with regard to location of production but the "protectionism" equated with national borders has, in reality, been strongly challenged through the increased globalization of capital.

One of the ways of analyzing the economic and political claims of postmodernist theorists and neo-conservative supporters of the "free market" and trade liberalization is to empirically examine the ways in which such theoretical assumptions are played out on and through the material levels of people's lives. Such an examination is not an either/or positioning but rather one that allows us to view the ways in which the cultural, social, and the economic act on and through the subject in order to produce certain identities and material consequences. In this instance the results continue to produce material effects through consumption. This issue of consumption has become a minefield within the cultural studies literature as various theorists (McGuigan, 1997) critique what they regard as an overemphasis on "positive" effects of media consumption—the active consumer—while ignoring the overall ec-onomic and political context within which such consumption takes place. As Jim McGuigan contends: "we have the idea of a 'cultural' or 'symbolic' economy which consists of exchange relations and significatory flows but with little discernable rela-tionship to something like a 'real' economy that may have a measure of determinacy, however mediated, upon these exchanges and flows" (p. 140).

While recognition of the ways in which identification with a brand is an impor-tant aspect of the ways in which youth are encouraged to consume, such recognition is not enough to account for the construction of desire among youth. Therefore, it is useful to analytically explore the language of the students to understanding how they make meaning in relation to their patterns of consumption. Exploration of their dis-courses can allow access to the ways in which youth subjectivities are produced through construction of desire that leads to the consumption of material goods.

This issue of the relationship between the audience and the reception of media has generated much discussion, particularly within the arena of critical cultural stud-ies. Virginia Nightingale's book *Studying Audiences* (1996) charts quite succinctly the tension that has emerged and the binary between an emphasis on the audience or on the text, a parallel binary echoed in the theoretical positioning of political economy and pleasure.

In the context of this study, the students are the audience and the texts are the televisual, aural, and print images produced in the United States that are received and consumed by black youths in Canada. Such images offer school youth the op-portunity to review and pursue a variety of differing subjectivities in general and black subjectivities specifically. In terms of theoretical analysis, much of this area of work falls into "audience reception theory." Such theories within cultural studies have at the heart of them the postulation that the audience receives the media in a variety of ways, that the audience, unlike those conceptualized by Adorno and the early critical cultural theorists, is an active one. Hermeneutics and literary theories have helped to undermine the acceptance of one reading of the text. For structural-ists the meaning lies behind the text via semiotic analysis, while for poststructural-ists the meaning is never final but always deferred to some extent, illustrating how the text is polysemic with meaning emerging from the process of interaction. I also recognize the critique that has been posed by authors such as Virginia Nightingale, who argues, "the activity of audience need no longer be conceived as responsive but can now better be understood as symbiotic or interactive" (p. 145). In particular the work of Kim Schroeder is useful in problematizing the traditional encoding/decod-ing model adopted by early media reception theorists.

## Construction of the Study

No study can totally represent the whole of an issue or present an understanding that is fixed once and for all. As such, this study is a reflection of a specific group of African-Canadian students living in Alberta, Canada, in the late twentieth/early twenty-first century. The study cannot be said to represent the way in which all self-identified black students use media to make meaning in their lives. It also needs to be noted that any reference to groups of black students is a reference to a "representation." It does not automatically and unproblematically refer to and reflect a pre-existing material reality. Instead, as McRobbie notes in relation to her own work, the study "constructs and gives an identity to a social group" (McRobbie, 1997, p. 176). It is also worth noting that narratives from focus groups or individual interviews are not just taken as true or false representations but rather should be seen as "actions arising from interaction between interviewer and interviewee" (Jensen, 2002, p. 240).

Yet, although the data generated are not generalizable across all African-Canadian student populations in Canada, the experiences of the students can highlight the ways in which identity formation develops in relation to racialization and media culture. The recognition of this shifting web of identity can aid not only in understanding differing social groups such as African Canadians but can also lead to an understanding of the nuanced ways society operates in relation to its parts. The descriptor African Canadian draws on the work of George Elliott Clarke (1996), an African-Canadian social critic and writer who argues that the term refers to:

> persons and expressive cultures, located in or derived from Canada, possessing, to some degree, an ancestral connection to sub-Saharan Africa. The phrase encompasses, then, recent immigrants to Canada from the United States, the Caribbean, South-America, and Africa itself, as well as indigenous, African-descended community. (p. 118)

The discursive tensions with regard to understandings of what it means to identify as black can be explored in the discussions of who can identify themselves as black and who cannot. Is a black identity based on skin color alone or on an ideological positioning? In this research the answer would seem to be much more complex with identity being produced as something that's borrowed; as much a temporary "cut" (Barker, 1999) as a fixed essential entity.

> Our social identities as black, white, man or woman do not only describe who we are but imply norms of actions. Thus we develop moral identities that are gendered and racialized and nationalized. It is through the identities that we understand who we see ourselves to be; this implies group loyalties and memberships, which imply what we ought to do and how we ought to be. (Ferguson, 1996 in Garry & Pearsall 1996)

Early on in this study the decision was made to concentrate on students of African descent. This narrowing of referent has proved both advantageous and problematic. Constructing a specific group based on geo-historical/political and kinship categories has meant that other social groups within the school were not interviewed. This is to some extent problematic because if, as suggested by poststructuralist literature, we form our identity in relation to "others," then the black students identified by this study form their identities not only in relation to media culture but also in relation to fellow students. Although the latter limitation of the study is recognized, nonetheless time constraints mean that only African-Canadian students are discussed as opposed to the wide variety of racialized groups who make up the school population. Further, the study, unlike many concerning the educational experiences of African-Canadian students, does not identify what percentage of students might be failing or succeeding in the education system. Although this might appear to undermine this study's direct usefulness to educators, the study does indicate the complexity of students' identity formation in relation to media culture and the ways in which negotiating such complexities can intersect with their academic lives. As well, the study can give teachers an insight into the world in which the students live and perhaps indicate the ways in which the cultural is important in terms of academic success.[3] It should also be noted that although media culture is the focus of discussion, and music, music magazines, television, and films are highlighted in the interviews, newspaper consumption was not discussed directly nor the social relations of viewing videos at home.

The conceptualization of the study was the direct result of a previous project on the perceptions of schooling, peers, and popular culture among high school students in two Edmonton schools (Kelly, 1998). The earlier research was exploratory in nature and revealed the importance of media culture in terms of meaning making within the students' lives. Although the focus of the initial exploratory research was black high school students and perceptions of their high school experiences, the study revealed that the boundaries between the school and the outside world were often blurred for youth. In particular, the world of media culture seemed to offer a point of "border crossing" between school and the "outside" community (Giroux, 1997). Another impetus for *Borrowed Identities* was that at this specific historical juncture, youth culture is important among school students, and paramount within this category is black youth culture. In some ways black-mediated identities are being made available for "borrowing" by youths from all ethnic backgrounds, regardless of how they are divided by time and space.

Since my study is concerned with understanding the meaning making of the students in relation to their identity and media culture, it was therefore important to find a method that seeks to be ideographic rather than nomothetic in emphasis. Thus the emphasis is on using a qualitative framework to develop an understanding and interpretation of the ways in which the youths under discussion make meanings in their lives rather than developing causal laws that can then be applied ahistorically to all schools and social contexts. Such an understanding of qualitative research draws on symbolic interactionism and phenomenology (Mead, 1934; Schutz, 1972) for its philosophical orientations. The latter delineates qualitative research as processes that highlight how people construct and interpret their worlds and thus make sense of their lives (Merriam & Simpson, 1995). I am concerned about understanding meaning and grasping the youths' definition of the situation but one also needs to view with caution a paradigm that becomes "predicated on the empiricist's picture of social reality [and] omits something most important, namely, intersubjective, common meanings—'ways of experiencing action in society which are expressed in the language and descriptions constitutive of institutions and practices'" (Taylor 1971/87, p. 75 cited in Schwandt, 1994, p. 20).

The research, although concerned with interpretation and meanings attributed to televisual and aural texts, also tries to "avoid the reduction of meanings to free-floating discourses" or the "positivist imperative of reducing them to structural variables" (Morrow, 1994, p. 294). John Thompson's (1990) *Ideology and Modern Culture* and his "depth hermeneutic" framework as a methodological approach is useful. This methodological framework allows us to understand the research participants' perspectives while at the same time being able to locate those perspectives within a wider political, socio-economic, and historical framework. In many ways the framework offers a way to counteract relativism evident within interactionism and offers a degree of depth to research. Such a depth-hermeneutic framework consists of three phases. The first is related to the development of a social-historical understanding of "blackness" and black identification in Alberta and Canada in general. The second phase involves analysis of the students' discourse as narrative; while the third can be seen as interpretation/reinterpretation of previous social-historical and discourse analyzes in relation to each other. Norman Fairclough's (1992; 1995) work on critical discourse analysis has also provided insights into the ways in which text, discursive practices, and social practice operate intertextually.

The taped conversations are examples of discourse and as such recognition is given to Fairclough's (1992) understanding of three aspects implicated in the constitutive effects of discourse:

> Discourse contributes first of all to the construction of what are variously referred to as 'social identities' and 'subject positions' for social 'subjects' and types of 'self'. . . . Secondly, discourse helps construct social relations between people . . . and thirdly discourse contributes to the construction of systems of knowledge and belief. . . . These three effects correspond respectively to three functions of language and dimensions of meaning which co-exist and interact in all discourse—what I shall call the 'identity,' 'relational' and 'ideational' functions of language. (p. 64)

## Researcher Identity—Looking Within

Unlike other research methodology, with qualitative research the primary instrument of data collection and analysis is the researcher. As such, it is important to recognize the role that my own subject position plays in the construction of the research question and population as well as the collection and analysis of the data. As Patti Lather (1991) argues, formulation of a research question may reflect one's raced, classed, and gendered positions within society. To argue that value-free factual research is possible in social sciences is to insist on a "fact/value dichotomy [which] simply drives values underground" (p. 51). However, this is not to suggest that there is an automatic alignment between a person's factual position and their value position. Although the purpose of this study is to gain an understanding of the students who participated in the study, the study also involves the construction and formation of my own identity as a researcher, academic, and black woman. Positioning of myself as a black, middle-class, heterosexual woman with experiences of living as an immigrant in white-dominated societies recognizes that knowledge and meanings are produced from a specific social and political understanding of the world. We all have a standpoint from which we speak (Collins, 1990; Hartsock, 1998) even if we do not recognise it as such. Therefore, subjectivity should not always be feared, for "subjectivity can be seen as virtuous, for it is the basis of researchers' making a distinctive contribution, one that results from the unique configuration of their personal qualities joined to the data that they have collected" (Pershkin, 1988, p. 55). Although explaining/reflecting on such a standpoint and how I came to choose this research question may reveal the filter through which my research on media culture and identity formation was constructed, it does not provide a complete guide to the embedded bias that results from such a positioning. For post-positivists such as Patti Lather, the recognition of self in the research process goes a long way to undermine a naïve empiricism that makes the effort to leave subjective tacit knowledge out of the "context of verification." Thus, inquiry is increasingly recognized as a process whereby tacit (subjective) and prepositional (objective) knowledge are interwoven and mutually informing (Lather, 1991, p. 66).

As Denzin and Lincoln (1994) argue, the researcher enters the research process from "within a distinct interpretive community, which configures, in its special way, the multicultural, gendered components of the research act" (p. 11). The research process can be seen as affecting not only the subjects but also the researcher. Gaining access to the school setting and the students serves to highlight a consistent tension among discourses of qualitative research, researcher subjectivity, and the demands that emerge from the organization and structure of schools. For "gate-keepers" to educational settings (i.e., Faculty of Education, the administrators, and teachers), research in schools should first be instrumental with a direct application to schools, second, produce a report within the school year, and third, be in a language that is accessible to a non-social theorist. However, such gatekeeping can at times be in tension with the expectations of an academic conducting inductive research that develops slowly from the research process!

Data included newspaper clippings of items that referred to youth, media, racism, or racialization, copies of magazines that the students read, various genres of rap music, dance hall reggae, and various programs of Xtend*DaMix* and *RapCity*. In line with developing a social-historical analysis of "blackness" in Alberta and more broadly Canada, a search was made of archives for magazines and newspapers that might give an inkling as to the ways in which racialized, gendered, and classed "asymmetries are systematic and relatively stable." The latter analysis helps to elucidate the broader social context within which the students interact with media and form their identities. The pre-entry stage of research is a dual-edged process that involves seeking official permission, while at the same time unofficially going through a process of identifying a school that might fit the research profile of my study. Although, theoretically, a number of schools fit such a profile, many schools were unwilling to participate in a project because of the topic of my research. As one principal indicated, "I like my students to think of themselves as the same." Such a color-blind statement, while laudable on the surface, in actuality subscribes to a discourse that Virginia Chalmers (1997) identifies as "sameness with different color" (p. 72). Although the principal wanted the students to be color blind, many of the students interviewed in this present study and in my previous research did not see themselves as color neutral, either within or outside school. For the students, racialization is a point of difference that cuts across the official "color blind" atmosphere of Canadian society and schools.

On the macro level the result of this liberal color-blind attitude was a lack of official records on the composition of ethnic groups within schools. Because no official records are kept, it was difficult to ascertain the percentage of black students who were enrolled in the school. The study relied on students' self-identification as being of African descent in order to gather a subset of the African-Canadian students at an orientation meeting. Gaining access to the students was done via a teacher who informed students about my research and the date of the meeting. Those in attendance consisted of male and female students of African descent, with family ancestry in the Caribbean, continental Africa, and the United States. The students varied in age from fifteen to eighteen years old. Whereas the eighteen year olds were able to sign their own consent forms, those students under eighteen had to also obtain the consent of their parents.

After the orientation and while waiting for the consent forms to be returned, a number of visits were made to the school to observe two school-based cultural events. The following extract from my research journal highlights, using Richardson's (1994) codes, the ways in which representation of cultures is always in relation to something else and that a specific reading of a social situation is always in context and cannot be guaranteed. The school is laudable as it positions itself as multicultural and open to representations of students' cultures via a festival of cultures. However, my journal[4] queries such representations:

## Journal Extract: Culture Jamboree, Wednesday 24 February

*Today I visited the school to watch the "Culture Extravaganza," an annual emphasis on national culture. At times the school attempts to offer a public space wherein students "experience" each others' cultures. Food stalls are set up in the school, and these displays are varied and well supported by the students, who mingle and buy the different dishes. As part of the festival, students also put on a display of dances that are viewed as representative of their culture of "origin." (ON) The rationale for this sharing of cultures is based on the liberal premise that by sharing, one is opening oneself to a process of acceptance. However, what was interesting about the display was the way in which some cultures were represented via "folk" culture, with representation based upon specific ways of dressing, specific forms of movement: a representation of a tradition, history, time, and effort. For others, in this case the self-identified black students, representation was much more problematic. How can black culture be represented? Is it located within the continent of Africa? Is it located in the United States? Or is it not located anywhere?*

*I was particularly interested in the ways in which the sense of the "relational" affected the reading of the cultures. I watched the Scottish dancers in relation to a group of African Canadian girls.*

Observation Notes made on site:

*3rd dance. Scottish dancers. Dressed in traditional Scottish dance costume — waistcoat, kilt and leggings. The dance is choreographed, energetic, and looks professional. Well received by audience. Bagpipe music.*

*4th dance is by a group of black girls. The music is sort of ?? traces of Caribbean rhythm. Five girls dressed in everyday clothes, tones to black and white. Some dressed in trousers, Capri pants, or shorts. Mainly moving and "winding." The winding part brings cheers. Also notice that some of black boys are shouting comments, particularly the young man with the cane rows.[5] Wonder who he is? (PN)*

At times, the reflexivity undertaken in the journal enabled insight into the ways in which representation of an identity was not static and linear and was, therefore, problematic.

The concept of intertextuality "the necessary relation of any utterance to other utterances" (Jensen, p. 186) is important in terms of recognizing that social identities are constructed in relation to existing identities. Access to discourses on African-Canadian identities is important in terms of recognizing the complexities as well as the push and pull factors that affect the processes of identification.

## *School Climate*

The school site remains a common location within which the students interact and play out various identities. As such, the school acts as a site for discourses of style and music to meet and compete leading to the production of racialized, genderized, and sexualized identities. These social differences are recognized differently by administrators and youths within the school environment, with some differences being highlighted while others are denied or muted. Schools are physically bounded institutions (walls, desks), possessing distinct hierarchies and social structures and producing specific identities, e.g., student, principal, counsellor, classroom teacher. Schools, through the ethic of competition and selection, impose difference upon their students, but racialized differences are denied and subsumed in official curricula. Differences related to academic achievements are highlighted and reinforced. So it is that Cameron McCarthy's (1997) concept of nonsynchrony is useful here in identifying the ways in which students may coexist within a school environment but do not always share a similar consciousness.

The school that the students attended [Unity High] is a large urban high school in Edmonton, Alberta, with between 1,500 and 2,000 students, in grades 10–12 ranging from fifteen to eighteen years old. It attracts students from a variety of ethnic groups and is often described as multicultural. In selecting this school, various factors came into play: the ethnic composition of the school, the willingness of the administrators to allow access, and the willingness of the students to participate in the study. Geographically, it is located in a part of the city, where the population is a mixture of white-collar and blue-collar workers. Many of the students who attend the school are children of upwardly mobile professionals. They are attracted to the school because of its academic reputation and its ability to transfer students onto higher education—i.e., its effectiveness at social reproduction. Among the students interviewed, this bias, in terms of socio-economic status, was evident, since many of the students came from homes where parents had accessed post-secondary education and where education was seen as a valuable tool for economic mobility. Although there were students whose families would be considered of lower socio-economic status, the common sense understanding was that there was a degree of socio-economic sameness.

> **J:** Similar economic status? Explain that a bit more.
> **Denzil:** Middle-class area. That big grey area of middle class.
> **J:** You consider yourself middle class? How do you determine that?
> **Denzil:** Just compare yourself to the people with more money I guess. I don't know.
> **J:** So you define yourself by comparing yourself to?
> **Denzil:** I am not a trailer head, I am not a mansion. . . .*

The students' narratives often indicated recognition of differing discourses operating in school that contribute to the production of differing selves and schooled identities. At times these school subjectivities are produced through differentiation in access to types of knowledge. For example, the school has a variety of programs, including a special academic stream for students whose marks suggest that they will go on to post-secondary institutions and university. Leon describes the differences between the academic and regular program and how they contribute to distinctions between students based on "how" and "what" the teacher "knows" about a specific student.

> **Leon:** The only thing I see that's different in [Academic Challenge] that's probably different from other things is that the teachers treat you differently.
>
> **J:** Oh, in what way?
>
> **Leon:** Like they just think [pause] you are some kind of Einstein. //You think so?// Yeah. They generally think students in [Academic Challenge] are very, very, hard working. Maybe they are, but that doesn't pertain to me. I am not that hard working. And they just treat you like that. Like it's not a big deal, but they just treat you differently. They say stuff and they expect you to know it. They do stuff [pause]. Okay, do this. Like I don't have a problem with all that. But I know it's just a different mode because I hear different stories.

Thus, the general student population is streamed into differing levels for their core subjects of English, mathematics, social sciences, and sciences at grades ten, eleven, and twelve. Two of the students interviewed were part of this academic challenge program.

At other times formal design regulates the physical and material experiences within the school and contributes to contestation of the production of docile schooled subjects. Physically, the school is laid out on one floor with a central area within which students gather for social events. This student-defined space is located near to the school office and, as such, provides a "natural" opportunity for the teachers to "gaze" on the students as they socialize; the school administrators are only a "call" or a blink away from any trouble that might erupt. Students themselves were not unaware of this possibility of being within a Bentham-type panopticon (Foucault, 1980), even though partial. One student drew my attention to this when he described where he "hung out" when not in class and why he choose such a location:

> **Marcus:** I don't like to chill . . . right in front of the office . . . I just don't like them [teachers] watching always talking to me about something. . . . If we stay down there [by the door] we can see them when they are coming.

Corridors and lockers become focal points and sites where students mix and socialize. Yet often it is within these "freer" social spaces that students feel most closely monitored and most often challenged. One student's narrative recalled such an incident of conflict in the corridors:

> **Melvin:** I am not causing like a big disturbance and then he [a teacher] is like . . . "You guys shouldn't be in the hallways." Like he wasn't even paying attention . . . I am like "Ok, well look I am just going to my locker to get my stuff." And then he is like, "Why is she with you?" And I am like "Oh, because we both are going to my locker to get my stuff." But then he is like, "Oh, you guys are causing." I am like "Look, I've been in this hallway for about a minute and a half because of you. I could have just went, did my little thirty-second thing, got to my locker and took off. But you have to stop in the middle of the hallway." And he is like "Oh, but you guys are wandering all over the place." I'm like "Did you just see what I just did . . ." then he is like "Oh, are you getting lippy with me?" or something. And he is like "Let's go to the office," so I was like "Ok, let's go to the office." I was like "You want to go to the office and battle this, we'll go and battle this."

For some students, as described in the narrative above, this monitoring can result in admonishments as they challenge the authority of the school. As well, students are expected to have an identification card that is created during the enrolment procedures at the beginning of the school year. Students must carry this identification card at all times and present it, on request, to staff.

At lunchtime, various co-curricular activities, ranging from music through drama to athletics, are available for students. However, among the students interviewed, few were involved in school-initiated activities. The closest school-related activity was the "step-team"[6] that was organized by a group of girls interviewed during the study. Since the step-team was not organized through a school club, many of the girls felt that it was not really a legitimate school club and, therefore, not under the control of the administration. The latter scenario highlights the issue of social control as it intersects with a racialized identity. For the girls interviewed, the ability to control access to the dance group was important in producing a black-identified space for black students.

Sociologists in the United States, United Kingdom, and Canada have frequently identified the ways in which participation in school sports is often used to reinforce the symbolic representation of black males as concerned with "body" rather than "mind" (Solomon, 1992). However, within this study, although many of the students were interested in sports and seemed to have had successful sports careers in their junior high years, many of those interviewed had little involvement in high school sports. Observation of team photographs displayed in the school hallways suggests that only a small number of the African-Canadian students represented the school in organized sports. The following focus group narratives indicate the dynamics involved in the process of selection and rejection from sports teams. The perceived racialized dynamics to which the students allude is that black students are considered good at running but not at some of the other sports.

**Student 1:** School can ignore you for a year but then when track comes around [uproar]
**Student 2:** We don't get on the other teams, how come at track time you want us? (female focus group)

The reasons cited for this lack of involvement in school teams varied from economic structures—prohibitive cost—to not being able to submit themselves to the discipline and requirements of the sports coach. One interesting narrative presented by a young woman indicated that the gendered nature of school teams was prohibitive in terms of her gendered subjectivity:

**Student:** I'm not very good at joining sports teams and stuff 'cuz usually it's like [pause]; girls are girls, boys are boys. I can't work with girls.
**J:** Can you not?
**Student:** No. I try and like [pause]; Ok, boys get violent. But it's to the point of where they push you. They shove you on the ground whatever? Girls are like going for your eyes. . . . Like they think stupid things. If you are on the field they scratch you. [pause]; It's stupid. Like the girls just go out so that they can scratch other girls while they are playing. Like get the ball away and stuff [pause]; it's stupid.

Although the School Council was a student-based organization with elected positions, none of the students interviewed were involved. One student indicated that the organization lacked the ability to truly represent the students, as its role was confined to social activities rather than representing the views of students to those in the education hierarchy. This can be seen as a tension between discourses on democracy and discourses on authoritarianism:

**Denzil:** No, I found the students don't have much rights in what goes on in the school. "You have to do this you have to learn this, and you have to learn that's how it is. Don't argue."
**J:** So do you think you have a right to have your voice heard?
**Denzil:** Yeah.
**J:** On what basis?
**Denzil:** We have to learn it. I mean we are going to run the country when these people pass on. When these people retire. They may as well listen to us.

As noted above, few of the black students were involved in school-based clubs and organizations. This situation was not uniform for all ethnic or racialized groups, many of whom were represented in a variety of photographs on the school walls.

For many students, high schools are institutions that they are coerced into attending. In particular, the link between schooling and certification provides a strong economic incentive for attending high school with the objective of achieving a high school diploma. Life without such a high school diploma offers a dismal prospect economically. In this sense, the group of students interviewed was highly motivated to succeed economically, although they often questioned the ways in which the school organized the curriculum and knowledge production. As well, the built-in element of compulsion increasingly highlights how relations of power become sources of conflict within schools between teachers and students and among students.

The "hidden curriculum" (Jackson, 1968), through values, attitudes, or principles implicitly conveyed to pupils by teachers, plays an important role in preparing students to adapt themselves to specific regimes of power (Foucault, 1980). Linked with Foucault's notion of regimes of power, the school seems to act as a site where disciplining of the self is an important factor in producing specific schooled subjectivities. Students' ability to keep time by arriving for school and lessons "on time" is important in enabling them to present/position themselves as "good" students. Attendance is also a part of producing this specific schooled subject. Non-attendance can produce consequences that result in exclusion from school. The following narrative indicates the pressure that develops into a process of exclusion from school:

> Well, pretty much I just didn't like do what I was supposed to do. Like pay attention to my schoolwork 'cuz I don't know. High school was such a big world and then I just started meeting people like click, click, click. And like I don't know. And people just leave me slack and then like I wouldn't go to class. I wouldn't do this and I'd visit people I'd like to be with and they were at different schools or I'd do something during class or something. And like [pause] I just didn't go to class. And I didn't get really kicked out. Well, I got kicked out of [pause] a couple of classes, and then I had the rest of them that I'd like make like a special appearance at every once and a while.

In terms of discipline, the school booklet indicates clear rules that students should follow in order to show respect for authority. As one student indicated in his narrative, rule following can be difficult when the authority of the teacher is not recognized by the students:

> **Melvin:** I've got to put in like my info. If I don't put in my info, like then they are going to just keep on doing what they do. 'Cuz most of the time if you be like "Yeah, ok yeah," I end up in like an uncomfortable position where I am getting like even more angry. Because now [pause] I am moved to another table for something I didn't do, which is actually like saying to her [the teacher] "Heh! you just gave me a kick in my back side, why don't you just do it again any time you feel like it." Instead I'm like, "Hey, look I am letting you know what I just did, and I am putting down some ground rules because if you don't know, you better recognize this next time."

Similarly, for Gerald, a lack of respect for teachers can also result in "deviant" behavior that challenges authority and discipline. Asked what would make him respect a teacher, he replied:

*What would make him respect a teacher —*

**Gerald:** Teachers that would act like they are my friend. . . . They know they are there
to teach you but at the same time they <u>act like they are a friend to you</u>. . . . They
don't act like they are above you. Even though you know they are. That's why you
respect them. When <u>they act like they are a friend, you respect them</u>. And that's
why you will do what they say. But not when they like [pause] act like they have
higher power to you. Tell you what to do, you have to take their orders. That's when
I don't respect them.

In those cases where rule following was severely problematic, resulting in harm to
others or self, a school community-based police officer was on hand to give advice
and assistance, as well as oversee crime prevention programs.

Dress style is important in terms of aligning oneself with specific subjectivities
and in complying with the expectations of the school authorities. As the school
diary stated, "clothing should be adequate for modesty, and must not be decorated
with images or lettering that would be offensive to students, staff, or the public."
Dress style, therefore, articulates with popular culture to produce subjectivities and
thus becomes an important site for representation of ideology (ideology interpreted
as meaning in the service of power) as students cohere with or contest the various
norms and values of schools and wider society. As well as racialized styles such as hip
hop, students also produce themselves as "preppy" and "alternative" through differing discursive practices.

According to official educational policy, schools are neutral environments
wherein the primary differences recognized are academic; differences in relation to
race, class, or sexuality are not recognized or analyzed in terms of their intersections
and production of differing schooled subjects. In some ways the latter is continuing
the pattern set by the English-speaking founders of the education system, such as
Egerton Ryerson, whereby the school was viewed as a place for common experiences, a common place where differences would be subsumed within an Anglo-
dominant norm. Thus, the school takes its mandate from Alberta Learning, a government body whose primary understandings and dominant discourses produce a
multicultural framework whereby schools are designated as consisting of students of
various ethnic identities which have no effect on their school lives. This understanding of ethnicity is based upon a "color-blind" attitude, where equality means
that everyone is treated without recognition of differences. So it is that the racialized, gendered, classed, and sexualized discourses that students position themselves
within are ignored[7] (Kelly, 1998). In recent years this silence around difference has
been broken through the Alberta Teachers' Association project on promoting Safe
& Caring Schools.

Contrary to the dominant ("colour-blind") discourse of many educators in the school
system, these students' narratives also positioned them and others, at times, as racialized subjects. Although the school would like to perceive students synchronously as

having an identical consciousness as "just students," the narratives indicate that they have racialized perceptions of themselves and others with whom they interact in school:

> **J:** When you say Brown what do you mean?
> **Doreen:** Pakistani and Indian?
> **J:** Right, so that's what people tend to call them?
> **Doreen:** They call them brown. I don't [know] why.
> **J:** So you have brown and you have black. What else do you have?
> **Doreen:** Whites, and like Orientals.
> **J:** Oh, Orientals. And Orientals is?
> **Doreen:** That's everything from like Asia.

A few students alluded to demarcation of areas according to racialized groups:

> **Etta:** Well, like people consider that [pause] I guess in the Hexagon they have little corners which if you look you can see them. Especially like they have a large East Indian group. And [pause] the Orientals are never really in the Hexagon. 'Cuz they actually have basically their own hallway on that side of the school. They have what you call [laugh] Chinatown . . . the whole hallway is basically Oriental. You'll notice it. It's really easy to find. [pause] That doesn't bother me. Really. I guess it would intimidate you if you didn't know anyone.

Although these areas were marked and noted within the narratives, racialized boundaries were not perceived as being strictly policed, and several narratives allude to interaction taking place between different racialized groups. In positioning themselves as racialized subjects, the students identified themselves as black and were, to varying degrees, conscious of blackness as a political category that could be mobilized and used discursively to their advantage. Several of the students indicated that there had been a decrease in the number of black students attending the school, and with that decrease, the dynamic within the black group had changed. Thus it has to be recognized that schools are not static institutions but often change in relation to the dominant groups, individuals as well as academic leadership involved. So it is that such changes and dynamics are also reflected in the types of data that are generated in this research; as the dynamics change so too will the data generated. African-Canadian students indicated that the school used to be exciting a few years ago with lots of black students with whom to interact, but now their numbers were decreased:

> **Etta:** See [Unity High] used to be the school talked about. . . . In the very beginning of the year it was so good. Even all last year I think it was fun. But at the very beginning there were so many people, and then those people would get kicked out for

skipping. And so you never saw them again. But then there were still those regulars that [pause] it was so bad 'cuz all the grade 12's and stuff. Then this year it's like [pause] it's all right [drop in energy, flat tone].

The implication in terms of the students' school lives was that there was a decrease in intra-group mixing, and in some ways group solidarity had been undermined. At issue also was the perceived attitude of the administrators, who were regarded as "policing" black students' actions to such an extent that some students regarded one administrator as solely concerned with finding out "information" with regard to other black students. As Phyllis described the situation, the "black" group was seen as visible and signifying trouble so that even if they were not responsible for some misdemeanour, it was assumed that they had knowledge of the circumstances:

> **Phyllis:** Uum [pause], It's like they kind a pick the trouble groups out, and they kind a separate you. . . . Like the black kids are known for trouble and that's what most goes on so teachers kind of listen in for the gossip and stuff like that. "I'll give you candy if you tell me about such and such."

Or for the following student in reference to his interaction with administrators:

> **Roy:** I stay far from them. [They] wanted me to tell on my friend, [they] invited me down to the office . . . I don't really like it.

Other student identities also come to the fore in the school environment so that the narratives reveal gendered, classed, ethnic, religious, and sexualized identities. The following student indicated how his religious identity intersects with the norm and values of some teachers and the institutional discourse of inclusion and sameness. For him, the solution was a disciplining of the self, a situation reminiscent of what Foucault identifies as "technology of the self":

> **Wayne:** Like everything that I am doing like there is always a biblical [pause] thing that come through. So I write all those things in my essay, but I just, [pause] I don't, I have to like use my brain. I don't put too much because some of these teachers like, if they are not like a believer, some people don't like to hear you mention the word God to them or they feel upset or whatever, so. I don't want to put too much of that in case that teacher is that kind of person.

The school day is broken down into two halves, morning and afternoon, with further demarcations into "periods" that last about one hour. Demarcation between morning and afternoon sessions is achieved via a period for lunch that lasts about an hour. To reinforce the idea of knowledge as fragmented, learning is contained within subject areas. The teaching that takes place is bounded within such time and subject constraints.

Curriculum is represented as neutral and is developed and controlled by Alberta Learning under the authority of the governing political party. Recently, Alberta Learning has made attempts to link its curriculum with other prairie provinces under the descriptor of Western Canadian Protocol. However, up until the period of data generation, the curriculum, in the name of neutrality, does not provide knowledge that would take account of or offer an understanding of the racialized, classed, and gendered identities of students. In the narratives, the issue of curriculum and its lack of recognition of their racialized identities was evident.

> **Denzil:** Yeah. I asked him [a teacher]. "How come there is no black people in history?" He is like "Oh, I don't know. I guess they didn't do anything." He said something along those lines. I was like [pause][look of amazement] there's got to be something. So I just started doing research and found out a whole bunch of things. Like, like [pause] the street light and all those things invented by a black person. Everything.
>
> **Etta:** Oh, Gosh. Not in school. [pause] They never really go through that stuff. They really don't have much of anything black in the curriculum at all. They don't even really consider it actually if you want the honest truth.

In this section of the chapter I have presented an overview of the social context and structures of the school through the narratives of the students. This type of social analysis is useful in providing a sense of how the students regard the school and authority.

### African Canadian Identity

This section dwells on the political and problematic construction of identity—especially in relation to the concepts of "nation" and belonging. The starting point for this discussion is the link between the descriptors "African" and "Canadian" and the ways in which the students associate or disassociate themselves from the terms; it also highlights the links made by the students between identity, nation, ethnicity, and belonging. This latter examination will then enable readers to understand the ways in which a sense of belonging intersects with and contours the students' identification with a national identity. The students are categorized as African Canadians, in that at least one parent is of African descent; however, this is not necessarily a categorization with which the students themselves comply. Many of the narratives indicate that there is a great deal of slippage in terms of self-identification, with "black" appearing as a more consistent point of identification than "African" or "Canadian." In particular, the concept of nation in relation to the students' understanding of themselves as Canadians or other nationalities is highlighted.

The students see themselves in a myriad of ways in relation to Canada as a nation and Canadian as their identity. For many, "Canadian" is a contested term, an identification not easily made, and one that most definitely connotes white subjectivity (Schick, 1995). Thus it is difficult for those constructed within Canadian society as "non-white" and, therefore, "Other" to position themselves with ease as Canadian. Historically, construction of dark bodies as "Other" has been prevalent in the dominant discourses and understandings of nation, citizenship, and identity. For example, if we examine the cultural and economic formation of Alberta as a province at the turn of the twentieth century we find that from 1907–1912, various strategies were employed by the immigration authorities in order to discourage blacks from moving to the Canadian west from Oklahoma.[8] Alberta was foremost among the provinces fighting to stem the flow of black immigrants. Official organizations in Edmonton, such as the Board of Trade and the Imperial Order Daughters of the Empire, gathered petitions of protest to send to Ottawa (Shepard, 1997; *Edmonton Daily Bulletin*, 1911). The basis for their disquiet was racism and a belief that blacks were unable to live peacefully together with whites. The dominant Anglo-Celtic groups viewed blacks as biologically unassimilable and inferior.

Analysis of archival documents such as newspapers, government documents, magazines, and minutes of political meetings during this period of immigration reveals differing and competing racial discourses that intersect with regional, gendered, and political allegiances. The most consistent discourses drew on biological determinism and Social Darwinism to construct Anglo-Celtics as biologically different from and superior to blacks and other unassimilable groups. Through these racialized discourses, the dominant white group constructed blacks as their binary opposites. In this relation, whites were opposed to nature, while blacks, it was assumed, aligned with nature. Such a process naturalized and fixed differences between black and white by reducing the culture of black peoples to nature (Hall, 1997).

Discourses of race constructed blacks as antithetical to the budding capitalist environs that dominant groups in Canada wanted to cultivate. Blacks were posited as opposite to the thriving, hardy, and self-reliant northern Europeans. They were perceived as "lacking," initiative with a "sense of humour and predisposition to a life of ease [that] render[s] [their] presence undesirable" (Cooke, 1911, p. 11). For black women, stereotypes were gendered and racialized, as concern was expressed about the ability of such "unsuitable" bodies to produce future potential citizens who did not conform to conceptions of the "Ultimate Canadian" bred of the "best stock that could be found in the world" (Cooke, 1911, p. 11).

Such discursive practices played out through existing regionalized, classed, and gendered discourses. For example, addressing a "representative gathering" at the Conservative party club rooms in Edmonton, Mr. C. E. Simmonds of Leduc highlights how some white inhabitants encoded "race" within existing regional animos-

*[handwritten: people of Alberta were against Black immigration 1907-t]*

ities and as part of a general response to non-preferred immigrants, i.e., Chinese, Hindu, and blacks. In contrast, the preferred group consisted of northern Europeans who were considered easily assimilable, of hardier stock, and likely to thrive in Canada's northern climate. According to Simmonds, immigration should reflect personal rights, and individuals should be able to choose whom they live with. Under no circumstance did he want his province to become "Black Alberta" via a black invasion, and as such he blamed the eastern-based Liberal government for being out of touch with western sentiments:

> I can only see one way out of this difficulty . . . and this is to put the present government out of power and bring in one who will listen to our pleas. . . . Way down in Ottawa they do not think of the matter as seriously as we do, and therefore the interest is lacking. (cited in Shepard, 1976, p. 107)

Women were no less tainted with racism, and the Anglophile women's organization, the Imperial Order Daughters of the Empire protested black immigration and black male immigration in particular, by claiming that black men were a sexual threat to white women. This argument illustrates the ways in which subjectivities often operate at the intersections of social categories.

Although responses of the Prairie Provinces to immigration varied, this was more by degree than scale. Most provinces were against black immigration on principle, whether from the United States or from the Caribbean.

Those black immigrants who made it into Alberta between 1907 and 1911 formed the core of the early black settlers,[9] Between 1901 and 1911, Alberta's population increased 5.5 times, from 73,000 in 1901 to 374,000 in 1911. The 1911 census placed the numbers of blacks residing in Edmonton and Calgary at 208 and 72, respectively. These pioneers settled primarily into four isolated rural communities: Junkins (now Wildwood), Keystone (now Breton), Campsie near Barrhead, and Amber Valley, twenty miles from Athabasca (Carter & Akili, 1981; Hooks, 1997).[10] Populated by groups that had fled persecution in Oklahoma, Amber Valley was the longest-surviving black community with its own baseball team, its own school, and its own church—a self-contained community. Of all immigrants who took out homesteads from 1905–1930, 45 percent failed to complete the government conditions that would give them title (Palmer, p. 107). However, black immigrants faced added pressures. According to Thakur (1988) and Palmer (1990, p. 84), the reason for the failure of most of these communities was a lack of infrastructural development, isolation on marginal lands, and racial discrimination. Many of the settlers returned to the United States. The rest resettled in Calgary or Edmonton and their surrounding communities, leaving only a few settlers on the pioneer homesteads. This group remained the dominant black group in the province until the second wave arrived.

With the relaxation and opening up of the immigration laws in 1962, and again in 1967, the Alberta black population was increased with immigrants from Caribbean countries such as Jamaica, Trinidad, Guyana, and Barbados. These revisions of the Immigration Act that finally took place were prompted not by any major desire by government and immigration authorities to further develop a "racially" pluralist society but rather primarily by economic and political expediency. The federal government realized that Canada would not be able to rely on its traditional source for skilled immigrants, namely, Europe. In Alberta, this loosening of the immigration laws coincided with a demand not only for skilled oilfield workers but also workers in construction and building trades, welding, and pipefitting. The latter was the impetus for the second large-scale immigration of peoples of African descent to Alberta. This group of immigrants was diverse in terms of geographic origins and occupational skills, many being "technicians, tradesman of all kinds as well as clerical workers (N. Darbasie, personal communication, September 2002).[11] These workers from the Caribbean were later joined by students from the Caribbean and Africa who would graduate from the University of Alberta and go on to enter a wide spectrum of professions. In the 1980s and 1990s, these groups of diasporan blacks were joined by blacks from African countries, who were fleeing war or trying to make a better life for themselves and their children. According to 1996 census data, 24,915 blacks lived in Alberta. Allowing for variations in the figures, this would translate to approximately 2 percent of the population in both Edmonton and Calgary being black. Of the black population in Edmonton, 4,280 were born in the Caribbean and Bermuda, while 6,620 were born in Africa (Black Women Working Group, 2000; Statistics Canada, 1996; Torczyner, 1997).

This latest period of immigration was also marked by an increased political self-organization. Cultural groups such as the National Black Coalition of Canada (NBCC) and Council of Black Organizations (CBO) provided a link with their homeland for many new immigrants as well as a forum for challenging the racialized state of Canadian society.

Ironically, the influx of the newer immigrants from the Caribbean and the continent served to subsume the early African-Canadian pioneers. Because of the numerical dominance of this new wave and the lack of knowledge of an earlier black presence in Alberta, there was initially little formal attempt to be inclusive and build the community. Blacks from the Caribbean were often regarded as representing the universal in terms of black groups. This historical overview situates the ways in which blackness can be understood in relation to the development of Alberta in the past century, because the way students understand their place within the Canadian nation draws on this historical tradition. Student understandings are "contextualised social phenomena, they are produced, circulated and received within specific social-historical locations" (Thompson, 1990, p. 22). Furthermore, Canadian traditions are located within the colonial relations of British and American domination and dependency. To adequately identify these understandings today means highlighting the pervasive influence of the American media on adolescent culture, both in the way in which blackness is perceived within Alberta and as it is positioned in relation to the global representations emanating from the United States via Madison Avenue and Hollywood.

This diverse population, a result of differing immigration patterns, was reflected in the student sample for the research. The percentage of black students in the high school from which the research sample is taken is difficult to ascertain because the school board does not identify its students on the basis of racialized identities or ethnicity. However, a safe estimate would be that the black student population is less than two percent. The 14 students interviewed and discussed within this study come from a variety of backgrounds, with nine students having one or both parents who emigrated from one of the countries of the Caribbean—Jamaica, Barbados, Trinidad and Tobago, and Guyana. Five students have an affiliation with one of the countries in Africa. Also significant within the group were students who might be described as being of "mixed origins." This concept of origins is, however, problematic because it implies a biological-racial self, thus reinforcing the concept of race. As a partial answer to this problem of classification, I have chosen to identify such students as having "mixed parentage," whether that be in terms of race, ethnicity, or continents.

With the above contextual and conceptual concerns satisfied, the chapter now analyzes students' narratives with regard to how they position themselves in relation to Canada as a nation. If as suggested by poststructuralist theorists our identities are formed in relation to an "other," then it would be insightful for our study to be able to examine intertextually how Canadian identities play off against the more "glocalised" identities produced through media consumption. As Foucault argues, subjectivities are produced through historical and social discourses.

In the twenty-first century this process of othering continues and is at times reinforced through multicultural discourses that are dominant in Canada. Rinaldo Walcott (1997) provides a cogent argument for this positioning:

> The multicultural narrative is constituted through a positioning of white Anglophone and Francophone Canadians as the founding peoples of the nation, with "special" reference to Native Canadians. All Others exist and constitute the Canadian ethnic mix or multicultural character. Thus the colonizing English and French are textually left intact as "real" Canadians while legislation is needed to imagine other folks as Canadian. (p. 79)

A clear example of how this distinction between "real" and "other" translates into policy documents can be viewed in a 1998 draft document developed by the Social

Studies officials at Alberta Learning.[12] Within the document it was evident that identities were not regarded as complex or as operating at intersections.

This discursive tension between "real" Canadians and "other" Canadians reinforces the sense of "black" and "Canadian" as binary opposites. A binary articulated through the idea of "just come"—an idea that is "crucial to the nation-state's construction both of black invisibility and hyper visibility" (Walcott, 1997, p. 42).

As stated earlier, the students see themselves in a myriad of ways in relation to Canada as a nation and being Canadian as their identity: symbolic, continuous, translated, and contextual. Their discourses are aligned with common sense understandings produced through discursive practices. In terms of symbolic continuity, the youth perceive national identity as aligned with certain symbols that have a lasting effect. For some students, they are Canadian by virtue of place of birth, and, therefore, identification with an origin outside Canada is a bureaucratic procedure. For others, identification is strongly aligned with one or another parental country of origin. Therefore, it is not surprising that overall, the students' narratives displayed differing and often-ambivalent orientations towards the adoption of African Canadian as a point of identification.

In a similar vein, the following extracts highlight the ways in which the discourses of identity change according to the context and the raced subject positions of the participants. For this student, identification is managed and performed:[13]

**J:** Do you see yourself as African or Canadian, or . . . West Indian, or Caribbean?

**Etta:** What do I identify with the most? /Yeah/ Well, first thing that pops into my head I guess must be I feel more like [Martinquane]. When I am here in Canada, I feel that I am [Martinquane] than anything else. To me if I am Canadian I identify with [pause] to me like identify with like white people. /Right/ But if I am in [Martinique] . . . I am Canadian. That's how it is. 'Cuz they know that I am not from there. They know what family I'm from whatever. But I am born in Canada, so I am Canadian. And for me it is a little different, because technically I am half-African . . . . But maybe I am biased with the whole thing. I do not see myself as an African.

For this student the situation is not straightforward. It involves a process of self-reflection and, to some extent, double-consciousness as she reads the social situation to take account of the perceptions that the other person has:

**J:** You wouldn't call yourself a Canadian?

**Etta:** Not here I don't suppose. Well I always go. . . . 'Cuz I am born here so I don't want to lead anyone [on]. Usually I say I am born here. But obviously my mum's from [the Caribbean]. 'Cuz usually . . . that's what people are asking. I figured that out. 'Cuz they don't expect [pause] to hear that you are Canadian. They just know what they want to hear. Like whether you are born here or not. I've learnt that. 'Cuz some people always ask you. If I say, "Oh, I am Canadian?," they will say, "Oh well where are your parents from?" Or something like that. They ask you a further question. So I usually always put in a one sentence. Depending on who it is.

**J:** Who it is?

**Etta:** It depends I guess like [pause] I don't know. If a white person ask me normally I'd say [pause] 'cuz I guess normally I do say I am [Caribbean]. 'Cuz Canadian to them [pause] most of them don't understand what that means. But to a black person, especially if they are not from here. I usually tell them I am born here, but where my mum's from 'cuz that's what they want to know.

Context and ethnicity of the audience can modify this complex process of identification and negotiating of a descriptor. Thus, the need for collective identity and fragmentation of identity varies according to social situation. Euda's narratives below indicate when fragmentation of collective might be necessary and when she would not necessarily call herself black:

**Euda:** If I was with a whole load of black people, I would then become a [Barbadian]

These narratives also reveal a problematic positioning resulting in specific discursive practices that Foucault identifies as "technologies of the self." This intertextual reading of identity and what it means to be Canadian in some ways supports a more open-ended pluralist definition of identity; one that changes according to context, a reflection of the intersubjective nature of interaction and identity:

Thus, the above discussion ascertains that context is important in determining whether the students construct black identity as an "outernational project" or not. At times they regard black identity, as a singular construct contained by state boundaries. At other times they do not (Gilroy, 1995).

The lack of African-Canadian symbols becomes an important factor when placed in relation to the media definitions of African American that the students were exposed to. The narratives indicate that the proximity of the United States to Canada and the plethora of images of blackness that emanate from the United States, come to play a part in the ability of the students to define themselves as Canadian. Thus some students perceived African American as an identification that was as relevant to their sense of self as that of African Canadian.

Often everyday meanings develop in relation to other cultural formations. As such, the narratives often drew on the United States in terms of defining the meanings and representations of blackness and black identity that exist in Canadian society. For Denzil, the proximity of the United States resulted in some leakage of U.S.-defined "black" culture into what could be defined as black Canadian. At times this leakage comes to define other perceived black cultural formations as subordinate to that of the United States. Speaking about the influence of the African country from which his family emigrated, Denzil suggests that it offers little in terms of understanding the meanings associated with blackness in Canada:

> **J:** Are there things about your Mum's culture that you bring to being black?
> **Denzil:** There's nothing about the culture. 'Cuz being black quote, unquote is being black American.
> **J:** So is there a black Canadian identity then?
> **Denzil:** No, er [pause]. When you say African American, it encompasses like black people in North America.

However, in putting this latter perspective to Melvin, another student, a different response was garnered. For him, there is a clear distinction drawn between African-American and African-Canadian identity, with representations of Canadian blackness being identified as more syncretic. In addition, Melvin calls on culture to reinforce the multicultural discourse dominant in Canada to both understand meanings surrounding culture and to differentiate Canadian culture from that of the United States. For him, it is the ability to mix with students from other racialized groups and the consequent construction of syncretic cultures that provides the "difference from" the United States:

> **J:** What would you think if someone said to you, "Well, there isn't an African Canadian culture" . . . and that what we have here in Canada is African American culture."
> **Melvin:** Oh no, no. Well it's just like there is like [pause] Canadian and American and it's all different. And people learn differently from different environments. And that's how you like mold and shape like the culture . . . in different places. Because you are going to react to different stuff different ways. 'Cuz I am sure that I wouldn't even be the same person if I lived down in the States.
> **J:** You don't think so?
> **Melvin:** No. My mentality would probably be different especially if I was like meeting different people through the schools . . . like being black [pause] . . . 'Cuz I know people from the States that just like . . . used to just chill like with pure black people. . . . Well, I am not saying I didn't do that before, [in school] but like I like still did chill with whoever. But then they used to like "cuss off" like other races too and they would always be like stuff going off against them. And like here I still like . . . go through and do whatever with every race. And they kind a like single themselves out that way.

While Gerald agrees that there is a slippage between the signifiers "African American" and "African Canadian," his narrative also goes on to specify that this slippage is primarily around youth culture:

**Gerald:** I can't. I can't really explain it. It's just like there is no [pause], to me I've never seen any thing that's like African Canadian. Like everything that black kids identify with [pause] that I know about is like African American. Like rap is African American, all the movies you watch are African American movies, clothes you wear, [the] styles are African America. Everything is like American.

Thus, Gerald's identification with blackness is primarily through youth culture, a youth culture that is linked to the United States. His recognition of youth culture as an important part of black identification is in line with recent theorization of black youth culture. Although the identification of students as black would appear to be a generic descriptor, the narratives indicate that the conception of black identity under discussion is specifically a youth identity. This point was also evident in the way that Gerald constructs blackness as related to dress and youth culture:

**J:** So give me an example of someone who you think dresses black? On the media or somebody that you know?

**Gerald:** All the black people except for people like old men. Like Denzel Washington. I always see him in suits and stuff, like basically anyone else, see Snoop [pointing to The Source cover page on the table], that's dressing black.

Or, take for example, the ways in which this young man asks me to elaborate and differentiate in terms of whom I am referring to when I speak of black culture.

**Melvin:** It all depends. Like [pause] . . . you mean black people as a whole? Or different age groups, or—

**J:** Oh, right. . . . You would make a distinction then? Age groups then? The culture would be different for the youth rather than the. . . .

**Melvin:** Yeah because . . . still when you are like young you are not like down into nothing like deeper in life. So you just like go with like the things that everybody is into and stuff . . . that make the things that black people are into. Like we talk the same and like, you know, listen to our music and what not and "do our thing." And like I am sure when you get like older, it like comes more visible that there is like different symbols and like different things that like represent [pause] your black culture. But like, um, it's not really recognized to me at this moment. So I'm still digging deeper into life. Like I've just begun.

Also evident within Melvin's narratives is that black identity is not an innate state of being but rather a social process of becoming which is heavily influenced by peers. He represents himself as "youth" on the way to becoming and adopting a differing "black adult" identity based on differing meanings and symbols. The construction of identity indicated by the narratives is one that draws primarily on U.S.-based youth culture and is open to change as one moves through adolescence to adulthood. This construction of black identity through youth culture is the focus of analysis in Chapters 3 to 7 of this study.

Of relevance in both Gerald and Melvin's narratives is the way that the discourses construct not just African-American identity as similar to African-Canadian but specifically African-American youth identity. These similarities are recognized and weighted as part of a yearning for African-American youth styles. In linking the two descriptors with regard to black identity, it becomes evident that similarities between the two are based on consumption of specific youth style. Media culture, music and style in particular are identified as important markers of black identity. Frank's narratives clarify how he sees these two identities of black American and black Canadian as fluid in relation to each other:

> **Frank:** They like try to do the same things. Everybody wants to do what other people do. Like "rappers do this," then everybody wants to do this. It's like [pause] want to listen to rap music and stuff like that.

What is evident from the above presentation of student narratives is not only that African-American youth culture is aligned with African-Canadian youth culture but also that some use "black" interchangeably with African American and African Canadian. "Black" is used in a way that makes the term interchangeable between those whose heritages are in differing geographic areas and reinforces slippage between the signifiers African Canadian and African American. The point of constancy that links these differing geographic areas would seem to be a conception of black identity that is linked with phenotype and age and a trace of historical memory as much as anything else. Substantiation of this postulation can be found in the following extract that self-evidently defines hip-hop as a black cultural form:

> **Gerald:** 'Cuz basically it's made up of black people!

## Summary

This chapter has identified the terrain on and through which the research object has been constructed. Factors that come into play in order to define the research area include the specific historical period in which we are living as well as the growing influence of media and the easy to access U.S. popular culture. My position as a black woman is important in terms of developing a sense of the intertextual. In reading the subject formation of these school youth, intertextually it is evident that construction of Canadian identity as synonymous with whiteness and the visual dominance of African-American youth identity act to reinforce the articulation between African American and African Canadian. The next chapter examines Gerald's closing phrase in light of Lawrence Grossberg's comment that, "the most basic experiences one has, the things one believes most confidently because they are the most obvious, those are precisely what power and ideology have produced" (Grossberg, 1997, p. 260).

# CHAPTER 2

# Diaspora as Collectivity?

*Consciousness of diaspora affiliation stands opposed to the distinctively modern structures and modes of power orchestrated by the institutional complexity of nation-states. Diaspora identification exists outside of, and sometimes in opposition to, the political forms and codes of modern citizenship.*

GILROY, 1997, p. 329

## Introduction

In this chapter we examine the ways in which the students regard themselves as similar to and different from other blacks. Through the students' discourse, their common sites of identification will be ascertained. Their narratives highlight racialized experiences, historical memory, and, in particular, musical choice as a resources for the production of symbolic meanings that can then be used to produce or contest relations of dominance.

The chapter looks at individual conceptions of culture and identity as they relate to notions of the African diaspora and black collective consciousness. In problematizing and exploring this sense of diasporan consciousness, I highlight the ways in which the students position themselves in relation to not only the diaspora but also what Paul Gilroy identifies as a "dynamics of remembrance and commemoration"— a positioning that can lead to a sense of consciousness not dependent upon a nation state for fulfillment. Enactment of such dynamics of remembrance would allow the students to use their experiences within a white-dominated society to articulate a discourse of "blackness" and "belonging" that crosses geographic borders.

Exploring the concept of diaspora as a starting point towards understanding collectivity that spans geographic boundaries allows blackness to be placed in relation to other national and ethnic identities. Diasporan identity is a transnational identity, according to Stuart Hall:

diaspora offers a basis to reassess the idea of essential and absolute identity; and offers a way to imagine a more complex ecologically sophisticated and organic concept of identity than offered by the contending options of genealogy. (Gilroy, 1997, p. 339)

## Hybridization

The idea that identity is not from our essential selves, not present at birth but instead derives from a social context implies fluidity and hybridity of identity. This ability to change our identity and to see it in relation to other identities is where Homi Bhabha's "third space" becomes relevant. If we can view our identities as relational, then a process that he identifies as "translation" can take place. Chris Barker argues (after Pieterse, 1995) that hybridization can be divided into two types—structural and cultural: Structural hybridization refers to a variety of border zones, "while cultural hybridization distinguishes between cultural responses ranging from assimilation, through forms of separation, to hybrids that destabilize and blur cultural boundaries." While both types of hybridity would indicate a degree of boundary crossing, they do not represent the "erasure of boundaries and we need to be sensitive to both cultural difference and to forms of identification that involve recognition of similarity" (Barker, 1999, p. 70). Although hybridity denotes fluidity rather than fixity, Stuart Hall argues that he cannot adopt a totally postmodern referent towards identity. For him, the way in which he is trying to think questions of identity is slightly different from a postmodernist "nomadic."

> I think cultural identity is not fixed; it's always hybrid. But this is precisely because it comes out of very specific historical formations, out of very specific histories and cultural repertoires of enunciation, that it can constitute a "positionality," which we call, provisionally, identity. It's not just anything. So each of those identity-stories is inscribed in the positions we take up and identify with, and we have to live this ensemble of identity-positions in all its specificities. (Chen, 1996, p. 502)

One of the most insightful areas of work with regard to hybridity has been Gilroy's theorization of the concept of diaspora. As a concept, diaspora is seen as a human scattering of peoples from their original site and location. In terms of a general understanding, Gilroy (1997) argues that:

> Slavery, pogroms, indenture, genocide and other unnameable terrors have all figured in the constitutions of diasporas and the reproduction of a *diasporan consciousness*, in which identity is focussed less on equalizing, proto-democratic force of common territory and more on the social dynamics of remembrance and commemoration defined by a strong sense of the dangers involved in the forgetting the location of origin and the process of dispersal. (p. 318)

Afrocentric theorists such as Molefi Asante view the diaspora as a point of cultural unity: "a panethnic unity of all black people of the diaspora, pointing to the origins of African people in the 'spatial reality of Africa'" (McCarthy, p. 249). In contrast, cultural theorists such as Paul Gilroy argue that culture, like identity, should be regarded as fluid, not resting essentially within a specific group. Specifically, he undermines the claims of those who would see African-American culture in absolutist ethnic terms. For Gilroy, black American culture is related to a broader grouping of blacks residing geo-spatially in what he terms the Black Atlantic Diaspora. His conception of a transnational formation that links the Caribbean, Africa, Europe, and America is considered a more insightful unit of analysis for the study of black culture. Gilroy draws on historical analysis of the development of the Enlightenment to reinforce his argument that the ship was an important transporter/purveyor of a diasporic black culture across the Atlantic region. At the same time his argument develops the idea that blacks were an integral part of the formation of the European Enlightenment project. Slavery and issues related to freedom and democracy were the foundation of European society.

Gilroy (1997) gestures to the sense of fragmentation that is inherent within the concept of diaspora, viewing it as a space to move the concept from a descriptive level to an analytic level. For him, diaspora "points towards a more worldly sense of culture than the characteristic notions of social, landscape and rootedness" (p. 328). One needs to think of identity formation in terms of "routes" rather than "roots," to rethink black identity as an "outernational project" rather than a singular construct contained by state boundaries. Marie Gillespie (1995), in using Gilroy's conceptualization of diaspora in her ethnographic work on Punjabi youth in London, argues that a "diasporic perspective acknowledges the ways in which the identities have been and continue to be transformed through relocation, cross-cultural exchange and interaction" (p. 7). Similarly, using diaspora offers the opportunity to re-read the relationship between identity and location, between nationality and geographic origin. It allows for a shift in "attention from notions of geographically-bound contexts that develop in chronological sequences to notions of regions bound by a discursive 'field.'" Further, such a reading allows analysis of the political and the social aspects of identity as well as the ability to view the way in which representation of sameness and difference become part of meaning making and everyday culture. Diaspora helps us understand the intersections of ethnicity, class, religion, and gender in identity formation. It also helps us explore to what extent the students have an "overintegrated" or "pluralistic" sense of self in relation to their diasporan community. In other words, where and when do they use boundaries of blackness as markers of difference? As well, the concept of diaspora, with its connotation of sameness and differentiation, provides a fundamental theoretical means to grasp the contemporary politics of identity and identification. Leroi Jones/Amiri Baraka called this "a changing same" in his rich discussion of African-American music and its relationship to both selfhood and community (Gilroy, 1995, p. 26). Further, Herman Gray (1995), in supporting Gilroy's conceptualization of "changing same," argues that this view of:

> blackness as a cultural trope is alert to, but not blinded by, the socially constructed character and context in which different notions of blackness is made meaningful. African American, black Atlantic and African traditions do survive and exist in popular forms and practices through which they are socially organized and made culturally meaningful. But they are not as some neonationalists and Afrocentric advocates would have it, frozen in time in some original form to be preserved and revisited and resurrected as a source of authentic affirmation and guidance. (p. 151)

Gilroy's concept of the "Black Atlantic" extends an understanding of the African diaspora and reinforces the notion that culture is hybrid rather than absolute as some Afrocentrics would pose. Such a process of cultural hybridity indicates a complex theoretical position, since it undermines any claim of black American culture as absolute while also recognizing that commonalties were developed historically between Africans of the diaspora. Arguing that the ship was the vehicle of communication among blacks of the diaspora during the nineteenth century, Gilroy (1993) develops an analysis that "ships were the living means by which the points within that Atlantic world were joined. . . . [T]hey need to be thought of as complex cultural and political units rather than abstract embodiments of the triangular trade" (pp. 16–17). Gilroy's work suggests that one should view the formation of culture as rhizomatic (Deleuze & Guattari, 1987), "routes" rather than "roots." Such an understanding of culture recognizes the various ways in which culture is syncretic rather than absolute.

However, while hybridization is a useful concept, it should also be recognized that the concept is itself problematic. While it fits within a theoretical paradigm that is more tolerant of fluidity than fixity, it also reinforces and implies the meeting of distinct, separate, and homogenous cultures. Thus, within the confines of this study, the students already bring hybrid cultures with them to any situation of social interaction. "The concept of hybridity is acceptable provided that it is recognized as a discursive device, a way of capturing cultural change by way of a strategic cut or temporary stabilisation of cultural categories" (Barker, 1999, p. 71).

## Experience as Translation

While the earlier narratives identify the adoption of Canadian identity as problematic and not the source of easy identification, so too is the adoption of an African identity problematic. Experience emerges as an important aspect of the way in which diasporan students come to view themselves in relation to the continent of

Africa. For students with Caribbean heritage, the narratives suggest that there is no innate desire to return to Africa, the "source of origins." This problematizing of a "return" is similar to a process identified by Homi Bhabha as "translation," an exploration of identities as transformative processes in the interplay of history and politics. For Wayne, recognition of his diasporan experiences means that there is no simple identification with African origins. Instead, he viewed himself as:

> **Wayne:**  Black Jamaican. [laugh] I know that my fore-parents are from Africa, but I am a black Jamaican. My mom wasn't born in Africa; my dad wasn't born in Africa. I was born in Jamaica. So I know that my origins come from Africa. But I am a Jamaican black [pause] Caribbean Black.

What Wayne identifies is a discourse that recognizes his past yet does not see an easy return to that past. As such, his origins in Africa are subsumed under his reflections on Jamaica, his last "port of call." In this context, translation means:

> those identity formations which cut across and intersect natural frontiers and which are composed of people who have been dispersed forever from their homelands. Such people retain strong links with their places of origin and their traditions, but they are without the illusion of a return to the past. They bear upon them the traces of the particular cultures, traditions, languages and histories by which they were shaped. The difference is that they are not and never will be unified in the old sense, because they are irrevocably the product of several interlocking histories and cultures. (Hall, 1992, p. 310)

In a similar vein, the following student identified the problematic nature of "translation" and the difficulties of a straightforward identification with geographic area. For Doreen, born in Canada, length of stay/rootedness outweighs identifications. It is difficult to identify with a memory and a past Africa and yet also difficult to identify a Canadian present:

> **Doreen:**  Oh if people call me African I am like, "Oh I'm from [St. Lucia]" . . . I don't like to say Canada. It's just a habit. And everybody always thinks you are from somewhere else too.

As with Doreen, Etta also indicates how the process of "translation" affects her ability to adopt the subject position of African. Again, the United States is drawn on as a counter position to explain the ways in which blackness is codified with rootedness:

> **Etta:**  That they are basically American, but they are black. If you got as far back as your descendants. If you go back and back and back. They are still American. And

if you go really, really, far back, then you will get African. Whereas with me, how would you put it? You don't really consider yourself to be African if you have some-body that's from the West Indies.

What Etta is alluding to is the difference that results from a process of translation.

This process of translation is evident in the students' narratives that highlight the ways in which ethnicity articulates with relations of power to highlight specific cul-tural differences within the black-identified group. This issue was evident in several references to intragroup differences that are smoothed over with humor and jokes:

**J:** When you say it sometimes comes up as a joke. Explain that to me.
**Gerald:** Like [pause] like my group. Say like there's Africans and say there is Jamai-cans and then there is like Africans, [they] like to make fun of each other.
**J:** In what way?
**Gerald:** Like each other's countries. Make fun of Africa and then they'll make fun of Jamaica.

Or in a similar vein:

**Omar:** It's like, well, I don't know? Like to all the black people. I think inside they re-alise that that's where they are. That's where like all their roots are. Whether you are Jamaican whatever you are. That's where your roots are . . . I think some Jamai-cans fail to realise that. /Fail?/ Yeah. 'Cuz they always want to distance themselves from Africans.
**J:** How do you see that?
**Omar:** Well, [pause] phew, lot times. Like when we had, even if it's for fun, for jokes. Like I have a lot of Jamaican friends. And you get into these discussions where you start making fun of each other's cultures. Like, "Oh yeah, you Jamaicans are always fishing." "You Africans are always hunting and this and that" And so you like, you fail to realize that you are both the same! That [the] only difference between you two is what part of the world you are standing on.

Omar's narrative highlights the unity of blackness that is again based on the concept of historical origins, a consciousness that is historical and pan-Africanist.

Although Omar's narratives attempt to negate the process of translation and dif-ferences in order to achieve a sense of political unity based on biology, this notion of unity soon becomes problematic for students who declare themselves as black but who are of mixed heritage, African and European. The following narratives indicate the problematic nature of a return to the Africa continent for children with a hybrid identity, for them there is no automatic return and acceptance waiting in Africa. Saaka relays his initial reception on the continent:

**Saaka:** I'd get teased a lot 'cuz . . . they knew I was different. All they had to do was hear me talk and to look at my skin, it was lighter than theirs so they knew I was different. I'd get teased a lot. Also at the same time lot of people could see I was different and want to be my friend. But then lots of kids would bug me too.

Or this student, who also returned to another country in Africa:

**Nelson:** And they always call me foreigner and stuff like that and I was like, I didn't know what it meant at first. I asked them [adults], they are like, "It means foreigner, don't worry about it" and I go "Yes" [they said] "They are little kids, they don't know." But . . . [pause] everyone was good to me there. They were all very nice to me. Like the family name there is big.

Adopting African as a general descriptor for those from the African continent and those translated by the diaspora was problematic for one participant. For this student, peoples of African descent are complicit in homogenizing Africa when such a descriptor is used too freely. For him, one should identify a specific country where one's heritage lies:

**Saaka:** I don't like when people say . . . they are African. "What country in Africa are you from?" When people ask me if I am African, I go "No, I am Nigerian." They ask, "Where is that?" "Africa." They go "Oooh." No one knows anything about Africa because it's never taught. [Nigeria is the biggest] country in Africa and no one can find it on a map. It's like Americans [laugh] Americans don't know anything about Canada.

This narrative highlights the ways in which one can align one's self with discourses of subjugation through one's unwitting use of language. The narratives illustrate the ways in which peoples of African descent can also come to use and reinforce discourses that homogenize Africa and represent it as a country rather than a continent with a variety of cultures. Saaka's ironic laugh is also enlightening as it recognizes that Canada is also in a similar position of erasure in relation to the United States.

## Common Sites of Identification

The comment by Gerald at the end of Chapter 1 indicates that the color of peoples designated as black is important in terms of being able to claim black identification. The body acts as a signifier to connote specific meanings as embodiment becomes linked to the ways in which boundaries are created around sameness. The narratives indicate that phenotype is an automatic signifier for blackness. Gilroy (1997) describes the rationale for such a state as:

where separation, time and distance from the point of origin or the centre of sovereignty complicate the symbolism of ethnic and national reproduction, anxieties over
the boundaries and limits of sameness may lead people to seek security in the sanctity
of embodied difference. (p. 333)

While the discourses would suggest that dark skin equates with identification as
black, the narratives of some students problematize this automatic correlation. At
times, the ability to be seen as black was not as straightforward as suggested by the
body but was complicated by cultural understandings as well as lived experiences
within a geographic region identified with blacks. The narratives reveal that at
times, discourses are competing and often fragment the construction of a sense of
blackness as based solely on skin colour:

**Omar:** Oh, even like, I consider like there is these two brothers they are from Guyana.
I consider them black. They look more brown. They speak [patois] things like that.
I consider them black.

Because of their cultural expressions derived from the Caribbean, those students
whose heritage was on the Indian subcontinent via the Caribbean, could, but not
automatically, be reproduced as "black" through recognition of discursive practices
that draw on history and culture.

So how do the students' narratives construct students whose physical attributes
might not cohere with a common-sense understanding of "black" yet are of African
descent? For some students who have mixed heritage—one parent of European descent—passing/being accepted as black was not always automatic but was instead
dependant on the extent to which their phenotype cohered with other dominant
signifiers of blackness. If they did not look like the dominant representation of
blackness, then their claim to being black might well have to be legitimated. One
student who was of mixed heritage and whose appearance did not cohere with the
predetermined conceptions of black indicated how he negotiated this social situation when interacting with a new group of black students:

**J:** So how do you stake your claim then?
**Bob:** I don't, really. I just wait [they say] "You're black." "Oh," I'll go, "My dad is." "Oh,
Okay."

For Bob it, was a matter of waiting to be challenged and then laying out one's African heritage. His basis of legitimation is bio-political based on his father's African
heritage.

Within other students' narratives, discourses on mixed-heritage students constructed various formulations that drew on gender and parenting to identify the degree to which a mixed heritage student might identify with blackness. For Etta, the

gender of the black-identified parent was a decisive factor in determining a child's psychological orientation towards a black self. She describes how this process worked with a friend:

> **Etta:** I know she is half by her skin colour, but I always thought of her as being black. Because her mum is . . . totally [Caribbean]. That's how she is raised, and you can even see the attitude in her. Like just the way she is. And like sometimes, like a lot of half people they turn out to be perfectly fine, not a problem, you know. They have no problem with like who they are whatever. But a lot of cases they do have a problem. They don't know who to identify [with]. And I see that most if the guy is black and the mum is white.

However, the narratives of another student, Phyllis, who argued that the influence of her non-black mother was also important in enabling her to identify herself as black, indicated the problematic nature of Etta's comments:

> **Phyllis:** I paid attention to more of the black side. My mum has always kind a pushed me to the black side. . . . Like she likes the fact that I acknowledge my white half I don't like [pause] exclude her from anything you know. Like if anything I excluded, it wouldn't be my mum.

As well, embedded within Etta's narrative is an assumption that the mother is the primary caregiver and therefore more influential in terms of the acquisition of a sense of self. Such a view reinforces the idea that the transmission of culture is unproblematic. Little account is taken of the ways in which enculturation/socialization is neither automatic nor predetermined but is, instead, fragmented by relations of class, ethnicity, and religion.

## Double Boundaries

The literature on identity indicates that as part of maintaining a boundary, cross-racial dating is often perceived as taboo, as muddling the binary opposite black/white. Many of the students indicated that they did not have any concerns about either themselves or others dating across racialized groups. This may have been a reflection of the number of students who were of mixed heritage as one such student indicated:

> **J:** What about tensions? Does that ever create tensions between different ethnic groups?
> **Denzil:** Not really. [pause] Only the really ignorant kind of . . . stupid people "What are you doing?" like that. It's sooo backward. "What are you doing with that white girl?" "What are you doing with that Chinese girl"?

However, such an acceptance of cross-racial dating was not unanimous among the whole student population as indicated by the following narrative from the wider sample of students interviewed:

> **Marcus:** I am not bothered about dating them. But when it comes down to like seriousness, like the rest of my life, having a kid I have to take care of, then that's different . . . I'll go for a black girl.
>
> **J:** How is that?
>
> **Marcus:** I can't see my self with a half-kid, straight curly hair, light complexion. Can't see myself like that. Get up in the morning, with a white face beside me, can't see that.

Marcus's narrative indicates that the positive response of other students to my questions might well have been with regard to "dating" rather than a long-term relationship. Despite claims that neither of the two genders were concerned about cross-racial dating, the young women indicated that if they did have a relationship across racialized boundaries, it would be noted and remarked upon by males. Males, in return, also indicated that girls were sensitive on such issues. What emerges is the way in which, in terms of gender, relations of both the young women and young men construct women in racialized ways that reinforce stereotypes of black women as "tough" and independent minded, while white women are seen as "soft" and easily manipulated. The latter narratives are evident of one young woman's positioning within such discourses:

> **Euda:** Black girls don't take it . . . we speak our minds all the time.

Often this comparison is constructed in relation to other racialized groups of women. The following narrative reveals such genderized/racialized discourses at work:

> **Doreen:** As far as I am concerned girls that are not black spoil [them], girls from other races put out for black guys and then they expect to get stuff from us whenever they come back. Like they want every single thing, they want to buy them. And like listen, I am not one of those girls that go out and. . . .

Or for another student:

> **Eulyn:** Well I'll tell you my perspective instead. . . . They are um [pause], well, they're kind a dumb, right. In the sense that they will do anything //uumph// for a guy right. And [pause] I don't know. It's hard to describe.

What the latter does is to construct non-black women as passive, dumb/innocent, naïve, and in some ways hyperfeminine. If one places this construction of non-black women in a binary relation, then black women emerge as assertive and street smart. Such racialized constructions of gender can also affect the ways in which young men represent themselves and young women as dating partners:

> **Marcus:** 'Cuz most white girls are too easy to control . . . do whatever you tell them . . . black girl she will stand up for herself . . . she will not let anyone walk over her, she just takes charge.

Such an assessment of potential dating partners is an interesting one. Young men living in a patriarchal society with a preference for women who are perceived as "independent-minded," able to take charge—attributes not traditionally identified with the hyper-masculinity that they encounter in youth culture, is unexpected.

The narratives indicate that although the majority of the students exhibited a willingness to identify themselves as black, finding common signifiers of black identification and its representation in everyday practices was often problematic. While one student was able to identify symbols as a common source of identification, naming such symbols proved elusive:

> **Melvin:** Black culture? //Uh huh// As in how black people like [pause] have like [pause] symbols that like would mean it's their culture? //Yeah// Ah, yeah. I'm pretty sure. Yeah. What symbols it would be though I don't know.

Another student's narrative implied an identity that is ascribed as much as achieved; a black identity that is determined and constructed by bureaucratic descriptors that are seemingly imposed externally upon the self and without choice. He answered my question, "What does it mean to you to be black?":

> **Gerald:** It's the way society looks at you, not what you think of yourself. [pause]. That's how I see someone being black. If society thinks you are black then you are black. You don't have a choice.

Gerald's comments indicate there is a bureaucratic/political element that acts as a coercing influence in the construction of ethnic and racialized identity. The latter is similar to Isajiw's (1999) concept of "double boundaries," "those from within and those from without, self-identifying and being identified by others" (p. 176). In the present it is difficult to escape such categorizations, as the state increasingly comes to recognize "needs" on the basis of identities and social identities become more political (Gilroy, 1987).

This recognition of black identity as constrained by political and bureaucratic practices can also be seen in Omar's narratives:

**Omar:** The easiest way to say is the thing that separates itself from everybody else. 'Cuz I think that's what the black people are trying to do. As much as all the black people are saying, " Oh, how we want equal rights." They really want to be separated from everybody else. They don't like it when other people are like, how you say [pause] like doing the same thing as they are. . . . That's basically it. It's like what the French people are doing almost.

**J:** Oh, you think so?

**Omar:** Yeah, well almost. It's not to the point where it's political. But almost.

For Omar, black identity connects people through a desire on the part of blacks to be separate from others, a desire orchestrated through music and language. Part of this desire to be separate is based on an understanding of culture as property and a social resource. Such an understanding of culture leads to a fear of any sharing that might dilute and consequently weaken culture as a resource. By inviting others to participate in one's culture, one also opens up the possibility of a social rejection on the basis of being too strange and exotic. Etta alludes to such a situation at another high school that she attended. There, the construction of a white norm meant that other racialized students were thus constructed as "other than" the norm. She explains her reluctance to share aspects of black culture such as stepping:[1]

**Etta:** And it's kind a like you feel kind a [pause] not ashamed, but like no one is going to appreciate, anyways 'cuz there is nobody there. [pause] That's your kind or whatever. Like here it doesn't really matter. 'Cuz everybody appreciates everything. So there is so many of everybody else. You are already part of. There it's like [pause] it's almost all the same kind of show. And if something else different comes across. Everyone is like "Oh?" Because the majority is white anyways.

Omar articulates a similar point with regard to sharing black culture and experiences in general:

**Omar:** Like sometimes [pause] you are afraid of what the other, the outsider, is going to say about it. So you don't want anybody to have a big image of what you believe in. So you just kind a distance it from other people. You know the type of thing like that. But you always want them to like it. So in a sense you want them to learn about it, but you don't want them to have a negative thought about it. So it's like. I don't know [pause] That's all I can really say. Like you just don't, you don't [pause] it's like your shelter. You don't want people to like look at it and say, "What is this! This is rubbish." You want them to say, "Yeah that's good. I never knew."

Thus external social factors as well as internal psycho-social factors construct black identity.[2]

*Historical memory and knowledge*

At times the students' identities become linked with a sense of historical memory and knowledge as a means of developing a sense of black collectivity. One student made use of historical memory in order to suggest a unity in origins that is often not recognized by those born in the diaspora and from which they often try to distance themselves. For Omar, whose family has consistent links with Africa, recognition of that continent was a matter of respect:

> **Omar:**  It's kind of like Africa is [pause] it's where it's like most, like some people they realise that's their true roots. And then some people maybe do realise it but just distance themselves from it. Because I guess like the technology is not great. Like, for materialistic things, nothing like cultural or anything like that it's just materialistic. They say, "Oh 'cuz like Africa is not in the twentieth century yet." They have most of the Third World nations in on there, stuff like that. So people don't want to put themselves in the same class as that. See they want to distance themselves. They're "Oh, in Jamaica we can get these Nike things or that. You can't get that in Africa." "Oh fine" "Who cares? "You're from there!" "Your ancestors were born there at one point in time." So, I don't know. People [pause] just don't . . . appreciate the Land [Africa] as much as they should I would think. Even me, I sometimes don't.

In other words, the development of technology and, through it, access to commodities becomes a marker of "progress" within the worldwide economic hierarchy, in which the continent of Africa ranks low. Another student, Langston, did not share this perspective of historical memory as unifying; instead, he used historical memory of slavery to reveal differences in the experiences of those who were enslaved and those who remained in Africa. Further, in recognizing such differences and comparing the African diaspora as the dislocation, he finds that continent more interesting:

> **Langston:**  Like I know about black American history, like I know everything basically, but it's like I come from a much more interesting view. Like way more interesting. Like African history is pretty interesting, like very interesting. Like the slave ships and bringing from Africa to America where they worked as slaves until so, so, date. Lincoln freed them and there was a civil war. I know all that. But where they came from? The stories behind them are really interesting. They have folk tales. I would have liked to live way back in those times.

Or for Eulyn, this past has an effect on the present:

> **Eulyn:**  Because when we were slaves, back in the day. I mean, the stuff that they put us through and then to say "Well, it's Okay you know. It's the past, whatever don't worry about" and it's kind of annoying.

In another instance, historical memory and knowledge of black experiences become important resources in the formation of black subjectivity and identity:

> **Denzil:** That's a common link in every black person. They feel. They feel for their slaves. They feel for everyone who fought for the civil rights and everything
>
> **J:** So even though you haven't experienced, it you still feel for them?
>
> **Denzil:** Right. 'Cuz without them, where would I be right now? I would probably be picking corn. Picking cotton or something.

In continuing the narrative, he indicates the importance of parental influence rather than biological essence in cultivating this sense of historical memory, black identification, and black consciousness.

> **J:** So how do you gain that understanding then?
>
> **Denzil:** My dad, my father really put into my head. He drilled it into my head. I was young, but I did a lot of research on my own on black history [or] whatever.

This idea of blackness as historical consciousness that leads to separation was also evident in the narratives of some students involved in a step team based at the school. For these students, historical memory and present-day racialized bodies were linked in order to become a source of power, to exclude those who were regarded as not being the bearers of such traces of racialized memories. At times, historical discourses are drawn on to give legitimacy and meaning to the idea of blacks having a form of cultural practice that requires knowledge of black history in order to understand and fully participate. Culture is posed as experience and knowledge, as a thing, a commodity that is the basis of understanding and legitimacy:

> **J:** Explain to me again the bit about having white people on it?
>
> **Eulyn:** I just think [pause], I don't think they know enough about it to say that
>
> **J:** When you say "it"—
>
> **Eulyn:** About the history behind it.
>
> **J:** . . . and they need to know the history to be able to do it?
>
> **Eulyn:** Yeah. And also it's our culture you know. It's fine if you want to watch it and stuff. But it's something we can say we have we did it you know.

In a similar vein another student saw black culture as the primary rationale of the group, as something that is rooted, that can be possessed, and should not necessarily be shared with or imitated by non-blacks:

> **Joy:** That's our culture. I don't like people trying to get in it.

From Eulyn and Joy's narratives, we can see how a shared history becomes an important boundary marker of black collectivity. Participation of non-blacks in this specific black-identified activity is channelled and monitored on the rationale that not just an understanding is required but also a *rootedness* in a specific historical formation. A sense of collective "blackness" is used to exclude those who do not possess such an understanding. Eulyn's narratives also suggest an understanding of culture that is supportive of Omar's critique of black culture as based upon maintaining a difference from mainstream culture.

Maintaining a sense of collectivity through the unity of the step team was not always easy, and often points of contestation emerged. Not all students supported this use of culture to maintain a difference from non-blacks. Another student, Euda, was more ambivalent about the social dynamics of exclusion based on a lack of knowledge of black experiences:

> **Euda:** Still a lot of people don't have the courage to join . . . [the dance group] I think that's Okay; it's not like I can do anything about it. So I don't say anything.

However, this sense of collective blackness was not just racialized, but also gendered, with none of the young black men involved in the activities of the group. The rationale for this fragmentation of a perceived black activity along gender lines was identified by one of the young women as due to issues of masculinity:

> **J:** Do the boys have anything to do with the step-team?
> **Etta:** No. They would never have anything to do with it. That's how they are, "rough." They are too "rough" to be on a step-team. They'd be too embarrassed. Yeah we asked them. We begged couple of them. They are like . . . they even laughed.

While youth involved with the step-team constructed a sense of unity through historical discourses, religious subjectivity was also a point of contestation with regard to the step-team providing a place for black unity. Many of the members of the team classified themselves as religious or as attending a church. At times, conflicts emerged between supporting their church and supporting the step-team. At such times one student stated that church was always given primary consideration. As she explains it, her religious affiliation gave her:

> **Eulyn:** Stability [pause] and [pause] it gives you something to look forward to, you know. Like [pause] a purpose in life kind of.

However, for some religious denominations, public dancing and displaying the body were regarded as inappropriate. In the following narrative, Etta illustrates how she was able to use the portrayal of the step-team as a black/African-identified activity in order to quell fears of stepping as a morally inappropriate activity:

First she had a big problem with it. I wasn't allowed to do it. But I tried to convince her that it's not dancing. It's just "stepping" . . . but my mum finally got the idea that it was more like an African history step thing. Not "whining up"[3] and stuff like that. That, she has a problem with, same with Joanne's mum. And that's [another] problem too. Some of the girls still want to add in reggae and stuff. And if my mum came and Joanne's mum came, we would be in this whole lot of trouble.

At other times, historical memory was seen as irrelevant to the present in terms of collective identity. Instead, a memory of slavery was viewed as a tool to deny individual black responsibility and action/inaction in the present day. Juliet illustrates how, she thinks that collective history and memory is used negatively as a tool by blacks to deny individual responsibility in the present:

> **Juliet:** Like come on, man, get on with it. You know those people in the States. They get me vexed. "Oh slavery this, slavery that." "Shut up!" It happened ages and thousands, centuries ago. Like get over it!

For this student, collective memory does not outweigh individual responsibility. Blacks who have not achieved success in education or the labor market are represented as fully responsible for their own fate. As interviewer, I attempted to probe the student's answer by posing a further question:

> **J:** Sometimes it's difficult though, no?
>
> **Juliet:** How is it difficult? Like come on . . . they are not making it any better by just sitting down not doing anything. Why don't they try to make a difference and get up off their butt and go and try to get an education and a proper job? I don't get it. Like don't go on about it I say.
>
> **J:** What about racism in the United States?
>
> **Juliet:** They talk about that too much too.
>
> **J:** You think so?
>
> **Juliet:** Yeah? //In what way?// Maybe . . . I really think, I think everybody just needs to get racism out of their head. That's my opinion. I think everybody needs to stop thinking about it. And stop jumping to conclusions.

For Juliet, the gap between history and consciousness is filled by a dominant neoliberal economic discourse that negates the role of history. Historical memory and knowledge is used as a source of power in social relations, not just between black and white students as in the example of the dance group but also in social interaction between black students. In the following narrative, one student identifies a feeling of isolation from the sense of community that can be developed around historical memory. For her, the variable that separates her from the black group is "knowledge" of black experiences. She describes her experiences at a social event:

**Euda:** I felt uncomfortable because I thought there would be other people there, not just black people. I feel intimidated when I am around all these people, and they are like expecting me to know this and that. I know about my parent's culture, but I don't know like everything.

## Links in Everyday Experience

Some of the students regard identity as based on experiences that link individuals based on blackness. Some students, in recognizing commonalities, used social descriptors rather than biological affinities in order to make links with other blacks. For Joy, common experiences among blacks were often dependent on external forces and definitions:

**Joy:** Calling each other names, you know [pause] racial names and stuff . . . and their opinions of like other people are the same. They have gone through the same experiences that you have. Like the hair bit. . . . Or being called racial names at school, that type of thing you know. Or [pause], yeah, like the family discipline. That's the things I can look at [pause] and, oh yes, dancing, liking the same music, going out, same kind of dressing, same kind of style. Um [pause], same kind of guy choice. All of that.

Or

**Denzil:** There are certain things that a black friend could identify with that your other friends can't. In terms of not getting a job, not getting a job because they won't hire coloured people or whatever. Any kind of discrimination white people can't really identify with. Life is harder if you're coloured. It's that simple.

**J:** And that's what you think gives you a commonality with other sort of coloured and blacks?

**Denzil:** Anybody who basically isn't blonde hair, blue eyed, has it harder in life.

Because of differing understandings of raced experiences, some students are likely to choose as confidants those who are most likely to empathize with or acknowledge their experiences. As Denzil continues, at times differing racialized identities can undermine the process of understanding:

**Denzil:** I have one friend that's very um [pause] not so much racist as he is a [pause] what's the word? [pause] He's, he's kind of like he has to be efficient, has to be this, has to be that, and kind of that's the way it is and accept it kind of thing. And he'll always say, well black people are this. They lead the crime whatever, whatever. But he doesn't talk about how it's a product of the white man's government and all this stuff. He neglects to see everything else. He is British, very proud of his Britishness.

And so he is always talking about how great England is but he doesn't. . . . There are so many things that are not that great about England.

Thus the difficulty of some friends in recognizing raced experiences within Canadian society can be compared to bell hooks's (1992) argument that the mainstream of society " believe[s] that all ways of looking that highlight difference subvert the liberal belief in a universal subjectivity (we are all just people) that will make racism disappear" (p. 167).

## Music as a Resource of the Diaspora

Throughout the narratives, various sources of commonality are called on in order to indicate the ways in which blackness as a cultural form unifies the students. While such sources varied from food, strict parents, to common dispositions on life, the most frequently stated source was music. This postulation with regard to the unifying force of music is not unknown among the discourses of blackness that circulate within white-dominated societies as a measure of authentic blackness. Paul Gilroy (1995), in discussing the relationship between music and cultural identity argues that:

> music dominates popular culture. It is central to [a] . . . consideration of cultural identity because of its global reach, and because it is repeatedly identified as a special area of expressive culture that mysteriously embodies the inner essence of racial particularity. (p. 25)

Although the narratives construct music as a source of unification for black peoples of the African diaspora and continent, the choice of music assigned to the category "black" drew primarily on genres that are regarded as having their origins in the African diaspora rather than Africa itself. Thus r&b, jazz, rap, calypso, reggae, and soca were all identified as signifying blackness in their musical forms. In the following narrative, Euda identifies her breadth of musical preferences:

**Etta:** I like Usher, but I wouldn't like buy the CD; I'd like tape it off some one. Uum, I like. . . . See to me, rap is good. When I say rap is good, maybe it's not a good thing. But I like rap. [pause] If it is not [pause] just straight rap. Like if it has like music. Like Mase is kind of a good rap because . . . it's rap but his style, the way that . . . it has a kind of flow; it has to have a style. It depends on who is in it. And it depends on if it's one group or more that one group. And it doesn't really matter either way just as long as it's a good group. I don't like hard core rap. Nothing to it. I guess you could say? I like rap like Mase. I like Foxy Brown is okay 'cuz then they have singing and a rap. It's good 'cuz it's catchy as you could say. Biggie was, I have to say his thug stuff was really good. And when they feature a lot of artist and stuff, that's cool.

Or as Phyllis indicates:

> **Phyllis:** I can listen to almost anything. Just usually if I am going to listen to music by myself though it's usually r&b or reggae. But if I am going to go out somewhere I am kinda accepting. Like I am not very picky. As long as there is music in my ear, and I have my friends there, I am okay.
>
> **J:** So R&B though, you said if you were on your own?
>
> **Phyllis:** Like if it's me and a couple of friends, couple of my girl friends whatever, we were just chilling and listen to r&b and stuff.

Interestingly, very few students identified musical forms from the African continent as of consistent importance in their listening repertoire. The following student's taste in music was not typical of the participant in the study:

> **J:** What music do you listen to?
>
> **Merle:** Rap of course. R&B. Um [pause] Nigerian music, I love Nigerian music. It's so moving. It's like, you have your rap and your r&b but then when it's like um [pause] like at a Nigerian function. . . . It is so fun 'cuz it's like moving you know. It's fast and I also like jazz. I like um I am not really into blues that much as jazz, but I really like jazz. And classical helps me study. I use it sometimes. But hardly.

For students with direct family links to the continent of Africa, there was no automatic alignment with music from Africa as a whole or from the country where their parents were born. Where access to genres associated with Africa were acknowledged, it was often via parents rather than the airwaves or digital pulses of mass media. Thus, the spaces where the students had access to such music were often private rather than public. As one student revealed about a parent from west Africa:

> **Toni:** No he doesn't listen to any music? Like he does sometimes. Like he has some tapes of . . . King Sonny Adeh, like some other Nigerian artists, but he doesn't really listen to them. He will occasionally. Say like he has some friends over, he will like play [them].

Music described as black seems to be primarily from North America and the Caribbean, with few of the students being regular listeners of music from any countries in Africa:

> **J:** Do you ever listen to music from continental Africa?
>
> **Omar:** Well my parents do. I listen to it. In the car, my dad, he plays a lot. Um [pause] I used to go to like [pause], pot luck parties with my parents, things like that. That's what they used to play. I listened to that. I don't listen to it by myself, but when it's there I do.

Unlike rap, r&b, and reggae, music from the African continent is limited in its general availability. In comparison to the numbers of students who could access rap and r&b and reggae via *MuchMusic* or MTV on cable or satellite or via audiotapes sent by relatives in the Caribbean, few mentioned any comparable public spaces within which they could access or consume African music from the continent.[4] As a result of this comparative lack of easy access of music from the African continent, consumption is often confined to private spaces of homes, cars, or ethnic-specific functions rather than public spaces such as television and radio. One of the consequences of this lack of public space is that there is no consistent public dialogue among the students in relation to music from Africa. Unlike reggae and rap, there is no community of supporters among the students to open a dialogue about such music: to move its use from a private domain to a public domain. It may also be that these students do not consciously align cultural production within Africa as black, preferring to align blackness with production/reproduction within white-dominated societies. This ready willingness of youths from continental Africa to identify with North American blackness is not new. Ibrahim's (2000) research on Francophone African youths in Ontario, Canada, argues that, "continental African youths find themselves in a racially-conscious society that, wittingly or unwittingly, and through fused social mechanisms such as racist representations, asks them to fit racially somewhere" (p. 120).

### Diasporan Fragmentation and Music

Nationality intersects musical choices identified as black and thus fragments any primordial claims of black homogeneity. Musical identifications emerge as an important point of contestation in terms of perceived collective nature of black identity.

Used in differing ways for maintaining intragroup differences, some students draw on musical choices as a means to identify themselves as similar to or different from their black peers and other racialized and social groups. For students whose parental origins are in the Caribbean region, soca and calypso were listening choices alongside reggae and rap. Reggae also had appeal to other students whose parental backgrounds were not in the Caribbean but who interacted with peers from the Caribbean. However, it was problematic to identify these Caribbean variants as musical genres adopted by all black students. As this student indicates with regard to reggae:

> **Phyllis:** I would say it would have to depend. Because most African people I talk to don't like reggae. //Oh really?// Then you talk to a lot of people from the islands, and they don't like anything that Africans do either. So it would depend on where you are from? Because [pause]; most people identify with reggae, calypso, this and that. Right?

Although reggae was identified within some student narratives as a form of black music, there was no uniform or easy acceptance of this musical form by all black students. Students identified themselves in general with reggae as well as with individual artists such as Buju Banton, Mad Cobra, Shabbah Ranks, Beenie Man, Bounty Killer, and Red Rat. Although students designated their choices as just "reggae," in actuality the latter artists are aligned with a subgenera of reggae, namely, dancehall. Dancehall reggae has developed most extensively in Jamaica, where according to Nelson George, "dance hall is so dominant . . . that indigenous hip-hop groups on the island have little chance to blossom" (1998, p. 205). Although not often acknowledged, in terms of lyrics and contents dancehall and rap, especially gangsta rap, share similar orientations toward gender and violence.[5] Stephens (1998) argues that:

> this "new" reggae was a type of "low" cultural production that was much more difficult to aestheticise than Marley's music. The crude lyrics tend to be mainly about gun culture, sexuality, and "slackness," and were expressed in a thick Jamaican patois that is extremely difficult for an American audience, white or black, to decipher. This was also a more threatening form of reggae music for white audiences because it could not be removed from the very live black bodies who produced, consumed and enjoyed it in the ritual spaces of dance hall. (p. 162)

In continuing the discussion on reggae, Michelle Stephens (1998) argues that reggae as a genre has become a site of contestation in North America. She further argues that symbolic of this tension has been the way in which reggae musician Bob Marley has been commodified during the 1990s as a "natural" mystical figure with universal appeal across race: a reading that negates his more radical "roots" and "culture" positioning. For Stephens (1998), dancehall reggae has emerged as "a very different contender for Marley's throne," with a strong challenge to the direction which modern reggae was taking (p. 161). In some of the narratives, this contestation was evident as Marley was regarded as much more universal, regardless of national heritage, open in terms of lyric interpretation, while dancehall lyrics were much more difficult to access and had to be worked at.

One student, Melvin, identified himself specifically with dancehall reggae rather than other subgenera of reggae. His narratives reveal not only his linking of dancehall reggae with gangsta rap but also the ways in which music is a symbolic social process. In the following narrative, Melvin discusses what he perceived as the similarities and the differences among "inspirational" reggae, rap, and dancehall reggae:

J: Dance hall? So what's dance-hall reggae?
**Melvin:** Well, the other reggae is like more common, but the contents pretty much differ.
J: What' s the difference between dance hall reggae and the other reggae?

**Melvin:** Well, most of the other reggae is more like cultural and political. While it still has a bit of political in dance hall too but it's like the type I am listening to is like kind a "gangsta reggae."

**J:** The equivalent of "gangsta rap"? So what does that talk about then?

**Melvin:** Well, pretty much all the same stuff like "gangsta rap" talks about. It talks about guns, um, violence, so and so forth.[6]

To some extent, Melvin identifies how dancehall reggae may well evoke similar responses among those who listened to gangsta rap. Other students also identify the ways in which reggae, as a genre, is similar to gangsta rap. But whereas Melvin saw such content as unproblematic, for the following student the lyrics, when deciphered, were problematic:

*Jamaican Dancehall (nasty!)*

**Doreen:** But some of the stuff they are singing is just pure filth. And they play it like on the TV and everything. But they say a whole bunch of nastiness on the thing, because people don't know what they are singing except for Jamaicans. Who can understand the reggae, you know. But as for everybody else, they are talking pure like nastiness on the thing. They are talking about genitals and everything. And people don't understand it 'cuz they are talking so fast, and you know they have their accents and everything.

This unacceptability of some reggae lyrics was also seen in the wider focus groups, as one participant indicated:

**Roy:** My mum doesn't really let me listen to new reggae. 'Cuz she thinks it's like garbage. But she likes the old-time stuff like Bob Marley.

**J:** What would she see as new reggae?

**Roy:** Like the dubbing part . . . I think like the way they talk, and she always think that my head is like always focussing on that.

**J:** And what would she like your head focussed on?

**Roy:** On school right now.

Below, Gerald's narratives indicate similarities between reggae and rap, not just in relation to guns but also with regard to the performer's construction of sexuality. In discussing sexual orientation, his narratives suggest competing discourses around the issue:

**Gerald:** It's in like lots of songs. Lots of rap songs, lots of reggae songs. Like how it's bad, and not acceptable. And, um, I don't know. We still accept it though.

The black male identity constructed through reggae is heterosexual. In 1992, Buju Banton's homophobic lyrics in "Boom Bye Bye" caused a controversy, as did Shabba

Ranks's comment of support that, "God created Adam and Eve not Adam and Steve." Chang and Chen (1998) argue that:

*dancehall (Jamaican) is ANTI-GAY*

the militantly anti-homosexual attitude of Jamaicans, men and women alike, is startling. . . . Indeed, a 1996 poll indicated that 96 percent of Jamaicans were against homosexual relationships being legalised. The dance hall is full of songs condemning homosexuality and no stage show goes without at least one ringing condemnation which inevitably draws a huge chorus of approval from the crowd. (p. 204)

As well as indicating the ways in which musical genres are seen as overlapping, Gerald's narrative also draws attention to the ways in which language, i.e., patois, fragments the perceived unity of black identity. For those students whose parents were born on the continent of Africa or in North America and who were not familiar with patois spoken in Jamaica, rap lyrics were regarded as more accessible than those of reggae. However, this explanation begs the question as to whether the language is not accessible or rap is more accessible is as a result of its wide access to audiences via the telecommunications industry. In contrast, soca, calypso, or reggae, to a lesser extent, is much less widely distributed via mediazation and the proliferation of cable networks.

## Production of Dominance of Jamaicans — Microphysics of Power

What Foucault terms "relations of power" are evident throughout the students' narratives. Although on the whole the students would see themselves as living within a society dominated by European Canadian culture, this was not the only point of domination experienced. Also evident was a contesting of the ways in which Jamaica as an island and Jamaican identity subsumed identities associated with the "smaller" islands in the Caribbean region. Jamaica and Jamaicans are often taken to represent the universal in terms of Caribbean experiences and the meanings of Caribbean blackness. The following students, whose families are from one of the smaller Caribbean Islands, reveal how Jamaican identity becomes intertwined with power relations to fragment not only black identification but also the Caribbean identification:

> **Eulyn:** They just . . . for one they think like [pause] their island is the best island and they just portray themselves really differently. In Canada, the Jamaicans think that [pause] you know that they are hot stuff. But I was told back in Jamaica they are nothing like that. They are nice, calm people [pause]. And [in Canada] they are really loud too.

Or for another student:

> **Etta:** So they [non-Caribbean blacks] don't understand much about West Indians like they have no idea. They've never been to [Barbados] or [Grenada] before. We had

to like explain to them. Of course they have heard of Jamaica. They always hear
about Jamaica [said with sarcasm].

At times, this issue of Jamaicans representing the universal in terms of black
experiences in Alberta and Canada is generalized to other social situations. In this
instance the issue concerns what type of dance group might represent "blackness"
and if such a group would be able to represent differing forms of black dance such
as calypso:

> **Doreen:** But I wouldn't put Jamaicans because I don't think they understand it. 'Cuz
> you know how they think they are better than everybody else. Like I wouldn't put
> Jamaicans in, no, seriously I wouldn't.

As stated earlier, the Caribbean region is a complex formation of islands and
countries that often becomes subsumed under the identity of Jamaica. However, as
Winston James (1996) argues, "divided by the distance of the sea—the distance
between Port of Spain (Trinidad) and Kingston (Jamaica) is equivalent to that from
London to Moscow" (p. 156). One of the primary mechanisms for promoting Jamaica as a universal rather than a particular island within the Caribbean is the commercialization of reggae music especially via representations of Bob Marley. This latter discourse is evident within several narratives as is the consequent positioning of
smaller Caribbean islands with genres of music other than reggae. By consuming different genres of music the students align themselves with different Caribbean countries and communities. This symbolic representation of Jamaica with reggae and
other countries with calypso or soca is active among many students, whether born in
the Caribbean region or not:

> **Eulyn:** Probably? Yeah. Like I think of reggae as Jamaican and calypso gets into like
> [pause] all the other countries down in the Caribbean. //uumph// I don't really relate
> Calypso with Jamaicans. I don't relate, yeah they listen to it they all listen to it. But
> it's just not the first thing that comes to mind.

Or as another student whose heritage is in the Caribbean region indicated:

> **Mirelle:** Reggae [pause] I would say mostly Jamaican, I would associate it with Ja-
> maica. I would listen to it. Mostly reggae I think about Jamaicans. And I think ca-
> lypso or soca with somewhere like Trinidad. Like with smaller islands like Trinidad.
> The small islands I would say.

Although reggae was presented as a popular genre of music, there were also demarcations in musical choices made between Jamaica and other Caribbean islands.
In some cases, a strong adherence to genres of island music other than reggae was

used as a marker, serving the dual purpose of indicating nonalignment with Jamaica as well as an alignment with "small islands." Thus, some students who wanted to maintain a distinction between themselves and the island of Jamaica aligned themselves more specifically with music such as soca and calypso from the "small islands." Such musical choices were also an opportunity to reinforce parental heritage and culture from these other countries and islands. Etta identifies how she makes this distinction. For her, the affiliation with calypso was also a way of marking difference from the "large island"—Jamaica:

> **Etta:** You know what? I think half the reason why I only like calypso is because calypso identifies more with the small islands.

While some of the above narratives position reggae as more pleasurable in terms of beat, other aspects of its construction make its adoption by all black students problematic. In comparing reggae to rap, the latter was regarded as a more uniformly accessible form of music in comparison to the more heavily patois-laden reggae. As discussed above, the dance hall reggae that has become popular over the past decade offers more dense lyrics than the inspirational "reggae" associated with Bob Marley. The following narratives illustrate the ways in which the discourse surrounding Bob Marley has placed his music within a different cultural space to that of recent subgenres:

> **Doreen:** He is a good singer. Lots of people like Bob Marley too . . . but he doesn't sing . . . like in the dance hall, you know those dance hall reggae? //Oh? // That's [Marley] just so deep and it's made just for the parties, and then there is reggae, they've got some reggae that's like Christian . . . yeah [pause] like . . . some circle people, and they have reggae that's like for religious things. Then they have reggae that's just for like dance hall like for youth, you know. Just to make them "go off" and like have fun at parties and stuff. And that's the reggae I like . . . like that one that you can "go off." 'Cuz it just gets you hyped whatever right. But Bob Marley [pause] he sings like good songs and he isn't singing it like where you cannot understand you know. He sings like regular [pause] you could sing along with. I like him though.

Doreen's narrative illustrates a positioning of dancehall reggae that identifies it with the descriptor "youth" rather than "adult," present rather than past, and further illustrates the ways in which pleasure intersects receptivity.

Reception of dancehall reggae by the wider group of black students was further complicated by language use. In particular, for students whose families were not from Jamaica or the Caribbean, translating the cryptic patois used in dancehall reggae songs was at times difficult. However, some were able to overcome this difficulty if they had access to friends who were familiar with patois and could translate the lyrics:

**Omar:** I am not Jamaican. So I just listen to the songs. I can't even understand what they are saying. //yeah// But I like the way it sound; you want to move, you want to dance to it and things like that. I can relate more to . . . like r&b than I can to reggae.

**J:** How is that?

**Omar:** Reggae will be harder. It's just that I can't understand what they are saying!

**J:** Because of the patois?

**Omar:** Yeah, I don't know what they are saying? I got like, I got, I wouldn't say a lot, but I have enough Jamaican friends to understand some of it. Like if they are talking like I know, I know for sure that there is one reggae song that I know all the words to. And then pretty much the rest of them I can't even hear anything.

Or another student whose heritage is in North America and the continent of Africa:

**Merle:** Probably 'cuz I have quite a few Jamaican friends. So they speak round me then I am like really? So I start to understand it. But my brother and my sister they know it like [pause] they know it. Like sometimes I will be like, "what?," and they will know what they are saying. Like my brother is really good. And he can put on the voice and everything.

Or Frank, whose heritage is in North America:

**Frank:** Oh, I've heard it. I can't understand it so I don't listen to. They always make fun of me. "Hey you can't understand that either," dong, dong dong, that's what it sounds like.

**J:** Do you listen to regular reggae? //No// You don't do that either?

**Frank:** Well I like it but I just don't, I can't understand it. If I am listening, I am listening to the beat or trying to get a word out of it. "I heard that one!"

Although the above two narratives highlight how the patois used in reggae is not received uniformly, and tends to fragment any perceived sense of homogenous black cultural formation; nonetheless social interaction that takes place among the students still provides opportunity for developing a sense of collectivity around musical choices as friends from the Caribbean act as cultural translators.

## Summary

This chapter has analyzed the ways in which the students orient themselves in relation to a collective black identity. This identification as black is accomplished in various ways through understanding the self in relation to Canadian identity and in relation to other blacks in the diaspora and the African continent. There is some evidence of the development of an "outernational" consciousness—a consciousness not aligned with the boundedness of the Canadian State. For many of the students with Caribbean heritage this consciousness is one related to identification with "blackness" rather than to the continent of Africa. There is for these students with Caribbean heritage no sense of a return to an "origin" represented by Africa. Any sense of a return that is envisaged is to the last "port of call." As Gilroy (1997) observes, "the memories of slavery are hard to maintain when the rupture of immigration intervenes" (p. 336). It is a Caribbean "culture" that they align themselves with and which they see as giving meaning to their identity. They make use of musical formations such as reggae, calypso, and soca in order to identify more closely with the Caribbean.

The narratives highlight how construction of a black group identity is shaped by media culture in general and more specifically by a hegemonic United States culture. It is worth noting that this media culture is referenced by the descriptor "youth." This United States youth culture constructs symbols that the students then have available for collective and individual identity formation. Youth culture provides an avenue through which students with heritage from the continent of Africa, the Caribbean, and North America can communicate. Using this conception of youth culture, the next chapter will analyze the students' narratives to ascertain if and how African-Canadian students receive United States hip-hop cultural products such as music. Overall, the narratives highlight discourses and discursive practices that would support Hall's postulation of "the end of the innocent black subject" (1996a).

# CHAPTER 3

# Music and Regimes
# of Representation

*In a mass-mediated image culture, it is representations that help constitute*
*an individual's view of the world, sense of personal identity and gender,*
*laying out of style and lifestyle.*
KELLNER, 1995, p. 60

## Introduction

In this and the three following data chapters, indication is given of how representation works intertextually to contour meaning through racialized regimes of
representation (Hall, 1997). By highlighting "regimes of representation," what
Stuart Hall (1997) identifies as the "the whole repertoire of imagery and visual effects through which 'difference' is represented at any one historical moment,"
(p. 232) one can identify how representations of blackness gain meaning when they
are read in context against or in connection with other media forms. Such representations offer students a potential source for identification as well as for the production of cultural forms and knowledge. Within the data chapters questions of receptivity are posed as to how the students receive youth cultural forms, and how these
forms intersect gender, economic status, sexuality, and parental authority.

The chapters also illustrate the ways in which the students are constructed
through what Foucault would identify as "truth effects." Issues of power and knowledge are implicated in the production of these regimes of truth. Identities are produced through certain discourses that enable and constrain who can say what and in
what circumstances. According to Foucault, "knowledge is produced and constituted at the particular sites where localized power discourse prevails." So it is that
through discourse only some students can be allowed to take on certain identities;

only specific students can be viewed as "authentic." That rappers are located within specific geographic locales seems to be especially important as consumption of United States products reveals the intersection between the local, the national, and the global.

As indicated in Chapter 2, American youth culture is seen as a primary source of identification—as the very blackest culture—the one that provides the measure by which all others can be evaluated (Gilroy, 2000, p. 181). It is this identification with black American youth culture that is at the forefront of analysis in this chapter and the following two chapters. I try to indicate the various ways in which media contour understandings of black identity as represented by and through youth culture. This latter exploration takes place via an analysis of the student' narratives in relation to youth cultural texts such as films, music, and music videos that are consumed. Of import is this distancing between the site of production and consumption of rap, what Giddens (1984) identifies as "space-distanciation." As well, the three data chapters identify how representation works intertextually to contour meaning via regimes of representation. Such representations offer students a potential source for identification as well as for the production and reproduction of cultural forms. Questions of receptivity are posed as to how the students receive youth cultural forms and how these forms intersect gender, economic status, sexuality, and parental authority.

Representations are not constructed in isolation but often work in relation to other social formations in order to develop what Stuart Hall (1997) identifies as a "regime of representation." The films that are watched, the magazines that are read, and the music that is listened to offer an insight into the ways in which students are able to create meanings from the varying media representations that they encounter. In speaking more specifically of music, Negus (1996) indicates the importance of such cultural forms when he suggests that a "sense of identity is created out of and across the processes whereby people are connected together through and with music" (p. 133). In a similar way, Negus's postulation concerning social connections can be extended into the areas of magazine consumption, television viewing, and adoption of dress styles.

In particular, highlighting media forms allows access to the accumulation of meaning across these forms of representations. By examining these dominant forms of media culture, we are able to identify how at this specific historical period, such a racialized regime of representation enables the consistent production and reproduction of a form of hypermasculine blackness.

This chapter draws on themes across media genres in recognition of the intertextual way that these discourses of representation are worked through by the students. It concentrates on those narratives through which the students construct musical preference. It tries to ascertain if Gerald's comment with regard to the influence of African-American culture on African Canadians (Chapter 2) is produced through other students' discourses. Concentrating on the relationship between Canada and

United States will reveal how these national formations operate as sites of production and how they shape the students' consumption of their products. All of this should tell us something about the students' identities, what they align themselves with and how.

Finally, cultural theorists have recently begun to recognize the role that pleasure plays in interpellating people into subject positions. This discursive analysis of their narratives begins with an overview of the socio-political placing of black youth culture and the hip-hop phenomenon.

*Hiphop = RAP, GRAFFITI, BREAK DANCING*

## Black Youth Culture

Over the past twenty years youth culture in general and North American black youth culture, in particular, has been dominated by the social formation of hip-hop culture. As a cultural formation, hip-hop consists of the intertextual relationships between rap, graffiti, and break dancing.[1] Although over the past few years the influence of graffiti and break dancing has waned, they were, in the early stages of this cultural phenomenon, thriving aspects of hip-hop's formation. Perkins (1996) suggests that the decline of break dancing was a consequence of corporate America's raid on hip-hop culture alongside the growth of video medium that replaced "authentic break dancers" with "'video hos,' 'fly girls' and 'fly boys'" (p. 14).

Although common sense understandings of hip-hop's origins are associated solely with the African-American community in the Bronx (New York City), its "roots" and "routes" are much more complex. As Nelson George (1998) describes the common sense myth:

> one of the prevailing assumptions about hip-hop is that it was, at some early moment, solely African-American created, owned, controlled, and consumed. It's an appealing origin myth—but the evidence just isn't there to support it. Start with who "invented" hip-hop: in its days as an evolving street culture, Latino dancers and tastemakers— later internationally known as breakers—were integral to its evolution because of the synergy between what the mobile DJs played and what excited the breakers. Also, Caribbean culture clearly informed hip-hop's Holy Trinity—Afrika Bambaataa, Grandmaster Flash, and Kool Herc. Two of them, Flash and Herc, were either born in the Caribbean or had close relatives from there. In Bam's case, non-American black music had been essential to his aesthetic. (p. 57)

Social, economic, and political factors were also at play in the United States during the early years of the cultural formation of hip-hop. Tricia Rose (1994) argues that much of this early development of hip-hop was undertaken against the backdrop of a "post-industrial city . . . that shaped their cultural terrain, access to space, materials and power"[2] (p. 34). In analyzing the narratives of the students, it becomes evident that the youth culture, as indicted in Chapter 2, consumed and produced by the students, derives primarily from the United States or is heavily influenced by the United States and hip-hop.

Bearing in mind the powerful influence of youth culture (Willis, 1990; Hebdige, 1979, 1988; Rose, 1994; Walcott, 1995) on adolescents, this dominance of U.S. cultural products is interesting when placed in a relation to a new geographic location, namely, Canada. In terms of access to representations of blackness that the students could either identify with or contest, the U.S. media would seem to exert a hegemonic hold over such conceptions in North America and the African diaspora. This dominance of the United States was alluded to either directly or indirectly in many of the narratives as illustrated here. As Gerald suggested in response to my query as to how he accounts for the dominance of U.S. media culture:

**Gerald:** 'Cuz they are number one.

**J:** Number one?

✴ **Gerald:** They are like the most powerful. All the movies, all the music, comes from there.

Gerald's comments provide a starting point for analysis as the students' narratives in relation to music and movies are highlighted to ascertain the extent to which his comments correspond with the lived experiences of the students under discussion.

### Rap Music Accessing and Reception

With the decline of break dancing and, to some extent, graffiti, rap music has come to symbolize the growth and longevity of hip-hop. At times, rap as a genre has achieved almost mythic proportions in terms of its supposed ability to cause social havoc and moral mayhem in youths in the United States and beyond. Development of groups such as the Parents Music Resource Centre (PMRC), founded by Democrat Al Gore's wife, Tipper, were important landmarks in the public construction of a "moral panic"[3] about the sexually explicit and violent nature of rap lyrics. The PMRC's subsequent 1984 victory in getting the music industry to apply sticker ratings for obscenity only served to reinforce the heightened sense of danger and possible moral corruption associated with the genre. Rap also received two other very public "outings" which helped to align it as subversive and harmful to mainstream society. The first was the public denouncement by Bill Clinton, during his presidential campaign in 1992, of female rapper Sister Souljah for "calling on black people to kill whites." Critics saw Clinton's actions as a political rather than moral indictment. For many, his response was manufactured to "reach out to the white Americans who thought the Democratic party would always cater to its highly visibly gadfly, Jesse Jackson, and the 'special interest group'—black folks—he represented"

(George, 1998, p. 173). The second "outing" was the very public trial of rap group 2 Live Crew for their misogynist and lewd lyrics on "As Nasty as They Wanna Be." Banned as obscene by a judge in Florida, the record's lyrics were defended by academic Henry Louis Gates as representative of a code of "black public knowledge." Gates argued:

> 2 Live Crew is engaged in heavy-handed parody, turning the stereotypes of black and white American culture on their heads. These young artists are acting out, to lively dance music, a parodic exaggeration of the age-old stereotypes of the oversexed black female and male. Their exuberant use of hyperbole (phantasmagoric sexual organs, for example) undermines—for anyone fluent in black cultural codes—a too literal-minded hearing of the lyrics. (Gates, 1990)

Not everyone in the African-American community welcomed Gates's pronouncements, and many criticized the underlying essentialism and sexism in his statements (hooks, 1994; Baker Jr., 1993). Nelson George in his book *Hip-hop America* challenges this public construction of rap as a socially and morally degenerate art form linked inherently and solely with the African-American community. For George (1998), rap and the wider hip-hop culture are not so alien from mainstream U.S. values. Instead, he cautions that:

> It is also essential to understand that the values that underpin much hip-hop—materialism, brand consciousness, gun iconography, and anti-intellectualism—are very much by-products of the larger American culture. Despite the "dangerous" edge of so much hip-hop culture, all of its most disturbing themes are rooted in this country's dysfunctional values. Anti-Semitism, racism, violence and sexism are hardly unique to rap stars but are the most sinister aspects of the national character. (p. xiii)

As discussed in Chapter 2, the students' repertoire of music listening ranged from soca, reggae, r&b, to rap. However, since rap has been the most dominant discourse during the 1980s and beyond, linking music and black identity in North America, this chapter highlights that specific genre as the focus of analysis. As well, within present-day Canadian society, there is an existing common sense discourse that positions rap as synonymous with black identity and considers consumption of rap music an inherent aspect of blackness and cultural formation. Thus, the students' narratives are analyzed in relation to the ways in which they access and position themselves within the various discourses surrounding the production and reception of rap music.

It is evident from the narratives that reception of rap music, as constructed by and through the discourses, is a complex entity that is filtered not only by identification with blackness, gender, and sexuality but also through the production of pleasure and access to economic resource. For those students who had part-time jobs or whose parents or caregivers are classified as being within higher socioeconomic groups, ready access to money was an important variable in the ability to purchase differing genres of music. Thus the students' ability to constantly access, purchase, and consume rap compact discs or cassette tapes was constrained by socioeconomic factors. As youths, not yet independent adults, some of the students did not have economic resources that could be diverted into purchasing music. At times this lack of resources led to creative ways to access music. The following narrative reveals one innovative way in which students are able to maintain knowledge of musical genres within their economic limits:

> **J:**  So where do you get the CDs, are they fairly available in the shops?
>
> **Gerald:**  You can buy them at any music store. But [pause] when I buy lots of my CDs, I buy them second hand. 'Cuz they are only like $6, I know the store. They have lots of CDs. So I just go through them, and I usually find a couple of CDs that I like that I pay like five bucks for. Instead of going to the store and paying fifteen. Like they might be a few months outdated, like maybe they came out a few months ago and then some one got sick of it and sold them to the store. But I usually find a couple of CDs that I like.

As well, those students whose funds were limited tended to draw on alternative social resources such as friends or siblings in order to consume or gain access to differing genres of music. Taping and sharing of music thus becomes an important mechanism for circumventing economic constraints and a way to increase music consumption. Taping of music occurred across all genres, from rap through reggae to Christian gospel. The following student describes the various ways in which music that is produced outside Canada gets disseminated across Canada:

> **Omar:**  Some people they have friends that live in . . . New York . . . where the music comes out new, and then it gets sent down here to them. And then . . . they make copies of, it and then it gets around; people hear it and you are like "Who is this?," and you find out and you go to the store and then you look for it or like on MuchMusic, even sometimes "RapCity." You listen to that and you like the song and you find out the artist. You go or, phew [pause], somebody travels somewhere and gets some new music; then they come back here and listen to it. Like it's all over the place.

Family and friends were also important sources. For Mirelle, her brother was a primary source of access to and sharing of recorded rap music:

> **Mirelle:**  I listen to rap. My brother is mostly into rap, so I pick it up from him.

Melvin's important source for access to new music was his friend [Robert]. In response to a question as to when he first encountered his favorite group of the moment, he replied:

Through my friend [Robert] . . . [Robert] had a tape, and he was playing it for me. And then I like listened to it. And I heard him and I was like "Oh he sounds bad," and so I just taped the song off of him and then I listened to it, and he had like a whole bunch of [the group's] songs. So I taped all those off of him.

Omar, Melvin, and Mirelle's narratives identify not only the complexities of gaining access to differing sources and genres of music but also the ways in which peers, family members, and others are important in mediating such reception of music. Such a social process highlights how musical tastes can, consequently, be contoured by interaction with sibling and peers. As well, such sharing provides opportunity for the development of individual aesthetic tastes that articulate with collective orientations. This process of "sharing" provides opportunities for reinforcing social interaction and exchange and increases the influence of music beyond those students who can afford to regularly purchase CDs. So for students who have siblings, the access to music is greater than would otherwise be the case. Students who had family and friends in other countries were also a source for gaining access to and expanding the listening repertoire of all students.

It is also noteworthy that the narratives reveal how consumption, i.e., liking and listening to music, does not always cohere with purchasing habits. Tricia Rose, (1994) in accounting for the greater number of rap sales to middle-class white youths in the United States, argues that "black teen rap consumers have a higher 'pass-along rate,' that is, the rate at which one purchased product is shared among consumers" (p. 8). For Etta, consumption and reception of rap music were contoured not just by sharing with siblings but also through personal preference for the visual rather than the aural repetitiveness of rap:

**Etta:** For rap I like Mase. As much as I listen to it, I don't buy a lot of CDs and tapes.
**J:** What do you buy then?
**Etta:** I don't really buy any CDs and tapes. Mainly because [my brother] buys a lot of them so I just borrow them. . . . Number two, as much as I like to listen to it. Why don't I buy a lot? Maybe it's the money. I would sooner tape it off.

There are a variety of venues through which students can access music associated with youth culture. Space and location are important in providing a structure for students to listen to rap and other musical genres. Such spaces can affect the ways in which rap music is received. The narratives indicate that hall parties and teen clubs provide such semipublic spaces where rap music can be accessed. These semipublic spaces can become sites for the expression of specific types of social formations.[4] However, as Gerald identifies, youth social venues were not fully "open" to all genres of music, and certain venues become associated with specific genres:

At a reggae party they'll just play pure reggae, but if it's just like [pause] like an average hall party . . . they will play mostly hip-hop, some reggae. Probably some r&b. Like a club [pause] they'll play [pause], depends what club. Like some clubs are different. Like Club Megamix, they play like hip-hop and reggae. And [other] different clubs that like play "techno," some rap.

Even in social spaces dominated by youths, there is a degree of censure of types of music that are perceived as appropriate and thus accessible. Social spaces become racialized at times, a process that is mediated by identification with different genres of music. Phyllis's narratives detail the ways in which even the descriptor "hall party" does not represent uniformity in musical taste and is a contested social space:

**J:**  Tell me about the music you could get at a hall party.
**Phyllis:**  It depends. Like if you are going to a black hall party, you are going to find a lot of reggae, "hip-hop" uum [pause], r&b, and stuff. But if you go to like, say, an Oriental party, you are going to hear a lot of like "techno," some rap [pause] you know like the odd reggae song that's been turned into "techno" or something. Sometimes you like it but usually it's kinda hard to mix them all together. 'Cuz like [pause] when you have a hall party, you make sure like a whole bunch of like different groups, it's like they try and play "techno," and then you get all the black kids sitting there going "Boo, shut it off, shut it off." Then they play a bunch of reggae, and then you get all the other kids going "Boo, shut it off."

Not all students were able to access youth cultural forms to the same extent and degree. While Phyllis's latter narratives might indicate the importance of a black hall party, this access was not uniform among all black students. As Mirelle illustrates, parental authority was often a factor in mediating access to different music genres available via hall parties. Here she constructs how she views hall parties:

**Mirelle:**  Actually, my mum doesn't let me go to hall parties. Only like when [pause] it wasn't even a hall party, it was my friend's birthday party she had in a hall. My mum doesn't like hall parties, because anyone comes in, there is no security, anything can happen. Alcohol can be served there, and it doesn't matter the age. 'Cuz it's in a hall or something. So my mum doesn't really like that. But she will let me go to like teen things at like clubs or something. But not too much.

In continuing her narratives, Mirelle seeks to rationalize an adherence to parental authority by representing going out as not something to be often undertaken. In this way conformity becomes rationalized as individual choice rather than an imposition of parental authority—a sense of Foucault's technologies of the self:

**Mirelle:**  I don't mind that though. 'Cuz, um, I don't like going out too much 'cuz then you don't [pause], um, you don't see the value in it. Like when I hardly went and I got to go, I'd be like, "Oh my gosh I got to go, I got to go." And I had a lot of fun. But then when you go too much, it gets boring and it's the same old thing.

*[handwritten: To what degree? In all faValies?]*

Parental authority acts as an important mediator in allowing access to music. As Merle's narratives indicate, one's age as well as the lyrics of the song are important *[handwritten: No - .]* factors in being able to access rap music in the home. In speaking of her parents she suggested that:

> **Merle:** They don't like that nasty stuff. Then again I don't really like get a lot of it. Like a lot of my own CDs they are like [pause] stuff that's clean. But like my brother, since he is older, he will get whatever he wants. And they don't really say anything. My mum is just like [pause] "don't listen to that." "Ok, mum." Just don't play it around them, that is. That's kinda bad, but it's true if you want to know the truth. [mutual laughter] Like the other day, it's funny, my brother had [pause] a CD in my room, and I was about to listen to it. Thank God I wasn't listening to it already. My mum saw the case, and it said on it "explicit lyrics." She is like "Are you listening to this?" I said, "No mum . . . of course not. I just keep these CDs [for Lynford] in my room."

Doreen's narratives, like Merle's, indicate the influence of parents and the censoring and consequent limiting of access of music for certain family members:

> **Doreen:** I like r&b, some rap is all right, but too much swears so. [pause] Oh, reggae is good too. Everybody in our house listen to the same thing. Yeah. Like my parents listen to like . . . all r&b, and my dad thinks rap is all right, and he watches it too. Like some days I come home, my dad is sitting down watching RapCity and stuff. So everybody listens to the exact same thing in our house. Like even . . . those that have swearing and stuff. As long as my brother isn't around we are allowed to play it or whatever. . . . It depends what type of music though; we can't have "mother this, mother that." But we can listen to rap, and my dad like he knows all that stuff. I don't know why; I don't know how. He just knows all of that? My mum and my dad are like singing along with the music.

## Music and Pleasure

The ways in which meaning gets represented in music are not just with regard to the content of the lyrics. The beats and combinations thereof also come to evoke pleasure and subjectivization. As John Storey (1996) argues:

> the pleasure of music is not the pleasure of the representation of something that has happened elsewhere (a reflection of meaning) but the pleasure of what is being made (the making and materiality of meaning). The pleasure and power of popular music is not in the performance emotion but in the emotion of performance. (pp. 106–7)

Social theorists suggest that in hegemonic and counter-hegemonic struggles, the production and regulation of desire are as important as the construction of meaning. The ways in which the body becomes both the subject and object of pleasure are important.

The narratives construct rap into differing subgenres such as positive, hardcore gangsta, and lovers. As Phyllis outlines:

> **Phyllis:** Wu-Tang and like [pause]; let me think here, Old Dirty Bastard. They are like hard core rap. They are kinda like hard core rap. They are like street rap kinda thing. They take like things that have happened in their lives. Like seeing their friends get shot. Or something bad happening, they take it and put it in a song, and they kind of express how they feel through the song. Then you have like LL Cool J. He is like the "lover rap" kind of thing. He goes on about "Oh yeah, I saw you at the bus stop" and this and that whatever. And he talks about girls and all that. Then in the middle you kinda have Puff Daddy where he kinda like takes, like he kinda takes his feelings from like loving someone and like feelings from like someone getting hurt.

For some students, rap lyrics were positive in the sense that they were a source of learning about self, society, and black identification. Such learning was related to the controversial use of the word "nigga" by some rappers:

> **J:** So how do you feel about that? About the use of the word?
>
> **Omar:** Like using the word "nigga?" It's almost—it's exactly what he says. They say in the song that people just use—a lot of black people just use it as like nothing. And that's the way I am too. I listened to it, I'm like, yeah, I'm like that too. We don't like pay attention to what the word is for. Like they say through the song is that we got to think about what the word was originally used for. People are like, black people now they just use it around the community like it's nothing. Like who cares, it's just a word. But they are trying to say, well, you've got to think like what was this word used for? What does it mean? Look in the dictionary, it means dumb, stupid, all those things. So that's what they are trying to say.

Students' identification with specific subgenres signifies something about the perception of self. One student indicated that for him the message in the rap song was important, and that his ability to hear a message made a distinction between himself and some of his friends:

> **Denzil:** I have a few friends, most of them they don't listen to rap the same reason that I listen to rap. The same way I listen to rap. They listen to rap because they like the music. They don't hear a message. They just hear the words. And they go, "They rhyme huh huh huh."

*(handwritten margin note: why do artos to use nigga?)*

Interestingly, Denzil's distinction between those who are able to hear the message within a rap song and those who are not was based not only on racialized understandings but was also intersected by class. The importance of conveying a message with rap was epitomized by several narratives that drew on Wu-Tang Clan as representative of a rap group that had messages within their lyrics. Nelson George (1998) reveals that:

*wutang*

[Al]though they in fact come from Staten Island, its nine members claim to belong to an ancient and secret sect searching for the thirty-sixth chamber of martial arts knowledge. While theirs is far from a coherent vision, the Wu-Tang have used their interest in Asian action movies to inject a sense of the mystical into hip hop. (George, 106)

Students who identified with Wu-Tang's lyrics were aligned with a variety of rap genres. In the following narrative, Melvin, who aligns himself with gangsta rap, identifies the rise and fall of the group:

**Melvin:** Wu-Tang? [pause] I love Wu-Tang. //Do you?// Yeah. Wu-Tang is probably the best group that came out [pause] . . . it's so sad that they went down like so quick. And the reason they did? I feel, I don't know, is because of Puff Daddy, who took away their thing. 'Cuz [pause] okay, Wu-Tang came out with 36 Chambers. And 36 Chambers is "wicked." Every MC in Wu-Tang has got some sort of different like style that like all put together sounds good, you know. Like the Riza, he is a like philosophising guy, kind of like a prophet. Method, Method talks about his own thing. Plus he has got the voice and the lyrics. Giza is like a wise guy, the only thing is like a [pause] a couple of them like //Cappadonna?// whew Cappadonna is wicked. His new CD is so. . . .

Noticeable within the narratives is the way in which the critiques of mainstream rapper Puff Daddy[5] now known as P. Diddy cohere with other discourses evident in other areas of the study. Omar, a fan of message rap, credits Wu-Tang with having "deep messages," a group that requires reflection:

**Omar:** It's like some hip-hop artist, they'll say something, and you just hear it, yeah you hear it. But then after, it takes me like a long time to understand the meaning behind it. //Right// There is like, the reason why everybody likes Wu-Tang . . . they have like [pause] like seriously deep message in their music. //Really?// Like if you pay attention to what they are saying. Like of course some of it is like what everybody is, stereotypes like "yeah they are just swearing; they are just singing all this." Some of it is true like that. But seriously, if some people took some time and listened to exactly what they are saying in the messages. It might take them a lot of time, but if they had the patience, they'd start to like it too. They'd start to appreciate it.

The way in which this student's narrative identified Wu-Tang as "open" to any racialized or social group was interesting:

> **Doreen:** They have been popular. They're like popular with every race. They are one of those groups; you know they are like popular with every race. They are like popular with like skaters, like they are popular with the heavy metal people too. I don't know how but [pause] 'cuz the music they sing. Like it mixes, like you could listen to [pause] like a party and everything, and it sounds good. But then you go to like [pause] like you could go like say [to] white people or whatever, and then you'll like hear them listening to the tune. And you are like "Holy," because the way they sing [pause] its just like . . . [pause] they sing the song [pause] for everybody, not just for black people. Some people just sing songs for black people and stuff.

Lyrics are an important part of accessing pleasure. Often this pleasure is contained not just within the words themselves but rather is evoked in the performance of the song/rap. It draws on aspects such as the "grain of the voice," the body of the voice, as it sings. As Storey (1996) suggests, "words are sounds we can feel before they are statements to understand" (p. 106). The narratives below identify how, for Melvin, the voice of the rapper "calls" him, in an almost Althusserian sense of interpellation:

> **Melvin:** His voice that caught me. Like caught me out . . . I don't know. I don't know how to explain it. It's like a child's high-pitched voice. But like [pause] the content was just different. So it's just something to do with the feelings in me. So I just listened to him. I don't see like that many people listening to it. So I kinda just like keep it to myself.

The narratives also illustrate how acquisition of the distinctive, in this case knowledge of a little-known rapper, can become a commodity increased by its scarcity. The importance of voice in evoking pleasure is not confined to rap but is also evident in the other students' responses to other genres of music. Mirelle indicates her attraction to/identification with jazz performers:

> **Mirelle:** Wynton Marsalis. I like both types. I usually like the jazz singer voice. The jazz singer voices, 'cuz they are all so full. And the way they like [pause] they'll change [pause] "double de boo bap," something like that. And it sounds nice but also when you just hear the instruments, like the saxophone or the trumpet or something. The drums are kinda nice too.

One narrative suggests that it is not only the lyrics and "grain of voice" that were the source of identification but that the appeal of differing genres was related to stages of adolescence. For Phyllis, as students got older, the ability of hardcore/gangsta rap to generate an identification faded:

**Phyllis:** I think it's just a phase. Like everybody [pause] even kids that I talk to out of junior high—now they are going through the phase where it's hard-core rap. Like killing people, and raping your girlfriend, and shooting up your mum, and this and that you know. And you get to high school and it's kinda like well, you know [pause]; that's over with. And it gets like the soft rap. Like LL Cool J and like Foxy Brown. They are kinda considered like soft rap and Jay-Z and stuff, you know. So it's kinda like a lot of people listen to that now.

## Gender

Phyllis's allusion to hard and soft rap highlights the issue of the misogyny and profanity contained and promoted by gangsta and hard-core rap musicians. Rap has been severely critiqued (hooks, 1992; George 1998) for its construction of gender relations, both in terms of its low level of support for women rappers and its use of misogynist language in hard core and gangsta rap. In terms of support for women rappers, many of the narratives indicated that women rappers were listened to and appreciated by both genders:

**Omar:** Uh! The beats and the lyrics. If it's a female rapper, and she has good beats and she has good lyrics, I'll listen to her. If she doesn't, I won't listen to her. I don't really care.

**J:** What about lyrics?

**Omar:** What makes good lyrics? Like, a lot of the things. What you say, the way it sounds, the way you present it, the way it flows. Like if it flows with the beats, then it sounds good. But if you, like, if the beat is going one way and you are singing another . . . then I can't stand it. That's basically it on female rappers.

A variety of female rappers were identified, especially Da Brat, Yo Yo, Missy Elliott, Queen Latifah, Mis Pen, Mia X, Salt-N-Pepa. The students' narratives reveal a complex positioning in terms of the ways in which gender is constructed and represented in rap music and videos. Women rappers are identified as often constructing their rap in relation to male rappers' lyrics, i.e., addressing their misogyny. As Omar's narrative indicates, when discussing Queen Latifah:

**Omar:** Queen Latifah, she is like [pause] the last CD I have of hers she is just basically, like, she was just talking about how she doesn't like it when, I don't know, the same situation when guys are talking about girls. It's just like she is talking about guys. In the way she, her perspective. And that's basically all it was about. I didn't see too much outside of that. She had a song about a guy where she was talking about a guy who was cheating on her. She had a song where she was talking about a guy who went [pause] who went too far trying to impress her. She had a song where she had [pause] she was talking about a guy who was like [pause] disrespecting her.

Other women rappers were identified with trying to outdo gangsta rappers by adopting a "bad girl" attitude based on explicit sex. Nelson George (1998) suggests that:

> Foxy Brown and Lil' Kim took Salt-N-Pepa's formula, made it more explicit, dropped in designer reference (Foxy favours Dolce & Gabbana, Kim sports Versace), and sold themselves as aggressive sex objects of desire. Whether they sell themselves as sex kittens or demanding lovers, the truth is neither of these MCs has truly explored in her music the complexity of being a young black woman in the 90s—certainly not with the nuance or insight the subject demands. (p. 185)

However, various social relations intersected this projection and reception of sexually explicit lyrics. One young male explains his listening preferences:

> **Gerald:** I don't really listen to her too much, but whenever I hear [pause] she is always like rapping about sex. [pause] Every time, that's all she ever raps about. Like every time I've heard her.
> **J:** What about Foxy Brown?
> **Gerald:** I've listened to her, but I don't really like her either. //Right// I think she is like the same as Lil' Kim.
> **J:** So you are not interested in sex?
> **Gerald:** No. That's all they rap about. Like that's like their whole concept. Just that.
> **J:** Whereas other rappers?
> **Gerald:** Yeah, like they could have that too, but like it's not all they will rap about. But for those two, that's like all I ever hear them rapping them about.

In comparing Lil' Kim with Queen Latifah, Mirelle indicates that the difference is based on respect:

> **Mirelle:** No. I think they are different. Queen Latifah has more respect. And then Lil' Kim is . . . not as [pause] she doesn't show respect. Well maybe she like [pause]. In her lyrics it's not respect. [laugh]

Similarly, Joy compares Lil' Kim with other women rappers in terms of lyrics:

> **Joy:** They are not as nasty. Like Queen Latifah, usually doesn't talk, kinda like that. MC Lyte, it kinda goes MC Lyte is not bad at all, I don't think. Sometimes she can be nasty, like swear and stuff. But she is not nearly as bad as like Lil' Kim. It's not always about sex, sex, sex. And same with Yoyo. Yoyo is usually like, she likes like a party scene, like dancing. That's what she will talk about and stuff, but not. . . .

For another student, Lil' Kim was again seen as a rapper whose lyrics were "nasty" and limited to rhyming about sex:

**J:** You said her lyrics were nasty? What do you mean by nasty? What does she rap about?

**Omar:** She is like, she is pure like, you can tell a hundred percent of her mind is on sex. //Oh right// And . . . money too. She likes money. So [pause] you put those two together and you start talking about that, after a while you get nasty. That's the way she is.

**J:** When you say nasty, you mean? Explain a bit more to me.

**Omar:** You just imagine what she is saying. You are like "Oh, oh what is that?" You know, like she'll say something and you'll imagine it and you'll be, "Ow." That's sick.

For Melvin, Lil' Kim compared unfavorably with another female gangsta rapper, Mia X, not just in terms of lyrics. He draws on gendered discourse to link creativity and physical appearance:

**Melvin:** Mia X from No Limit. And she is like pretty much a female gangsta rap artist. And she talks about like being like pretty much down with like whatever. Like her crew is going to do. So like she is like a female [pause]. Like Lil' Kim goes off on that a little bit too, but like [pause] it's more overpowering like. The less attractive the rapper is, like that female rapper, the better their lyrics are. So that's what happens.

These narratives indicate the ways in which gendered discourses are used in order to present a norm against which Lil' Kim is constructed as outside the norm. It is also interesting the way that some of these young men, in particular, listen to gangsta rap yet do not see it as particularly "nasty."

Reception of gangsta lyrics varied not just on the basis of gender but also in terms of religiosity. Such use of misogynist lyrics in gangsta and hard-core lyrics emerges as a point of tension within the narratives. For Langston, use of such terms as "bitch" is acceptable because it reflects women who exist outside their constructions in rap records:

**Langston:** Okay, like there is this song by Tupac [pause] like the title of the song is "Wonder Why They Call You Bitch?" You hear that and you think it's probably some derogatory term, derogatory rap about women. . . . But in this rap he talks about a friend. Like this girl is his friend, and she is the kind of girl that you know sleeps around. Like the song is "Do you wonder why they call you bitch? It's because you sleep around so much. All you ever think about is money—you try to get romantic to get their money. And that's why they call you bitch." That's what the song is about. I think that's enlightening. It is true; it's sad but it is true.

**J:** You think it is true!

**Langston:** No, like some women are like that you know.

**J:** Have you met any women like that? //Yeah!// Have you? //Yeah// Where have you met those?

**Langston:** Everywhere, they are everywhere . . . I know a couple. Like a friend of mine, what's his name? [Jo] right. Like this girl came into his house, like she is a friend of a friend. She came to his house and stole like, she robbed him blind. She took his pager, took his money, ran away. What are you going to refer to that woman as? Like I have a friend [John], like he was with a girl who openly confessed that she is only there for his money. Like I know a couple of girls who have sex like every day. Like girls like that—what could you call them?

Within the women's narratives, such misogynist terms and profanities were not as acceptable. The following young woman indicates why she positioned *Old Dirty Bastard* as unacceptable:

**J:** So what is it about Old Dirty Bastard that makes him hard core?

**Eulyn:** Um, he swears like every second word. //Oh really// Just some of the things he talks about. It seems pointless. You know already. You don't need to—you know.

**J:** Really what sort of things?

**Eulyn:** Like basically the stuff that happens in the States, about all the killings and gangs and all that kind of stuff.

**J:** And you think you know all about that all ready. //Mmuph// How do you know all about that then?

**Eulyn:** 'Cuz it's everywhere, you know. It's in the movies, it's on the TV.

The result, within the narratives, seems to be a contouring of the reception of rap genres that students identify with. This descriptor, in general, was associated with love as well as women. Langston positions himself as not particularly liking "soft" music, such as the Blackstreet, because of its perceived repetitiveness:

**Langston:** There's a lot of love going about. So [pause] it's nothing new. . . . It's just the same old, same old. Like a good song but [pause] just [pause] it's not that I am prejudiced against "soft music." Soft music is good. But everybody does it. What sparks my interest is what is different.

On a continuum defined by "hard rap" at one end and "soft rap" at the other, Will Smith consistently occupied the "soft" category of rap. As such, he was more acceptable to some students who wanted to dissociate themselves from harder forms of rap that consist of swearing and disrespect of women. As a choice in terms of rappers, the narratives below give an example of the ways in which he was positioned by some of the young women. As indicated in Eulyn's narrative above, there was little new to discover in ODB's music. It was predictable. In contrast, Eulyn and other young women viewed Will Smith much more favorably:

**Eulyn:** He is different from everybody else. He is old style. And he has even said himself that he doesn't like to, [pause] he doesn't like the way, um, other rappers demean their own women and stuff like that, so he doesn't [pause] do things like that.

*Beats in Music*

Originally, hip-hop consisted of the beats created by the DJ, before the addition of an MC rapper on mike. In relation to the study, the narratives reveal that while beat is important, students also indicate a need for variety. This beat is still important in helping students differentiate between different genres of music. Perkins identifies three waves of hip-hop that have washed over North America. The first wave is related to the initial growth of hip-hop, when the beat was most important. Break dancers filled in at the beat break in the records, while the MC talked into the mike. Groups such a Kurtis Blow and the Furious Five and Afrika Bambaataa are the most noted here. The second wave of rap can be pinned to the early 1980s. Perkins (1996) suggests that:

> the new personalities of the second wave—Run-DMC, L. L. Cool J, and Kool Moe Dee and Big Daddy Kane—epitomised a combination of street style and musical minimalism. More than any other single group or force, Run-D.M.C. catapulted rap into the mainstream. (p. 15)

Although Run-D.M.C. became the biggest crossover into the mainstream, they were also a band whose merger of "black urban street sound and slick pop overlay" was aligned as much with rock music as any other form of music. Nelson George (1998), in tracing the group's lineage, suggested that:

> Starting with "Rock Box" produced by Simmons with Larry Smith, Run-D.M.C. was promoted as a rock band.[6] There was a rebellious, nonconformist attitude in rap that Russell saw as analogous to the rock attitude he experienced hanging out at punk clubs like the Mudd Club, Hurrah's, and the Peppermint Lounge in Manhattan. (p. 65)

Perkins's third wave encompasses the growth of gangsta rap, which has come to eclipse more political message rap.

At times, the beats can make a difference in terms of reception. In the following narrative, Omar positions Tribe Called Quest as preferable to Wu-Tang:

**J:** Oh right. So what makes a Tribe Called Quest your favourite, where as Wu-Tang you appreciate but they are not necessarily your favourite?

**Omar:** They have every thing. With Wu-Tang, I like what they are saying, but sometimes the beats that they have, I don't know, I don't really like them that much. Or I don't like them, but after a while you are like "Eh, this is not bad." But when its Tribe Called Quest, pretty much everything they have ever put out I've liked. I like the beats, the lyrics, like they don't, like Tribe Called Quest is like one of the actual few groups that never talks about . . . being hard core and violent. //Not gangsta?// They are strictly positive. They are completely far away from being gangsta. They are just strictly spiritual.

Several students, primarily females with Caribbean heritage, indicated that they preferred the beat of reggae or calypso to that of rap, the main advantage being that one could move one's body to the beat. This differentiation may be due to the sample chosen, in that for many of the women, in contrast to the young men, the Caribbean was their geographic area of alignment. In the following narrative, Mirelle indicates a rationale for her preference:

**J:** So why would you prefer calypso over rap?

**Mirelle:** Calypso is more [pause] enjoyable to listen to. More dancey. . . . You can't dance to rap. Rap is more you bob your head. And you just shake your shoulder, like you move, you don't really dance and stuff.

**J:** So with calypso then?

**Mirelle:** You can like move your body, relax, dance. It's more [pause] . . . I could move more to it.

As indicated by the narratives, the beats, lyrics, and grain of voice can evoke pleasure in the listener, and at times, this pleasure seems heightened when all components come together. This coming together with heightened pleasure was captured in the students' narratives by the phrase "going off." For those moments of collective behavior, the "plaisir" and enjoyment can be seen as linked to the ways in which one shares an emotional experience. Melvin describes the sense of pleasure that going off entails:

**Melvin:** I can't say I really feel like any thing. 'Cuz music doesn't affect me that much. It makes me feel happy. If I hear like some guy with a good beat and then like [pause] I like the lyrics, "I go off" and then his voice, it's just like gets me excited, and I like get all hyperactive and stuff.

Repeated across the narratives, the phrase "going off" was used in a variety of settings. The metaphor "going off" is used in a variety of ways to describe and explain the emotional elements attached to listening to music. Often going off was experienced in relation to others, in a dancehall, but it could also be experienced while listening alone on a headset. It also implies a way of acting that is reliant upon previous knowledge and experience of a song. In some ways, it implies a social knowledge and familiarity that can lead to heightened pleasure. In fact the latter reinforces recent poststructuralist literature (Gilroy, 2000; Foucault, 1984; Butler, 1993), wherein the body has been identified as a site of meaning, as a form of language that plays a role in the politics of representation. The way in which the body interacts with the sound of music comes to be represented as a sign of pleasure or displeasure.

Doreen's narratives indicate that going off can be a collective as well as individual experience. Here, going off is a sign of collective appreciation:

**J:** I notice that when they touch the floor, people go "Eeh." Or cheer or something. Why is that?

**Doreen:** You know, because it just looks good [pause] right. Like when you touch the floor and stuff . . . I think it gets into it more. I know when I was in my dance group everybody would always "go off" when you touch the floor. It's just a thing in videos; [pause] you see them in videos.

Another student also identifies the collective social element in going off.

**J:** What sort of songs do you think that people "go off" to?

**Mirelle:** Songs that are common that everybody knows or they have heard before. Like when they heard it before it's more, it clicks with them, "that's my song." To me, if it's a new tune that I don't really know, I have to catch the tune. Then I can pick up the beat and dance to it. But songs that I usually hear then I'd be like "I know that song. And I can "go off."

For Omar, it was one specific song in particular that was able to conjure up the process of going off:

**Omar:** Uuh [pause] Ok it's like there's this Mobb Deep song. It's just like [pause] I like the way everything goes. The beats and the lyrics and the way like everything is put together [pause] I just like it. Every time I listen to it. I just like you know, like I have to sing to it type of thing like that. That's one of them. Just like, I don't know. The way everything just comes together in the song it makes like you know. You know how some songs you like 'em because the beat is good. And some songs you appreciate, because the lyrics they are like you know, they make you think. And when those two come together, you just like go off.

Going off crosses genres from rap to reggae to soca. The following narrative describes in detail how specific songs that are known create this sense of exuberance when listening to reggae:

**J:** So give me an example of a reggae group or a reggae song that you can go off to.

**Doreen:** 007. [laugh] "Who am I?"

**J:** Who am I? Who performs that?

**Doreen:** Bounty Killa [pause] No! It's Beenie Man, Beenie Man.

**J:** And you really like that? What is it that gets you off then?

**Doreen:** Oh my goodness. Okay. Now I started talking about that song, I want to hear it. No that song, it's just the how the DJ like [pause] mixes the [pause] mixes the tape, and then everybody knows what's coming on. Right. 'Cuz how the bass starts off. 'Cuz everybody is like "Whoa." Everybody just jumps on the floor with their bandanna in their hand, and then they start swaying it. Like it gets you hyped. Whenever like [pause] you know what song hypes up people when it's calypso. [pause] Big Truck. Have you heard it?

## Discourses of the Real

The narratives indicate a discourse which positions genuine rap as based upon "real" experiences in life and, therefore, more "authentic" than mainstream rap, which is based upon fantasy—a genre that is geared to a mainstream market and is produced purely for sales. It is evident that there is an ideological struggle going here with regard to the production of "truth." The latter is illustrated in the following narrative that creates a binary between mainstream rap and authentic rap:

> **Eulyn:** But there is the other mainstream rap that's just out there to sell. . . . They rap about something which nobody has ever experienced in their life. They'll say something like, "Oh, I have a car that I blew up yesterday." Yeah, they just talk about unrealistic things; you know they talk about things that people want to hear. Like "Oh I have so many women in my house . . . I drink champagne. I make this amount of money; I wear Rolexes; I wear big gold chains," you know. They talk about stuff like that. Everybody wants to hear oh everybody is kinda crazy about this Hollywood thing. And that's what commercial rap is. The mainstream stuff, that's the kind of thing that you hear everyday.
>
> **J:** And "true" rap?
>
> **Langston:** True rap is just [pause] the expression of one's self. You express yourself, your life. Many, many artists would say that rap is the greatest form of self-expression. It is the one form, the one form of music that the artist [pause] in every song in his album is telling you about his personal experiences.

This construction of rap is also seen in Tricia Rose's argument that "rappers speak with the voice of personal experience, taking on the identity of the observer or narrator" (1994, p. 2). For another student, the understanding of the "real" seems to cohere with the above student's interpretation of what is "true" rap in that it deals with personal experiences. This linking of the real and true in order to elevate certain forms of rap can also be seen in dominant discourses of rap in the United States. Perkins (1996) argues that:

> within the daily street reality of urban culture, black and Latino youth practice the value system of being "true to the game." Being "real" and true revolve around the concept of authenticity, not fakery. Public Enemy's rap "Don't Believe the Hype" celebrates the essence of being "real": "the book of the New School rap game/ Writers treat me like Coltrane insane / Yes to them, but to me I am a different kind /We're brothers of the same mind /unblind." (p. 35)

It is this ability to draw on personal experiences that makes the rap song more credible:

**J:** What is it you like about Master P?

**Frank:** He has a really good style to it. How he goes, he says stuff that can be related to real life. Like from previous experiences and stuff. He just got a new album out called "Master P., The Lie Is Done." He is in the new Source. He is the feature article in the new Source.

When asked to be more specific on what he saw as "real," Frank indicated that:

**Frank:** He used to be like a drug dealer. And a gangbanger, and one of his brothers died, got killed. So a lot of his songs are always about his brother and how his brother died.

Realism was seen as something that could be verified by comparison with the material world:

**J:** Can you? So what about the violence then?

**Omar:** Sometimes it goes too far, but when you, when you put it down to scale, it's like "Yeah, that happens." That type of stuff happens. Somebody is like, somebody goes, loses control over some'et that's stupid like you know, like money. Like when last year Marcus got shot over [pause] tracksuits or whatever the hell it was, it was like stupid. And so there is violence here. And some of the other stuff they talk about. Like girls talking about guys and guys talking about girls, you are like "yeah" that happens.

**J:** So it relates to your everyday life.

**Omar:** Like me, it's not every day. But I know people who do have that everyday life.

This understanding of realism is akin to John Storey's (1996) concept of empiricist realism whereby "a text is considered realist to the extent it adequately reflects that which exists outside itself" (p. 18). Again a struggle to produce "truth" and consequent power effect is evident.

### Old school vs. New school

Rapping can be viewed as a form of storytelling that makes use of rhyming and rhythm to produce narratives, often about personal accomplishments. Originally, such formations were based in the 1970s and early 1980s on raps and rhymes that were backed by musical samples to enhance their appeal at parties and community venues. The sound and construction of rap is very different at the turn of the 21st century. As with all cultural formations, rap has adopted and adapted itself over the years so that as we enter the twenty-first century, a uniform definition of this social phenomenon becomes problematic. William E. Perkins suggests that there are three waves to hip-hop and that within those waves various subgenres can be identified. This periodization of rap appears within the students' narratives as a space of contestation that allows them to position themselves in relation to discourses that surround the descriptors "old school" or "mainstream rap." Such dualism becomes symbolic as the students negotiate meanings in relation to the "real."

Further, it is no surprise to find that within the student narratives, rap is represented as anything but a homogenous genre, revealing instead a variety of subgenres that are important in terms of contouring subjectivity and identities. In line with this reading of rap as complex, Wesband (1995, p. 413) indicates five genres of rap that are drawn on in our analysis of the students' narratives:

> i) *gangsta*—machismo in orientation and includes gang violence drugs and the mistreatment and abuse of women often with explicit or sexual lyrics [e.g., Snoop and Ice T] heavy base is prominent; ii) *hardcore*—focuses on serious political messages aimed at the black community as a whole [Public Enemy]; iii) *reggae rap*—*ragga or Jamaican raga*—distinctive reggae style beat and rhythm with the lyrics spoken rather than sung [Snow]; iv) *female rap*—female vocalist emphasising gender solidarity and/or power over men. Strong beat, heavy bass [Salt N Pepa]; v) *East Coast or Daisy Age rap*—used to describe music of *De La Soul*—mellow sound drawing on Doo Wop, 1960s Soul and Funk. [*PMDawn, A Tribe Called Quest*]

These five genres, while not definitve, indicate the complexity of rap music and undermine any attempt to view it as homogeneous. Further, this complexity continues into the lives of the students as they identify with aspects of different genres in the construction of subjectivities—alignments that allow them to say something about themselves.

As Rose (1994) argues, rap draws its energy from the rapper's personal style, skilful use of words, and a reading of multiple social contexts. It also needs to tell a story to have a narrative thread. With the narratives, the issue of realism emerges as important and affects the positioning of self in relation to such a discourse (George, 1998). Lyrics come to define genres of rap so that some forms of rap become constructed as message rap (Wu-Tang) gangsta rap (Snoop), and political rap (Public Enemy).

In making distinction between the lyrics of gangsta rap and P. Diddy's more "playa"-oriented lyrics, Melvin constructs the following narratives. For him gangsta rap involves:

> **Melvin:** They like expand their stuff to a whole like different areas that they do. [pause] Like the building and, I don't know, whatever drug they are slanging. About just plain old thugging, like going out and doing whatever, and yeah, they talk about the money they make. And they talk about like um like killing off women

and doing this nonsense and that. And, er, like pretty much that's how it goes. But like Puff Daddy and them. They talk about lots to a certain extent only to sound like they are hard you know . . . but pretty much it's just about money and the girls.

Periodization was also drawn on in order to compare the past with the present and thus define the "real." Using this process of differentiation, the "past" was used to represent an ideal that is then posited in contrast to the "present." Positioning rap styles of the "past" and "present" as binary opposites thus allows present-day rap to be represented as "the other" and thus outside the boundaries of the self. For the following student, rap was not an attractive genre and was no longer "real" when compared to an earlier era of rap music production. For him, the subject position of Christian contests a reading of present-day rap lyrics as "respectful" and congruent with his own life experiences. It is not a source with which he could identify or draw inspiration. For him, present-day rap is a "fantasy":

> **Wayne:** I don't really get it. Some of the times I can't even hear what they are saying. Like most of their words are not . . . it doesn't encourage you; it doesn't do you no good whatever. Like MC Hammer, MC Hammer was a more respectful rapper because he raps reality and stuff. But those boys are just going on with their foolishness.

Ironically, this latter alignment of the "real" with MC Hammer goes against the grain of other narratives that position Hammer's commercially successful songs as "soft rap" and therefore "unreal." Rap critic Ernest Allen Perkins (1996) suggests that the "Hammer style might be compared to painting by number—a how-to formula lacking creativity, originality and spontaneity" (p. 38).

At times periodization and genre become intertwined with discourses of reality and commodification. The narratives suggest that the tension between "rap as reality" and "rap as a commodity" is being played out symbolically via the persona of Sean (Puff Daddy) Combs. In what can be seen as a classic discourse, i.e., strongly bounded statement that constructs ways of understanding and being, Puff Daddy, more than others, is constructed as symbolic of rap's move towards the mainstream via his recycled hits. Such a discourse of blame can be traced not just in the students' narratives but also in the magazines that they read, such as *The Source*, as well as more recently in general newspaper articles.[7] It might be that Puffy was the "crossover" into mainstream and as such did for capitalism what whites could not do—since their "aura" of authenticity was always debatable.

In the following narrative, the student identifies his alignment with the "old school," and assigns Puff Daddy as "new" rap. When asked which kind of rappers he likes, he gives the following response:

**Denzil:** All kind of rappers. Wu-Tang is like my foundation. I like West Side Connection. They also have good, [pause] they flow well and everything. KRS -One. All the older, all the old school guys. Cool Moe Dee, Curtis Blow, and all those guys, they are all "old school."

**J:** Who are the new school?

**Denzil:** Puff Daddy.

For another student, it was Puff Daddy's lyrics that were seen as lacking in realism and concentrating purely on his material possessions in contrast to a rapper such as Master P.:[8]

**Frank:** Lot of rappers rap about [pause] just whatever, and it doesn't appeal to me like, "Oh yeah. same o, same o." Like Puff Daddy and them, I like them, but all they rap about practically is how much money they have, what kind of cars they drive, it's like "who cares?"

**J:** So why is that not interesting for you? 'Cuz is that not what he has?

**Frank:** Well, it is interesting to me a little bit, but I don't find it as [pause] as I don't like it as much as I like Master P.'s I guess.

**J:** Does Master P., just talk about himself or does. . . .

**Frank:** He talks about everything, black people.

At times Puff Daddy's beats were also challenged in the students' narratives:

It's the same with Puff Daddy //Puff Daddy?// Well about the beats thing—just like how he takes like hits from the '80s and makes it sound so crazy and like takes like old school beats that like everyone like heard before and then like . . . a lot of like nostalgia like . . . and all this nonsense, and people start reminiscing and like listening to the beats again. That's all he does is making money off of recycled beats.

### Rap as Commodity

Discourses of commodification that emerge within the narratives highlight the ways in which blackness as a signifier articulates with a wider capitalist economic structure to produce racialized meanings in relation to rap. Keith Negus (1996) argues that music production and consumption is a business based upon a profit margin, and should be understood as a commercial enterprise driven by the profit margin (p. 37). Thus, any understanding of rap music has to take into account that music production is not purely a matter of aesthetics. It becomes part of a wider capitalist production, something to make money from. As such, production of rap becomes intertwined with racialized and aesthetic meanings that lead to positioning on issues that might, on the surface, be perceived as not related. Interestingly, a positioning of selves in relation to discourses of appropriation and commodification took place primarily in relation to rap. Few of the narratives reveal a critique of the ways in which other genres of black-identified music, such as reggae, jazz, or r&b, have been commodified by corporate capitalism. Nelson George, African-American music critic, argues that:

> white-dominated industry has instituted the conglomerate control of black music and that the pressure to "crossover" . . . has forced performers to modify their music to become acceptable to white audiences. This crossover is at times perceived as weakening the links of African American rappers with their authentic musical selves. (1998)

It is through this linking of blackness and authenticity that hip-hop and rap have been able to capture the sign of blackness as fixed. As hooks (1992) argues, a host of black men in the public domain "blindly exploit the commodification of blackness and the concomitant exotification of phallocentric black masculinity" (p. 102).

At times, discourses of commodification articulate discourses of realism to position rappers as "real" or not. For the following student, the issues of commodification are played out across the physical bodies of rap artists. Thus discourses on biology and aesthetics become intertwined and racialized so that subjection of the student to such discourses produces the social effect of constraining his listening choices. In this case, he finds it difficult to listen to rap music produced by a white artist. In response to a direct question as to whether white people rapping was a way of sharing culture, the following narratives emerged:

**Frank:** It's not sharing it really, but it's trying to. But people just don't allow it. They won't accept it. Most people won't //You don't think so?// No. Like remember when Vanilla Ice came out, he was all popular. When people find out he is white, everybody is like "oh" [subdued], then they stopped talking. I used to sing him all the time, and finally I stopped rapping him. And that's how it was.

Again, Frank's analysis identifies Vanilla Ice[9] as non-black and, therefore, not authentic/not real. The narratives also indicate the ways in which social pressure and other discursive practices can operate to discipline the subject within a specific discourse. As an example of the public discourse surrounding the acceptability of Vanilla Ice as a rapper, we can note the following rap penned by Del Tha Funkee Homosapien in response to "Ice" mania. "Ice is cool, but I can't stand Vanilla/Because he takes a style and tries to mock it/Ain't nuthin' personal G/But I am kinda into chocolate" (Perkins, 1996, p. 36). In questioning Frank more closely, he drew on an economic discourse with traces of Black Nationalism to highlight the material position of blacks as an economically disadvantaged group and therefore in need of support:

**J:** So what is it that makes a black rapper different from a white rapper?

**Frank:** I guess 'cuz you are like trying to support him and you be like [pause] I guess you feel that could be an opportunity for a black person to have a good position or get some money or something or something. But when you see it's a white person, your whole perspective just changes, I don't know why. //Oh really? // I don't know why. But I remember. I'd be embarrassed to sing and dance after I found that Vanilla Ice was white.

For Frank, rap is a symbolic form that has what John Thompson (1990) defines as economic value, " the value that symbolic forms acquire by virtue of being offered for exchange in a market." Thompson continues, "when symbolic forms are subjected to economic valorisation, they become commodities . . . symbolic goods which can be bought, sold or otherwise exchanged in a market" (p. 13). In this instance, the rappers can be perceived as selling "reality"—their experiences of poverty and violence. This ability to commodify experiences can also be seen in the ways in which it is easier for some bodies to be accepted as authentic rappers, while others are not. The following narratives identify how, for Omar, listening to and identifying with white rappers is a complex process that illustrates the economic intersections of race and class with political and economic unity. For him, this process of commodification was racialized with the definition of "authentic" black musical styles tied into "exchange value" within the larger white community. For Omar, a rapper's experiences are an economic commodity that can be sold:

**Omar:** Well the thing about rap is kinda different. Well, actually any type of music. Country music even. You know how there is a stereotype that a country music singer has to live in the country. Rap singer [pause] has to be black. It's not [pause] people take the stereotype too far, it's just the fact that rap music is about . . . zzz, oh, how can I explain it? [pause] talking about what you live. So . . . then, the reason that most of the rappers are black is 'cuz it was created like [in] New York, wherever. I think it was created in New York. But that's where most of the violent things that happen—that's where they are. That's why rap music is so violent nowadays. But that's why the rap culture is like that, because that's what those black people are experiencing. So for somebody to come from outside to make their own sell out of it; it's like [pause] you are trying to steal what they own. You know. So you probably wouldn't take to, you probably wouldn't like it too much. So that's the way I feel about it. The reason black people want to keep rap to themselves is because it's something that they all relate to with themselves. And it's not like there aren't white rappers.

This alignment of specific signifiers with specific types of music to codify such musical representations as authentic or not is not unique to rap. It can also be seen in other genres of music. Sim (1998) explains this social process as one in which:

"authenticity" can be seen to be constructed as one more style: values of truth and authenticity will be set up in the dress codes and style of singing of performers (folk singers do not wear pin-stripe suits), perhaps in the instruments they play (for example, acoustic instruments tend to signify such values better that electronic instruments). (p. 142)

As Omar continues his narratives, he also highlights that it is possible for other ethnic and racialized rappers to become in some sense "real":

**Omar:** There are a lot of white rappers. But the reason that they are accepted is because they go through the same stuff.

**J:** Right. So there are some white rappers that are accepted. //Yeah // Such as?

**Omar:** There is this guy called Milk Bone. Came out a while ago. I haven't—

**J:** Called what? //Milk Bone// well that's a good name for a white rapper.

**Omar:** I don't know. He was out awhile ago. I forgot. And there is a lot of like Spanish rappers too. Like Spanish Harlem. You ever heard of Spanish Harlem? //Yeah// Like there is Cubans, Cuban Lynx, stuff like that. Rap isn't just black. It's just that to be able to rap in that, to be able to be fully appreciated as a rapper, by all different, by all the rap industry, you should live the life that you are talking about. So like to try and take it from anywhere outside of that life is just like stealing a baby's candy or something.

**J:** So it's the life? // Yeah// that makes it what it is.

**Omar:** It's 'cuz everyone around the rap community can relate to what's being said. So if some urban kid with a whole bunch of money tries to rap for no reason, it's just like "What you doing? You trying to steal ours. Like this is ours, leave it alone."

Omar's narrative constructs lived experience as paramount in terms of being "real"; a positioning from which it is then possible to extrapolate that if white rappers "rap" about their experiences, then they might be acceptable to blacks. However, "experience" is not an "open" concept that allows easy adoption by middle-class white rappers, since the strength of the discourse lies in the recalling of experiences of poverty, violence, and gender relations. In the following narrative, class is constructed as a variable that can cut across racialized experiences and thus problematize the reception of rap:

**Denzil:** Getting the message is not being black; it's just getting the message is more personal. Nothing to do with the colour you are. 'Cuz I guess that if you were a poor kid growing, a white kid growing up poor, I guess you could hear the same message if you wanted to. It's if you want to hear the message or not. It's why you listen to the music I guess.

William Perkins (1996) positions himself in a similar way to the latter narrative. For him it is possible for white rappers to be seen as "real." He argues that 3rd Bass, now defunct, earned "the acceptance and praise of black rappers. . . . [C]omposed of two Brooklyn kids, MC Search and Prime Minister Pete Nice, who staked a claim to the black urban male style" (1996, p. 39). Perkins continues, "3rd Bass's attitude and rap style were shaped and nurtured by the cultural codes of black masculinity. Brash and speedy, rap was their way out, as they recalled in "Product of the Environment":

> In the heart of the city, you was born and bred
> You grew up smart or you wound up dead
>
> And your savior was a rhyme and a beat
> in a rap group
> A modern day production of the city street. (1996, p. 36)

Thus, as a genre rap music has a value that can be traded on the wider economic market. Although on the surface the tension is around authenticity, further analysis of the discourse suggests that what is for sale is the experience of blacks—a heightened representation that attempts to become defined as the "real." This definition of the real also reacts upon itself as a stereotype. The very images of phallocentric black masculinity that are glorified and celebrated in rap music, videos, and movies are the representations that are evoked when white supremacists seek to gain public acceptance and support for genocidal assault on black men, particularly youth (hooks, 1992, p. 109).

## Summary

This chapter has examined the music consumption of the students. In response to Gerald's comment in Chapter 1, that African-American culture is the dominant culture in Canada, it has examined the students' narratives to ascertain what sorts of cultural forms the students identify with, purchase, and listen to. The narratives reveal that the students position themselves in relation to what they identify as black music. On closer examination of the descriptor "black music," it seems to be performed by peoples of African descent and, in terms of production, based in the United States. Although there was a stronger musical identification by the young women with music associated with the small islands in the Caribbean as opposed to the large island of Jamaica, most of the music was produced in the United States.

In terms of music genres, r&b and rap were the most mentioned. The narratives indicate that from gangsta thorough to "soft" or "lovers," the students consume all genres of rap, from "message" to "gangsta." Misogyny is explored through their narratives to indicate how they place themselves in relation to and through various misogynist phrases that they use during social interaction. The chapter develops an understanding not only of how the students relate to rap but also how they code a musical genre whose main point of commodification is selling experiences vicariously. An analysis of the phrase "going off" reveals it to be a site of pleasure that students can achieve through participation in music—listening or dancing. This state of joy or bliss can also be achieved individually or collectively.

Beat of the music is important to those who listen to rap as are the lyrics. Many of the students indicate that it is the lyrics and the way that they relay a story that catch their attention in terms of listening. In terms of ascertaining what symbolic meanings are produced though rap, the students' discourses are analyzed to ascertain how they transfer phrases and codes from music to their everyday lives (see Chapter 8). Beat also captures the self when listening to dancehall reggae. A much heavier beat than that associated with Bob Marley's more "spiritual" reggae, dancehall is similar to gangsta rap in that both genres draw their legitimacy from relaying their experiences within specific geographic and social locations. Students from the Caribbean consumed this musical form most fully, although some students with no links to Jamaica or the Caribbean claimed that the heavy patois in which the lyrics are delivered prevented full consumption.

In terms of the overall thesis, the data presented help identify how rap is used in the everyday lives of the students, especially with regard to relations of domination. It ascertains how rap that is produced in Canada is consumed in relation to cultural forms produced in the United States.

The next chapter will analyse the hood genre of films and place it in relation to *Set It Off*, a female rebuttal of the "hood" genre. As well, it analyzes the students' narratives in relation to representations of blackness.

# CHAPTER 4

# Films and Regimes of Representation

*Films are not necessarily good because black people make them. They are not necessarily 'right-on' by virtue of the fact that they deal with the black experience.*
WILLIAMSON, 1996, p. 173

## Introduction

As argued in Chapter 3, representations connect meaning and language to culture. They are an essential part of the process by which meaning is produced and exchanged. This chapter continues to highlight a racialized regime of representation (Hall, 1997) via analysis of the ways in which the students perceive and receive various representations of blackness produced in film texts. Like rap music, films are part of that visual repertoire through which difference and blackness are represented at this historical moment. In conjunction with music, music videos, and other dominant representations in youth culture, they are part of a regime of representation.

Further, by examining the youth's reception of the "hood" movie genre which has developed in conjunction with wider hip-hop culture, the study is able to highlight how discourse constructs a specific representation of black youth identity that highlights male heterosexual identity. The phrase "the hood" has become a powerful signifier in present-day youth culture. It has developed consequent symbolic meanings that extend beyond the pleasure or displeasure of watching the movies. This chapter also discusses the influence of music videos as shown on television programs such as *RapCity*.

## Representations

Representation can be linked to meaning and language, through the way that various symbols are used to convey meanings. Thus, meaning is constructed by the system of representation. It is constructed and fixed, momentarily, by a code which sets up the correlation between our conceptual system and our language system in such a way that codes link the relationship between concept and sign. Codes stabilize meaning. If we agree that meaning is stabilized rather than fixed permanently, then logically we come to a position that allows words to carry somewhat different meanings. Meaning is perceived as not inherent in things and the world out there.

We share conceptual maps and have access to a system of representation via language in order to construct meaning. "The general term we use for words, sounds or images which carry meaning is signs. These signs stand for or represent the concepts and the conceptual relations between them which we carry around in our heads" (Hall, 1997, p. 61). Stuart Hall's (1997) discussion of representation is useful in terms of applying the concept to this study. He suggests that there are three main approaches to explaining how meaning gets translated through language. First is the reflective approach whereby meaning is thought to reside in the object, person, idea, or event, and language works like a mirror to reflect true meaning. Second, the intentional approach argues that it is the speaker or author who imposes meaning on the world, and, and, third, the constructivist acknowledges that neither approach in itself nor the individual users of language fix meaning within language. Within this study, the analysis is aligned more with the constructivist perspective than the reflective or the intentional approaches. In the social constructionist approach, representation involves making meaning by forging links between three different orders of things. These three different orders involve what we broadly call the world of things, people, events, and experiences: the conceptual world—the mental concepts we carry around in our heads and the signs, arranged into languages, which "stand for" or communicate these concepts (p. 61). It is also worth noting the social world does not exist *a priori* of discourses of representation. It can be argued, "what is out there is in part constituted by how it is represented" (Hall cited in Storey, 1996).

In linking youth culture to representation of blackness, the critical cultural studies literature has focussed on the political significance of how blacks are represented primarily in film and TV, news media, and rap music. Popular culture is now a major site of social, political, and moral discourse and debate. The construction of youth as a threat is often most acute for youths of African descent, especially in some cities in Europe and North America. Mercer (1994) argues that:

> the prevailing stereotype (in contemporary Britain) projects an image of black youth as
> mugger or rioter. . . . But this regime of representation is reproduced and maintained in

hegemony because black men have had to resort to toughness as a defensive response to the prior aggression and violence that characterises the ways black communities are policed. . . . This cycle between reality and representation makes the ideological fictions of racism empirically true, or rather, there is a struggle over the definition, understanding and construction of meanings around black masculinity within the dominant regime. (pp. 137–38)

The media, in the form of television, print, and music, are very much part of those practices. For Henry Giroux (1993), the media shape identity because we "inhabit a photographic aural and televisual culture in which the proliferation of photographic and electronically produced images and sounds serves to actively produce knowledge and identities within particular sets of ideological and social practices" (p. 19). Gray (1993) indicates that in some of the most notable U.S.

television shows, music videos and films, the construction of blackness and community is mobilised through various emblems of the imagined black nation, a mythic African past, and heroic black masculinity. These are expressed in the dress, hairstyles, language, bodies of young black (mostly) males who wear, speak and look the part of "real brother." From *Do the Right Thing* to *Boyz N the Hood*. (p. 368)

Though directors Spike Lee (*Do the Right Thing*) and John Singleton (*Boyz N the Hood*) would prefer to see themselves as having moved towards a stance which is "rebellious, sociologically important, entrenched in the Black psyche" (George, 1992, p. 5), these films have been criticized as portraying masculinist and nationalist representations (hooks, 1992; George, 1992; Gray, 1993). The significance of this is heightened if one recognizes that the films and television programs that the students watch and the magazines that they read can be viewed as representational systems, as part of the way that media attempts to convey meaning.

### Films

The students' narratives indicate that no commercially produced films portraying the lived experiences of African Canadians had been viewed by any of the students interviewed. This may well be due primarily to a lack of easy access to such Canadian-produced films as *Rude* or *Soul Survivor*. In comparing distribution patterns, both these films are not as widely distributed or as accessible to the public as other, more mainstream films. As well, the U.S. economic dominance of the Canadian film industry via multimedia giants constrains the Canadian film industry in general as it struggles to maintain a distinctive sense of self under the deluge from the United States. In fact, large media corporations control the films made available for general viewing and thus structure the choices available to students. Although the National Film Board of Canada has produced documentary films such as *The Road Taken* or *Speak It!*, highlighting the lived experiences of African Canadians, none of these films is discussed within the students' narratives.

Other films, classified as mainstream in the sense that they are watched by a larger segment of the population and are distributed more widely by large media corporations, are enjoyed by the students, despite such films' lack of overt black experiences within the plot. Among the variety of mainstream films cited in the students' narratives were *Titanic*, *Face Off*, *Donnie Brasco*, and *Braveheart*. It is important to recognize that although discussion entails the students' reception of specific film texts, this reception takes place within a socioeconomic structure contoured by globalized capitalism[1] (Morley & Robins 1995; Klein, 2000).

During the interviews a variety of films were discussed, either in response to open-ended questions or to more focussed questions initiated by the interviewer to elicit the reception of specific film texts. These discussions of films were undertaken in order to raise issues of receptivity in general and, more specifically, to discuss receptivity intertextually to discourses of blackness. Among the films discussed were *Set It Off*, *Soul Food*, *Boyz N the Hood*, *Menace II Society*, *Amistad*, *Waiting to Exhale*, *Being a Playa'*, and *Booty Call*, a variety of genres reflecting gender, sexuality, and racialized themes.

With regard to these films, the narratives highlight how issues of representations become linked with questions of "reality" in terms of the portrayal of African American experiences. In particular, the hood films evoked narratives that indicated a theoretical tension hinged on whether the constructed reality was mimetic of an external reality that exists in the United States. Joy's narratives lay out an understanding of the genre and its consequent influence on North American youth culture:

> **Joy:** *Boyz N the Hood* was good, so was *Menace II Society*. And then there was like all those kinda movies that kinda followed it. But *Boyz N the Hood* was like that first one that came out where like it was by John Singleton. That was kinda like the first one that like the reason that movie did so good, and why I think a lot of people liked it was because it was like a new idea. Just like when *Aliens* first came out. They like started that idea, and it was "bad." But then when people keep trying to copy it and make—it gets kinda repetitive. It's like the idea is done, tired. It's tired out. Leave it.

For many students, the constructions of black youths' lives in the United States, as portrayed in films such as *Boyz N the Hood*, and *Menace II Society*, were perceived as congruent with the "real" conditions that young black Americans encountered.

As Gerald indicates when speaking of *Boyz N the Hood*:

**Gerald:** What actually happened is what actually happens in the States.

Or, as Joy reveals:

> **Joy:** *Boyz N the Hood* was a very good movie. I liked it. It was sad, but that's how they have it down there. It was like realistic in some aspects, like the shootings and stuff. Like there's a lot of drive-by shootings down there, and I think that when that movie came out, it was like it kind a showed the public this isn't a pretty scene.

In a similar vein, Etta's narratives highlight the movies as good and realistic, thus enabling a sympathetic identification with black Americans:

> **Etta:** They are good movies. They are sad. I think it's realistic. It's sad. More goes on there [in the United States] than what we really know. We don't live in the States; we don't live in those areas, and we don't really see. Thing is, when you see them lots of people say, "Oh these are gangstas and stuff." They don't realise that these people felt that this is the only choice that they have. They don't know the background. Or the whole story. Lot of people put them down. And look down on them. And I supposed that you can for what they do, but they don't make much of—even in the States to help.

So it is that for Denzil the hood films were a source of knowledge, an eye-opener about the real United States, even if at times he saw the constructions as prone to exaggeration:

> **Denzil:** They're, they're good movies. They are eye-opening especially [for] white America. They go, "That's what it's really like?" And a lot of times it is. But some movies go a bit overboard. Like it's good to take a little bit of realism into it. But they are just trying to put all the sorrow and all the bad things that can happen in the hood into two hours and four minutes or whatever. So they are good movies; they can be almost educational. Yeah, they are good movies. I like them. I don't watch them for the sake of watching the movie. I watch them for something else.

As he continues to elaborate on the "something else" for which he watches such films, Denzil indicates a degree of ambivalence in terms of his identification. He recognizes that he cannot know fully what life is like in these innercity areas:

> **Denzil:** Just like, I don't know, identification. Something like that. Just to see what's going on. 'Cuz I don't, obviously. I don't live there, so I don't know what it's totally like. And at the same time that's not a very good way to try and identify—through a screen. You should go and live there. But I wouldn't want to.

For Phyllis, identification of realism within the film also led to ambivalence and the need to make a distinction between Canadian experiences and experiences in the United States.

> **Phyllis:** I guess, I guess for an American, like a black teen, it'd be almost accurate. 'Cuz that's like an everyday part of life for them. Like a lot of them live in the projects and stuff. //Right// Like maybe that is an everyday part of life. But for someone like me, that's not. So I guess for them it would be more realistic.

Not all students see the representation of inner city life in *Boyz N the Hood* as realistic. For Langston, the film's portrayal of the lives of black youths was "funny" rather than real. In response to a request to elaborate on his use of "funny":

> **Langston:** Funny peculiar and "ha, ha" sometimes. When you look at something that you have absolutely no idea why it's happening, it's funny to you. If it's real to you, it wouldn't be funny. When I watched it, it wasn't real to me. So it was funny, it was like "oh, good movie" It was a sad ending. Didn't make me cry or nothing. It was just, oh, sad the guy had to die when he was about to leave. It was nothing big.

For Omar, lived experiences were important in deciding on the degree of realism portrayed in *Boyz N the Hood:*

> **Omar:** I've never grown up in the ghetto, so I can't tell you whether it's realistic or not. But from what you see in statistics and stuff like that, it's probably true.

For him, other empirical evidence was necessary to substantiate the degree of realism in the genre.

What is evident through a sense of absence/presence in the narratives and the hood films, is that the black identity constructed by and through these discussions is a male black identity. The experiences highlighted within many of the hood genre are very much a masculinist interpretation of black life in the United States. Although the term "black" is used as a universal descriptor for the characters in the movies, the experiences that are highlighted are very much those of young males. Such masculinist orientations have been noted by cultural critics such as hooks (1992) and Mercer (1994), both of whom have suggested that male-centered genres such as *Boyz N the Hood, Menace II Society, Juice*, etc. offer primarily masculinist and sexist portrayals of women. Women are constructed solely as sexual objects and nurturers—there as background for the males to play out their roles. Further, Canadian theorist Rinaldo Walcott (1997) argues, "in these narratives of blackness, black women, gays, lesbians, and anyone who does not toe the line of narrowly-defined blackness are considered unimportant" (p. 124). This consequent and consistent erasure of women and gays not only reinforces the constructions of blackness as male and heterosexual but also contours understandings of reality. When analyzed, it was noticeable that many of the narratives referred to and linked discourses of reality and the real with representations of lived experiences of black youths in the inner city. In terms of giving meaning to various texts, this issue of reality was important. If linked with black identity, it allows us to analyze how the films that the students watch construct blackness.

This concept of "reality" becomes important in defining the acceptability of filmic texts for the students and is most evident in their assessment and reception of films such as *Set It Off*. Placing the student's narratives on *Set It Off* in relation to the more male-centered films in the genre highlights many of the tensions alluded to by Walcott (1997) above. Such relational analysis is important, since viewers often placed genres of film and television programs in relation to each other. As Tony Thwaites et al. (1994) argue, such an emphasis on genre is important because:

> In addition to counteracting any tendency to treat individual texts in isolation from others, an emphasis on genre can also help to counteract the homogenisation of the medium which is widespread in relation to the mass media, where it is common, for instance, to find assertions about "the effects of television," regardless of such important considerations as genre. (p. 92)

*Set It Off*, in contrast to male-centered films, portrays four female friends who live in the ghetto and are trying to survive economically. The story deals with the ways in which economic circumstances drive the women to rob a bank where one of them was previously employed. The story attempts to present itself as woman-centered response to the male-dominated hood film genre. Its representations, read connotatively, can be viewed as an attempt to stymie criticism that hood films portray women as epiphenomenal to the main action within the films, i.e., as objects rather than subjects.

Although the conditions of inner-city experiences represented via masculinist hood films were acceptable as "real' representations, *Set It Off*, the experiences of four young women living in the inner city, was open to much more scrutiny as to its realism. This questioning of the realism of *Set It Off* highlights the ways in which discourses of black youth culture have positioned black men and black women differently within a genderized discourse. The students who discussed the film positioned themselves in a variety of ways, but for many, the representation of women within the film was not seen as congruent with "gender reality" and actual experience:

> **Etta:** It was good, actually. Um, that was kind of sad. It was not really that realistic. But it was and it wasn't.

Or for Gerald:

> **Gerald:** Yes. The story line was like kind of hard to believe, like it could happen so.
> **J:** How do you think it was hard to believe?

**Gerald:** 'Cuz like four girls robbing a bank. It's just a hard thing to believe.

**J:** How is that?

**Gerald:** I don't know. 'Cuz it's probably never happened before.

**J:** How come?

**Gerald:** Just probably never happened. You wouldn't think of like four women robbing a bank and getting away with it. You just wouldn't think it would happen. But it could happen, so . . . .

Or for Omar:

**Omar:** Robbing a bank is not something you see a lot of ladies doing. So I think that's what that movie was supposed to be. I don't think there is any thing like any true meaning of life to it.

For Frank, the representations of women were incongruent with representations of women that he had encountered:

**Frank:** I liked it. But I thought it was fake, 'cuz first of all, I couldn't see Queen Latifah as a lesbian. And then four women like that wouldn't have the self-esteem to do that. It's not possible.

For Gerald, this incongruity between "known reality" and filmic representation did not affect enjoyment of the film, which, in comparison to *Boyz N the Hood*, was rated better. As he explains:

**Gerald:** It was just like—I don't know why I liked it; it was just like a better film I guess, better production and everything. The film was just better. To me, at least.

Unlike other students who like congruity between their known reality and the representation on film, Gerald found that the gap between the representation of his known reality and the filmic representation made the film more interesting. The pleasure for him is that the film goes against the grain of other films within the genre.

**Gerald:** That they put women that were like bad that would rob a bank just made it more interesting.

Although Gerald's narratives might imply a gendered receptivity of *Set It Off*, it was not a reception based on binary opposites, of male interpretation versus female interpretation. Many of the young women's narratives also indicate incongruity between their known reality and the filmic representation:

**Mirelle:** I thought it was pretty jokey. Four women try to rob a bank.

**J:** How is that jokey?

**Mirelle:** Not jokey, but like kind of like, um, like kind of "woody"? I don't know. I thought it was a good movie, personally, but it's just like any other movie when they want to rob a bank, I guess.

Highlighting differences is an important aspect in terms of meaning making and in making a distinction between categories. Eulyn highlighted various differences within the genre of hood films:

**Eulyn:** Compared to *Boyz N the Hood,* it's not as "rough" I guess. Because there was like, three of them were just girls who lived in like say a bad area. But they had like education, stuff like that, except for a couple of them. Compared to *Boyz N the Hood,* where there wasn't much education around.

The above narrative, while constructing black women as educated, relationally constructs black men as uneducated and, consequently, reinforces a sense of the importance of education in terms of making black women economically mobile and able to escape the inner city. The representations of black male identity are linked with uneducated roughness. Female identity is regarded as soft despite the criminal activity undertaken within the film.

This positioning of black male identity as different from and more disadvantaged than black female identity is also evident in Mirelle's narratives. For her, gendered and raced aspects were factors used to differentiate between the two interpretations and constructions of meaning:

**Mirelle:** Yeah. I think that movie is different from the rest of them. 'Cuz it could be like four white women robbing a bank, and they get caught the same way, and like one survives and. . . .

**J:** But you think that Menace was different. Couldn't it be just four white guys?

**Mirelle:** It would be different, 'cuz I think, I've never really pictured white guys growing up in a hood kind of thing. I know some of them grow hard and rough in different—but not the way black people—like made as if they grew up with the hardest kind of thing. They grew up to live, like a rough life. Tough, hard life.

The construction of black identity within these youth-cultural products orchestrates black male experience of the world through a more consistently racialized lens than that of black females. Etta's narratives highlight this predominance of black male experiences when, in discussing a scene in *Set It Off,* she uses the male experiences in the film to discuss the experiences of blacks in both Toronto and the United States:

**Etta:** Remember how they set him up? And the police just shot him down just like that? Things like that do happen now and then. Even in Toronto, like if you read, they had problems with it once in awhile where they want people to check into things. 'Cuz they don't think there is any reason for them to be killed. And when it gets that high, like percentage gets that high, like talking about the papers, sometimes I wonder myself why a sixteen-year-old kid would just kill. I can't see them being that much of a threat. Like sometimes it is true, they are. But when the percentages get that high, as opposed to other races especially, I begin to wonder.

The way that gender becomes subsumed to racialized meanings, that black women are represented as having more experiences in common with white women than black men have with white men, is also attendant within these narratives. Within the narratives, class as a social relation is erased and replaced by an overemphasis on black masculinity as a signifier for disadvantaged. Such understandings of oppression as a hierarchy can be traced to other discourses that are internal and external to the black-defined community (hooks, 1992). It is a contouring of meanings that positions black men as more disadvantaged than black women. What is also interesting is the way that in terms of identification, there is no clear gender demarcation. Both the young women and men adhere to a discourse of black male disadvantage in relation to females.

The narratives also highlight the ways in which films such as *Set If Off* are polysemic—capable of signifying multiple meanings. Whereas interpretations of reality and male identity might cohere within some narratives, interpretations by the students can also collide as they fill in textual spaces or leave gaps through which meaning can develop. The automatic acceptance of blackness and black identity represented through media images thus becomes much more problematic. In speaking of the reception of films, Manthia Diawara (1996) argues that "every narration places the spectator in a position of agency; race, class, and sexual relations influence the way in which this subjecthood is filled by the spectator" (p. 293). I would add to Diawara's set of relations, religious beliefs. Thus Eulyn, whose narrative positions her as religious, drew on such discourses to give meanings to the film *Set It Off*—meanings that the interviewer had overlooked. For Eulyn the most glaring representation in the film was the portrayal of rap musician Queen Latifah as a lesbian;[2] sexuality rather than gender was a primary factor in her critique of the film's realism. Positioning herself within a fundamentalist religious discourse contested her ability to accept lesbians as "natural." For her *Set It Off* was problematic:

**Eulyn:**  I didn't, I didn't really enjoy it [the film].

**J:**  Why was that?

**Eulyn:**  Because of Queen Latifah.

**J:**  Oh she was the one with the car?

**Eulyn:**  Yeah. She was portraying a lesbian. That's why I didn't like it.

**J:**  Oh didn't you? How was that?

**Eulyn:**  Because like she was actually portraying a lesbian, you know what I mean.

**J:**  She was acting out the part?

**Eulyn:** That's what I mean?

**J:** Explain a bit more.

**Eulyn:** Why I didn't like it? //Yeah// it's just wrong. I don't think it's supposed to be like that. And it's just the story was all kind of pointless. Cos they all get shot. And then she goes somewhere, and she is running the streets for the rest of her life with money. What's that?

However, Mirelle, whose narratives overlooked the sexuality of Queen Latifah's character, was willing, when asked directly, to accept Latifah's positioning as a lesbian in the film and identified different sexual orientations as part of portraying "reality" and "natural" life:

**Mirelle:** I guess they were just trying to portray like everybody had their natural life. Like one lady was struggling, trying to take care of her brother. One had a young kid trying to raise her up on her own, and she was like any other one of them. She was a lesbian.

In response to a query concerning how she reconciled her religious beliefs with such openness to differing sexual orientations she responded with a qualifier:

**Mirelle:** I think that's wrong. Like I don't believe in it kind of thing but I wouldn't judge them because I mean you just don't judge people by if that's how they are; then I guess I am not going to like clap for them but I am not going to like put them down kind of thing

In this instance, Mirelle's response indicates the existence of competing discourses around the issue of sexual orientation. Whereas her religious upbringing would suggest that lesbianism is "wrong," other more liberal discourses of equality compete with such an understanding to produce "ambivalence" in her response.

For Gerald, the ability to make a distinction between Queen Latifah's portrayal of a lesbian on screen and her off-screen persona as heterosexual enabled an acceptance of the film:

**Gerald:** I think she is a good actor in it. She just did a good job of acting. . . . I don't know it was kind of . . . like cos she was gay and everything. It's kind of like nasty. But like she . . . still did a good job of acting.

Yet, in contrast, Frank found that his ability to differentiate Queen Latifah's off-screen persona from her role made the film even less acceptable:

**Frank:** Ah . . . couldn't stand it. I can't imagine her like that. So that's why I like couldn't stand that. And that's like a stupid thing to add to the movie. What was the point?

Omar's narratives construct the addition of a lesbian character in the most receptive terms:

> **Omar:** It's not like it doesn't happen. There's a lot of lesbians out there. And she was black too. It's, part of ordinary life. But that's another aspect of life too, so you can't hate it . . . It's what happens.

The students' narratives also used the hood films relationally, to give meaning to other film genres and to construct what would be an ideal representation of blackness. Thus, Joy highlights this matter in relation to hood films and the more recent genre of youth comedy sex films such as *Booty Call* or *Being a Playa*. What would be an ideal type of representation of blacks within a movie?:

> **Joy:** One thing that I would like to see with a black movie is that it's not always about the shooting or something like that, but you know how you see a lot of white people, they always play in like movies like not necessarily an action movie but dramas, like we still have some dramas right, but I mean like even stories to do with corporate America. But I'd like to see black people put into that position. Something away from the shooting and the sex. Something totally different but just with black people. That's what I would like to see. 'Cuz white people do that. You see them with a whole bunch of movies, and people don't say nothing.

In a similar vein, Doreen's narrative constructs *Soul Food* as more positive in relation to the hood movies:

> **Doreen:** I think it made them look good. Because you know, you see some like, "Okay, I'll be ruthless." You know, "gangsta" movies—I really don't like that type of movies because they make black people, they don't look good. Like I don't like it at all. Because they make it look, and like, I know that maybe like when some white people see that movie or what ever, they'd be like "Oh, black people are just out to kill people now," stuff like that. I don't like movies like that, because there is too much killing, too much swearing. I don't like to see movies like that.

While the hood films were often discussed in terms of their representation of black life in U.S. inner cities, other films, such as *Soul Food*, and *Waiting to Exhale*, were constructed as able to represent the experiences of all women or families, not just black women and black families. *Soul Food* highlights an African-American family, and *Waiting to Exhale* the often-negative experiences of African-American women with African-American men. Phyllis, in discussing *Waiting to Exhale*, explains the universality of experiences represented:

> **Phyllis:** Okay, let me explain. It doesn't just portray like black women. 'Cuz not only black women have those problems. You know, like everybody has those problems.

Everybody is in love with someone, but they just can't have them. Sometimes it happens.

Or, for Langston discussing the same film:

**Langston:**  Yeah, it was a good movie. It was a true story. Not like, probably wasn't a real-life story, but it was true. It was realistic.
**J:**  Which bits were realistic?
**Langston:**  You know, like the woman with her man leaving her.

In ascertaining the meanings of hood films as constructed in the narratives of the students, one finds that the U.S.-mediated representations of black youth culture are not automatically and passively consumed by black youths in Alberta. Instead, meanings are constructed in varying ways that often intersect with not just gender and race but also sexuality.

## Television and Music Videos

Rap music videos offer a third aspect of the repertoire of imagery and visual effects through which difference and blackness are represented in the lives of the students. Again, rap music reception is highlighted to indicate the ways in which students position themselves in relation to the visual texts and thus secure certain subject positions. These televisual texts are against a background in which Canadian television is subsumed by U.S. television productions. Representation of blacks on Canadian television programs is infrequent, and exploration of these narratives is through television programs created for an audience in the United States. As one student argued, there are "not many Canadian programs, and they are not very popular."[3] Thus, representation of black experiences should be recognized as African American.

The narratives indicate that people view TV for a variety of reasons. For some students, it is an activity to be undertaken when nothing else is available. For others, it is a pleasurable experience not to be missed. Reception of television texts varied across and between genres and was often dependent upon the type of program and the social use to which such a text could be put. Soap operas such as *Young & Restless*, *ER*, and *Days of Our Lives* were, according to the narratives of the young women, in particular, programs not to be missed. The structuring of these programs as serials contoured their receptivity. Such programs were seen as both unpredictable and predictable. Such a position of ambiguity often adds to the appeal of such genres as "multiple enigmas are initiated, developed and resolved at different rates, and so the viewer's curiosity is in constant state of arousal" (Gillespie, 1995, p. 161). While Gillespie's postulation holds true for many students, some students indicated that they have learned the formula for this genre. It has become predictable to such an extent that it no longer causes a "constant state of arousal."

It is also interesting to note the degree of ambivalence in terms of the students' responses to television. Unlike the common sense understandings within society, which stereotype students as passive "dupes" "sucking up the dross" of television, the students' narratives were actually quite specific about what they liked to watch. Often, demands created by part-time work or schoolwork acted as constraining circumstances in their ability to watch television freely. In many ways the narratives suggest that television per se no longer offers an attraction as it perhaps did for an earlier generation of youth. Several of the narratives construct television as a medium that could be "taken" or "left"—a choice that intersects with the development of other media technology.

> **Phyllis:** I don't sit at home and watch TV. Like people like sit on a couch and vegetate and watch movies and stuff. Like yeah, I may do that on a weekend when I have nothing else better to do.

Or

> **Melvin:** I don't know. I watch TV because like if there's nothing else to do, I'll watch TV. Otherwise, I'll like even play video games or go out and play basketball or something.

Or

> **Frank:** I enjoy computers. I enjoy computers, like most people watch TV, I'll be on the computer. I like making programs or making web pages, stuff like that.

Past experiences of other mediums become part of the process of choice through which meanings of pleasure become identified with leisure activities. For one student, whose access to television was limited as a child, reading was perceived as much more satisfactory than watching television.

> **Etta:** My mum doesn't believe in watching TV. So we never had a TV, so both my sister and I, we kind of just always, always used to read. Like it was actually a habit. But now I have like my own TV, since like I work or whatever. So now I read less. But I still like to read. I actually like reading better than watching TV. Because TV, you kind of get tired and you are just sitting there because there is nothing else to do. But if you get caught in a good book. . . .

The students' narratives show that they watched a variety of television programs, ranging from re-runs of African-American sitcoms such as *Fresh Prince of Bel Air*,

*Cosby Days*, and Keenen Ivory Wayan's *In Living Color*. A few students noted that the number of programs centering on the lived experiences of African Americans had decreased recently in comparison to a few years ago.[4] There may be some empirical verification to this observation since recently, the National Association for the Advancement of Colored People (NAACP) has argued that the networks are not using black actors in prominent sitcoms (Haynes, 1999). Since many sitcoms are repeated year after year, some students still watch older programes such as *Fresh Prince of Bel Air*. In discussing the impact of shows such as *Fresh Prince of Bel Air* or *The Jeffersons*, Gray (1995) argues that they should be regarded as pluralist rather than assimilationist. His argument rests on the basis that "what makes these shows pluralist and therefore different from the assimilationist shows is their explicit recognition of race (blackness) as the basis of cultural difference (expressed as separation) as a feature of U.S. society" (p. 87).

The three programs watched by most students were *Jerry Springer*, *RapCity*, and *Seinfeld*. Interestingly, *Seinfield* was classed as a "show about nothing." This representation of the show as "about nothing" may well draw on the dominant media discourse and hype about the show. It is interesting because, as a show about nothing, it is not located consistently within a workplace, or family, or school—traditional sites for location of "sitcoms" as well as sites that define status of the individuals involved in the onscreen interaction. *Jerry Springer*, a "talk" show that consists of more fights and expletives than "talk," highlighted discourses on the constructed nature of realism in the program. Of the three programs, only *RapCity* has consistent representations of blackness, and, therefore, for the purposes of this book, only narratives highlighting this program are presented.

*RapCity*, unlike many of the programs that the students watch, is a Canadian product of the growing sophistication of satellite and television cable communication technology. In response to this thrust of late capitalism and technological opening up of Canadian borders, media mogul Moses Znaimer[5] founded the *MuchMusic* television channel in 1984 to play nonstop music videos in a similar way to its U.S. sister, *Music TeleVision* (MTV).[6] This enthusiasm to communicate back and forth beyond state borders is reinforced by a general culture of globalization and corporate capitalism. The latter can be seen as an example of the ways in which corporate capital is able to stretch geographic boundaries of the nation state to align more profitably with corporate structures and thus support the ideology of globalization. TV stations such as *MuchMusic* enable the rest of the world to be inculcated into a world of youth culture in general, and hip-hop in particular. The following narratives reveal the choices of programs made with regard to *MuchMusic*:

**Phyllis:** That's mainly what I watch. I watch Much Music a lot.

For Melvin, *RapCity* was his main choice in viewing the *MuchMusic* channel:

> **Melvin:** Well, like if *Rap City* is on, I'll like [watch] the station *Much Music* but like if *RapCity* is not on, no. 'Cuz they don't even like play rap on it. That's pretty much the only stuff I want to see unless they've got like a reggae video on or something.

The two *MuchMusic* programs discussed were *RapCity* and *XtendDaMix*. *RapCity*, by far the more referenced of the two programs plays primarily rap videos, while *DaMix* concentrates on r&b and reggae. Although produced in Canada, many of the music videos that are played originate in the United States. However, despite the strong flavor of U.S.-produced music, *RapCity* provided the most publicly accessible venue for Canadian rappers. As Gerald outlines, in response to a question as to how he heard about Canadian rappers Rascalz and Chocolair:

> **Gerald:** TV, watching *RapCity*.

Thus, Canada and the rest of the rest of the digitally accessible world was inculcated into the culture of hip-hop.[7] As an offshoot of rap music, music videos have become an important means of mediating images of youth culture. These images of dress style act as a form of layering that shapes representations of blackness in Canada. Rinaldo Walcott (1995) identifies the importance of music videos for expanding the ability of music to project certain meanings and images:

> The addition of image to music greatly expands the range of possible messages that may be conveyed by a pop song. Standing as it does at the intersection between popular music, cinema and television, music video is a unique manifestation of popular culture that demands a corresponding flexibility of approach in its analysis. (p. 8)

Music videos, when read intertextually, reinforce representations constructed via rap music, i.e., they reinforce a dominant image of black masculinity. In particular, music videos construct and reinforce the image of the "authentic" rapper as an African-American male rather than an African Canadian, male or female. Such linking is undertaken by focussing on specific signifiers during the playing of music videos. The males in the video's foreground are often placed in relation to specific backgrounds with friends—a positioning that identifies them as being in the hood. Tricia Rose (1994) has noted this placement in music videos and argues that:

> Nothing is more central to rap's music video narratives than situating the rapper in his or her milieu and among one's crew or posse. Unlike heavy metal videos, for example, which often use dramatic live concert footage, and the concert stage as the core location, rap

music videos are set on buses, subways, in abandoned buildings, and almost always in black urban inner city locations. . . . When I asked seasoned music video director Kevin Bray what comprised the three most important themes in rap video, his immediate response was, "Posse, posse and posse." (p. 10)

In the following narrative, Langston identifies the ways in which videos are constructed around an array of signifiers that reinforce rap's main thematic concerns of "locatedness" and identification with the hood:

**Langston:** Two thirds of the videos that rappers do show don't have anything to do with the song they actually are singing about. Like sometimes, like you might hear a song about—like sometimes they do go together. Like if it's not a story. If it's about a rapper saying something like "Oh yeah, I am rich," they are going to show big houses. If it's a rapper saying something about women, they are going to have a lot of ladies in there. But then again, there is a theme to the story. Like sometimes they just go stupid and just put any thing there. Sometimes the video's just an expression. It's more of a celebration most of the time. Like videos, two thirds of the times, were just a celebration of, you know, "Well, I made it this far all my friend; all my friends come into my video. Just show up." And they will be talking about something totally different.

For Doreen, rap music videos, construction of gender, beauty, and desire are highlighted. Her narratives identify the ways in which constructions of beauty and desire are often contoured by the relationship between the production of a videotext and its reception. For her, male reception of videos and construction of desire are mediated by:

**Doreen:** The videos are good. I just watch the videos for the dancing.
**J:** What about the ways in which the women are portrayed?
**Doreen:** [suck teeth] LL Cool J. I don't like how he acts in like those videos. 'Cuz he always gets some girl in some little piece of clothes. That ain't covering anything, okay? And you know what gets me mad? Girls in videos, right? Actually it doesn't matter. Okay, the girl, like a person who is famous, could be the ugliest person, and the girl is ugly and you see all these things. There might be a girl in our school who looks like her, right, and they look exactly alike. But because she [the girl on video] is famous, everybody thinks she is so sweet. And the girl in our school is called, "she is a dog, and she is ugly." I am like, why are you guys talking that way though? And they think that every black girl they see in the video is so pretty. Just because like she is in a video. She could be the fattest, like, ugliest girl, whatever, and they still think she is pretty just because she is on TV. I don't get that.

In the above narrative, Doreen describes how music videos evoke meanings through interaction between videotext and reader. Constructions of beauty draw on the glamour of the medium to contour women in certain sexualized ways, moving them from the category of ordinary to the extraordinary and exotic. Doreen's narrative also indicates an awareness of what Stuart Hall identifies as "preferred readings" in the construction of a videotext. She was able to identify the construction of a male gaze in music videos and how specific signifiers connote specific meanings. Her narrative challenges the automatic accessing of a specific reading of the videotext and, instead, indicates that to some extent she negotiates between preferred and oppositional meanings (Hall, 1980). She indicates the gendered codes that are constructed within music videos:

> **J:** So you can tell when it's a video made for a guy?
>
> **Doreen:** Yeah!! When you see pure girls standing up there, like jiggling up their booties in the screen. And you know when its for girls when you see some guy pouring water down himself [laugh]. That's the girl bit, "cool off." All these guys like singing mostly slow songs. Like guys singing, you know it's for girls. Like it's so obvious.

At times, reading music videos as gender coded extends into everyday lived experiences as explanation of social relations. In the following narrative, Melvin accounts for an acquaintance's dress style as a reflection of representations garnered through music videos. In response to a question on why he sees another student as identifying with music videos, Melvin identifies how videos reinforce representations of women as sexual objects and the social consequences of identification with such representations:

> **Melvin:** Oh, it all depends like what kind of videos like, um, she just dresses like, okay? 'Cuz there is East Coast and there is West Coast rap. And like pretty much there's more rap, but that's what separated them. And the East Coast ones wear sort of baggy jeans and stuff, with little like shirts that come up to there [midriff] and then big jackets sometimes, otherwise they are like holding up with something. And like that's what she is, like she is dressed like a mixture of both. Because the West Coast girl, they pretty much come out like half-naked. With everything like hanging out. They come with like G strings and stuff like. That's what she'll be sporting. Like warm weather, too. Shorts that like [sucks teeth] all that nonsense and big shoes.

As well, music videos were recorded, thus increasing further the gap between production and reception. The differing ways in which the video can be viewed evoking emotions repeatedly, are evident within Merle's narrative.

> **Merle:** Oh I watch them all the time [laugh]. I have to go buy it. Thank you for reminding me. I have to go buy myself a new tape. I record them because we have a stereo system in our family room. So when it comes on, we put on the super bass.

You turn it up on the speakers, because it's on both sides and it sounds so good. And then you just go back. If you don't have that song on tape, you can listen to it on the TV. And I don't know, I like it. You just see them and then they will be wearing new styles or something. Girls will get their hair . . . it will be like "Oh, I like her hairstyle, do my hair like that. Things like that." It's just fun.

The narratives identify *RapCity* as an important source for images of blackness. News reports and reality TV programs, such as *Cops*, can also be identified as part of a regime of representations that contour understanding of black youth culture. Phyllis identifies such a link between *Cops*, a reality crime show, and overrepresentation of blacks as criminals. In a sarcastic tone, she identifies what she learned about blacks on TV:

**Phyllis:** Unless you are going to get into, like the "Cops" thing, whatever. Then they show like every black case there is going.

However, for Omar, other "positive" representations of blackness exist on TV to contest those of *Cops*:

**Omar:** If you choose to watch all the bad stuff, you can do that. So you can learn just about any thing. Like there's shows like "Cops" [laugh]. Half the people they catch are blacks. So its like "Oh, okay. I guess all the black people are crooks." And then you can watch another show like, phew, "What's that?" There used to be a whole bunch of shows. Like the "Cosby Family" even. You'd be like, "Whoa, black people are nice," you know, well behaved, whatever. So you can learn anything.

Even the more "factual" news programs emerge within the narratives as conveying racialized codes (Koza, 1994). Thus, presentation of the news is read intertextually in conjunction with and in relation to other existing discourses and texts that flow within society. Eulyn highlights how this process of intertextual coding works for her when watching/listening to the local news:

**Eulyn:** But I guess, um, they just show the negative stuff, really.
**J:** You think so? //Uh huh// Give me an example.
**Eulyn:** Like we [blacks] are murderers, and robbers, and all that kind of stuff.
**J:** And this is on the news?
**Eulyn:** 'Cuz like if someone, like with that stuff that happened with Valley High. It was a black kid who stabbed the guy. It wasn't like, if it was a white person, I am sure they wouldn't have said any thing.
**J:** Oh, did they say it was a black kid? //Yeah// How would the [news] have dealt with it then? What would they have said?
**Eulyn:** They probably would have said, "Oh there was a stabbing at Valley High between, you know, kids or whatever."

This narrative also illustrates the ways in which meaning accumulates across different texts "where one image refers to another, or has its meaning altered by being 'read' in the context of other images" (Hall, 1997, p. 232). Such an intertextual reading also draws on the unsaid, the absence/presence, to give meaning to a social situation. In continuing our interview, Eulyn expands on how she uses the absence/presence of racialized signifiers to "understand" the context of a news item:

> **Eulyn:** Well, first of all, when I hear something, I am always thinking, "Oh, please don't let them be black." And then when I don't hear anything I am like, "Oh, they are probably not, then."
>
> **J:** So what sort of things?
>
> **Eulyn:** There is a bank robbery, or someone held up at Mac's.

Eulyn is identifying what John Fiske (1987) describes as the relationship between negativity, "otherness," and power. As Fiske sees it:

> There is, of course, a connection between elitism and negativity; the positive or "normal" actions of elite people will often be reported whereas those without social power are considered newsworthy only when their actions are disruptive or deviant. In representing the dominant as performing positive actions and the subordinate as performing deviant or negative ones, the news is engaging in the same ideological practices as fictional television. (Fiske, pp. 286)

## Summary

The chapter analyzed the narratives intertextually, highlighting the ways in which the meanings of images are read in relation to each other. The narratives suggest that the youth culture that the students encounter represents blackness via regimes of representation. Reception and consumption of magazines, movies, and music videos draw heavily on U.S.-based youth culture and other racialized and gendered discourses that exist within society. This access to predominantly U.S. youth culture adds up to a hegemonic representation of blackness for these Canadian youths of African descent. In some ways, the students' narratives reveal a disjuncture in experiences that Anthony Giddens (1990) identifies as "locally situated expressions of distanciated relations" (p. 109). By this he means that the students encounter cultural formations that place them in connection with an African-American youth culture that is not directly aligned with Canadian experiences. Across the varying forms of youth culture discussed, hip-hop was perhaps the most significant cultural form and presents a variety of symbols through which meanings can be constructed. A racialized regime of representation was highlighted to reveal how representations of blackness in films, rap music, and music videos reinforce the lived experiences of African Americans as representative and universal of blackness within the diaspora.

In looking at the hood films in conjunction with hip-hop culture, the narratives construct a specific representation of black youth identity that highlights male heterosexual identity normalized through discourse. As with all discourses active within society, this gendered and racialized discourse operates intertextually as students draw on other discourses within society to make certain meanings intelligible. Also evident are the ways in which Hall's encoding and decoding model of audience reading could benefit from the addition of an "independent dimension of aesthetic discrimination in audience readings" (Schroder, 2000, p. 233). The latter aesthetic discrimination, according to Schroder, would allow for the insertion of a continuum from immersion to critical distance and thus allow for the evident "commuting between positions on the continuum."

The next chapter will analyze the ways in which regimes of representation produce dress styles and the consequent use to which the students put such style.

CHAPTER 5

# Riding the P. Diddy Train: Style as Performance

*[We] . . . inhabit a photographic aural and televisual culture in which the proliferation of photographic and electronically produced images and sounds serves to actively produce knowledge and identities within particular sets of ideological and social practices.*

GIROUX, 1993, p. 19

## *Introduction*

Chapter 4 presented the ways in which the students encountered youth culture and films as part of a racialized regime of representation. This chapter analyzes the various ways that the students consume and produce youth cultural formations and meanings through dress style. It illustrates the everyday uses to which the students put their knowledge of dress style and music in order to produce an understanding of urban space: linking ideology and consumption as well as problematizing the tension between "space-distanciation" and representations of blackness. Further, the narratives illustrate how use is made of youth culture to reinforce a binarism that evokes a sense of "them" and "us," self and "other." Finally, the chapter outlines the way in which ideology, i.e., the fixing of discourse in the name of power, operates to shape the relations of consumption and commodification. Such a focus reveals the nuanced ways in which the mass media can act as a system of knowledge and power, reproducing and managing relations of domination along lines of race, class, gender, and sexual orientation. It reveals "how the meaning mobilized by mass-mediated symbolic forms is understood and appraised by the individuals who, in the course of their everyday routines, receive media messages and incorporate them into their lives" (Thompson, 1990, p. 24).

Desire for U.S. products are generated through the magazines that students read and music videos that are played in programs such as *RapCity*. Two main hip-hop magazines are read, *The Source* and *Vibe*. Analysis reveals how *The Source* is constructed as a male space, for young men to access the "real" knowledge on rap. This conception of "real" knowledge becomes anchored in U.S. rappers and consequently operates as a code to delegitimate Canadian rappers' claim to authenticity. The latter is reminiscent of Foucault's conception of power/knowledge. This is the last of the three chapters that examine the ways in which images of black youth get played out through the media via regimes of representations.

## Magazines

Magazines are the third aspect of youth culture examined to ascertain the ways in which media act as a repertoire of imagery and visual effects through which "difference" and blackness are represented during the late twentieth/early twenty-first centuries. A wide spectrum of U.S.-based magazines, ranging from the more general *Ebony* and *Jet* through *Sports Illustrated* to rap-specific *The Source* and *Vibe*,[1] were read by, although not always purchased by the students:

> **Student 1:** *Sports Illustrated* and stuff. *The Source*. Mostly I look for the basketball articles.
> **Student 2:** Shoes.
> **Student 1:** Some times the clothes and sometimes I will go for the car magazines.
> (Focus group of males)

In particular, the narratives reveal that the two hip-hop culture magazines, *The Source* and *Vibe*, are widely read. One student indicated the nuanced differences between the two magazines:

> **Doreen:** Actually, if it's about rappers, you have to go to *The Source*. If it's about r&b and all that stuff, then *Vibe* is like good. And they've got good clothes in *The Source*. But if you are looking for clothes, I suggest look in *The Source* because they have good clothes. All those rappers are advertising their clothes in there, advertising their shoes and all that stuff.

These U.S.-produced magazines are also drawn on to provide understanding and give meaning to rap in Canadian society. Both these monthly glossy magazines, in conjunction with music video representations, reinforce the construction of "authentic rap" for African Americans. These two magazines are equated by many students with possessing "the deep" knowledge about rap and r&b and are seen as somehow more authentic than others, especially when defined in relation to Canadian rap magazines:

**Melvin:** *The Source, Vibe*—there's more, I just can't remember. The other ones—they might be like Canada based magazines of rap. But the deep ones that you would actually go and look into if you wanted information are like *Source* and like *Vibe*.

Access to U.S.-based magazines emerges as part of a double process in the consumption and the development of preferred readings. As with many issues of social relations in Canadian society, meaning is constructed in relation to the United States. First, the consumption of rap information in *The Source*² and *Vibe* reinforces the U.S. position as the source of "authentic" knowledge and, at the same time, delegitimates Canadian sources. As a result, Canadian rap music is seen as imitative rather than innovative, mimetic rather than "authentic." The following narrative reveals a view of Canadian rap as "lacking" both numerically and qualitatively:

**Doreen:** No offence. Canadian music sucks, man. //It does?// Yeah. Oh come on, there is like—like nothing. There is only one player like that whole group gets like five groups, and they made like one whole video. You must have seen it on *Much Music*. It's like on all the time. [she is referring to a combined group of Canadian rappers]

As the narratives make clear, representations of rap are based on experiences in the U.S. The magazines bought by African Canadians reinforce and promote specific types of knowledge as more authentic than others. Reading is part of a social process. For some of the students, talking about and exchanging magazines provide not only opportunity for social discourse but also act as a mechanism for reinforcing the importance and symbolism of particular magazines as authentic representations. Through "school talk" and interaction at school, magazines become an important means of transmission for what Hall calls "regimes of representation."

**J:** So tell me a bit about *The Source, Vibe,* and *Jet*.
**Denzil:** They are all basically the same in that they bring rap news. Mostly that's what I read it for. And you see new clothes and new hair and stuff.

In reference to *The Source* magazine that her male peers read, Mirelle says:

**Mirelle:** Source 'cuz [its] mostly on the rap artists and stuff, so they [males] want to know what's going on. What's the latest music coming out.

Mirelle's comment identifying *The Source* as a "male space" is echoed in the following narratives from Doreen. For Doreen, the magazine provides information for guys, while allowing her to objectify male bodies:

**Doreen:** I read *Vibe*. I like *Vibe*. *Ebony* is my favourite. That's my favourite magazine. I used to get *Jet*, but I don't think they sell it in Edmonton anymore.

**J:** That's what someone else said to me.

**Doreen:** I like *The Source* lots too. That's like a guy magazine. Like all those guys read that. I just get it for the pictures.

**J:** Pictures of what?

**Doreen:** Of those black guys in there. Like some of them are good.

**J:** Are they? So what do you do with them?

**Doreen:** My whole room is like, covered with them.

Doreen is alluding to the polysemic nature of the texts and, in this case, the way in which meaning is never fixed but is open to interpretation. While she identifies *The Source* as a "male space," she is also able to claim it as a space for the female gaze. Although this gendered receptivity was not expressed within all the narratives, it highlights the important role that such magazines play in the representations of masculinity as well as the contouring of gender identification. However, not all female students were able to publicly and freely gaze on black male bodies. In the following narrative, one student indicates how her mother responded to discursive practices such as her display of pictures of a male singer on her bedroom wall:

If I put one poster up that she doesn't like, she will rip it off. She has done it before. She will rip it off. It doesn't matter if it's a good one. Maybe I was in a phase where I thought [the singer] was just really nice to have on my wall. It was small little one though, right. I just put three here and three there. It was nice. Looked nice. There was no background or any thing, just [the singer]. I came back home, they were all off my wall. She took them off.

Although both magazines are discussed in the students' narratives, *The Source* seems to be more popular, especially with the young men. Nelson George (1998) supports this postulation about the popularity of *The Source*. He argues that in 1997, "the magazine's relevance and vitality were confirmed when it sold more copies via newsstands than any other music periodical in America, averaging 317,369 copies per issue, compared to *Rolling Stone*'s 169,625. *The Source* continues on because it represents a keep-it-real alternative to the glossy, photo-driven coverage that has defined *Vibe*" (pp. 71–72).

In the narratives, *The Source* and *Vibe* were sites for the transmission of cultural meanings and understandings in relation to music and style associated with black youths. Interestingly, a number of the student narratives indicate that although they read the magazines, they did not purchase them. A variety of reasons were given for this anomaly. For one student, age was a factor in buying magazines, since one of the attractions of a "teen" magazine was that it enabled identification with an older age group and signified a certain kind of self and subjectivity. Thus she identifies how the purchase of magazines changes with adolescence and perceptions of the self:

**Phyllis:** I don't read many magazines really. I used to read like a lot of, like, when you are a kid you go through like a teeny-bopper stage when you read like *Dot* magazine and da da da magazine, whatever magazine, kind of stupid. And then, I don't know. Like just the little stuff like that I used to read. But now I don't really read much. Once in a while I read like *Seventeen*, or I read *YM*. Sometimes I will pick up a bop magazine because I will see someone, like a singer I like, on there.

Other students see magazines as too expensive. It is less expensive to browse through a friend's copy or thumb through a copy on the newsstand. As Eulyn explains:

**Eulyn:** I don't know. I just think it's a waste of time because you are going to read it once and then that's it. //Oh right// So it's better just to read about it for free. Then you don't have to worry about it.

Although many narratives suggest that they did not purchase magazines, students were nonetheless still influenced by the contents via social interaction and exchange with peers and siblings. Tricia Rose (1994) indicates that:

*The Source's* "pass-along rate" is approximately 1 purchase for every 11–15 readers. According to Bernard [an editor at *The Source*], this rate is at least three to four times higher than the average magazine industry pass-along rate. It is conceivable, then, that a similar pass-along rate exists among rap music CD and cassette consumption, especially among consumers with less disposable income. (p. 8)

For Wayne, it was neither age nor cost that was prohibitive but, rather, his religious belief that made reading or purchasing magazines with "worldly truths" highly problematic and thus because he assumed they had nothing to interest him. In response to my question concerning his magazine reading, he gave the following response:

**Wayne:** I don't read magazines [annoyed].
**J:** Do you look through them?
**Wayne:** Not unless I have an assignment.
**J:** How is that then?
**Wayne:** There's nothing that interests me.

At other times, students' receptions of magazine articles about rappers were coded as examples of "reality" in the United States: a reality that, although brutalized, can be translated through discourse as positive. Ironically, such articles of brutality and inner-city life reinforce discourses that actively produce and reinforce a myth of the American dream of "making it."

**Doreen:** Well, it goes like this. . . . You know what I like to see though, like about that magazine. How they are talking about how they were all like poor and everything, and it's like their dream comes through, because they got all rich after, and like everybody loves them up. And they are like—make pure money and everything. I like to see that type of stuff because it's "real." Like I stop and think, "I really feel bad for people in the ghetto, like I really do."

## Consuming Style

Magazine consumption is an important part of youth culture and is instrumental in developing and producing a sense of style as well as offering a point of identification. The latter can be illustrated by Gerald's comments with regard to an advertisement in *The Source*:

> **Gerald:**  Yeah, like we don't get that kind of stuff like in Canada. [pointing to picture of shoes in *The Source*] Like Lugz, like if we could, we would wear those too.
> **J:** Lugz did you say? What are those?
> **Gerald:**  You can't buy it. It's a type of name brand for a type of shoes. You can't buy that stuff here.[3]

Gerald's narrative leads us into the area of dress style and the ways that youth style is developed among the students. Without doubt, hip-hop style is and has been the most influential among students and youths across North America and beyond. The importance of dress style can be seen in Paul Willis's (1990) comments that "clothes, like musical tastes, are an indication of the cultural identities and leisure orientations of different groups of young people." In terms of this study, his comments would hold true, as the narratives position students within and in relation to discourses of style.

As the narratives reveal, hip-hop style and culture are not just a matter of purchasing or accessing magazines, listening to the music, or watching films and music videos. It is not just about consumption; it is also about production. It is about producing a sense of self. It is this presentation of the body that becomes important in signifying specific meanings and identities through dress style. Stephens (1996) argues "within hip-hop subculture . . . the styles and material culture of the subculture have been central to identity formation. That goes for the wearing of fake gold chains called 'dope-ropes,' oversized casual pants, the X Cap, to the high-top-fade hair cut, and other hip-hop manifestations" (p. 197). Throughout the narratives, consumption of hip-hop culture leading to production of identities was neither automatic nor uniform. Often consumption leading to the production of subjectivity was contoured by time availability, gender, and socio-economic status. For some students, adherence to the latest dress style and the latest forms of rap music was problematic, thus consumption was often partial:

**Gerald:** Like I am not really into hip-hop that much. Just like, not as much as most of my friends are. Like I don't know how much time they spend listening to it or watching it or reading, but I don't really have that much time to spend on it. So I don't know. Like I love the music, but I'm just not like into it as much as they are.

Or

**Etta:** Don't get me [wrong], I like hip-hop and stuff like that, but people—that's their life. People that actually do the killing and stuff like that is because they feel maybe that's almost their identity. People that couldn't get past the struggles of being black, I guess. Things like that bother them.

What these two narratives illustrate is that hip-hop is a cultural formation that requires knowledge and cultural understanding of the everyday experiences of those who are directly involved in the production.

As the narratives illustrate, common sense understandings among the youth construct hip-hop as a black cultural formation, where the signifiers "black style" and "hip-hop" are interchangeable. Although the students dressed in a variety of ways not necessarily identified with media-generated discourses on being black, it is clear from the narratives that the representations youth draw on for inspiration have much in common with hip-hop culture, often with a personal inflection. Some of the students referred to dressing in "baggy style" or having a "sporty style" as black, while others were cautious in generalizing about a connection. Throughout the narratives, the dress style that the students were cognisant of, and identified with, was one mediated by music magazines and music videos. Gerald struggles to articulate this point of connection between style and black identity:

**J:** So how would someone who is black dress?

**Gerald:** Well, there are exceptions. Black people don't dress, but like, I don't know, like the name brands that you wear, the shoes you'd wear, the way you'd wear it. It's like the styles that you'd have.

Or

**Phyllis:** Kind a like a sporty style, I guess. The track pants all the time and the Nike shirts and everything.

Or Melvin, in reflecting on his dress style:

**Melvin:** I still wear baggy clothes. Just for like comfort. Like baggy clothes, the like, jeans, like how would you say? Ok, when Exhaust first came in. Like Exhaust jeans.

I used to like sport those all the time. And like, the gold. I used to wear, I used to have gold.

And he continues:

> **Melvin:** Actually, you always have to have like nice shoes. Cos everybody, man, there's all these people I don't even know where they get their money from, but they've got like a million of pairs of like Nike this and all. And yeah like I used to, like, dress in all those shoes too. And like get all the nice new brands.

Gerald's, Phyllis,'s and Melvin's narratives are consistent in identifying black dress style with consumption of designer labels such as Nike and consequently the importance of branding in the production of specific subjectivities.

The narratives indicate that dress style as both consumption and production is often developed through reception of media images of rappers and r&b singers. In this way a desire is invoked among youth:

> **Gerald:** Oh I kinda see that the way we dress, we try to imitate people like Snoop and like other rappers.
> **J:** Such as?
> **Gerald:** Method Man.
> **J:** Who? What does he look like? What does he dress like?
> **Gerald:** I don't know if he changes his styles. Like, basically [he was] the first one that I seen to wear those like, you know, those fishermen hats with the rim around them? It's like a cap and it has like a rim going all the way round.

Or as Melvin's narratives highlight, there is a close, if not direct, relationship between rap music and hip-hop dress styles:

> **J:** Where did you see it?
> **Student:** Oh, they pretty much all have to come down to music. To rap, so you would see this on TV. Anything—dress, everything that comes down pretty much comes from rap. Any one who says it doesn't—it comes straight down, man.

As one student's narrative reveals, at times this link between a rap musician and a personal dress style involves not just a process of reception but also a process of production—the taking on of a style and making it one's own. The following narrative illustrates how a student identifies with the hairstyles of Buster Rhymes and Snoop Dogg. But it is an identification that is partial, as he changes aspects of the style to make it different:

Dogg came in with his cornrows like, then I got that. And I kinda stuck with that for a while. And then when you see Buster Rhymes going off with like his crazy hair going all over the place. Even though he's got dreads or whatever. I just like, do my hair all crazy.

One of the female students talks about deriving a basic style from a singer and individualizing it:

> If something looks good, I'll wear it. And put a hat to it or for my nail polish the same colour, make-up the same kind of, different things like that. I'll like add my little touch on it to make it me.

Although identification is made with rappers, this identification is not total.

## *Style as a Relation of Power*

Youth style is an indication of status and power. Dress style is an important resource that is used in combination with other attributes to define and construct specific identities and ways of presenting the self. It is a way of giving social meaning to the body. Intertwined with this understanding of dress style as giving meaning to the body are issues of geographic location and economic dominance: Edmonton in relation to Toronto and Toronto in relation to the United States. Edmonton was often seen as disadvantaged and marginalized in terms of receiving and producing the latest fashion trends. One student who had lived in the United States indicates this point:

> **J:** You have the latest clothes? So how do you know it's the latest?
> **Delroy:** Because you know what everybody else wears, "Okay, I haven't seen that yet." Like this FUBU shirt. //Yeah// My brother bought me this for Christmas. Nobody else had really seen one of those before, but they are starting to come here now.
> **J:** Oh, I see, right. So you think the U.S. is definitely ahead.
> **Delroy:** Yeah, we got it. We get everything ahead.

The narratives indicate that the degree of prestige of a given dress style is related to its location within or near to the United States. Students allude to the ways in which dress styles are diffused into different geographic areas in Canada. Styles in Toronto were seen as a reworking of the styles in the United States and were rated more highly than dress style in "dry" Edmonton. The following narrative highlights such a hierarchy:

> **Doreen:** They dress good. They kinda dress like them [singers in magazines] sometimes too. But the States has way better clothes and so does Toronto. Toronto has wicked clothes. Here. I can put it this way. I think Edmonton—it kinda sucks in a way. Because everybody's style like was in Toronto last year, is like [only] now coming down here.

In some ways, innovativeness in dress style in Edmonton was contoured by an exist-ing relation of dominance between Canada and the United States, especially as rep-resented in and through the consistent production and location of media culture in the United States. The following narrative substantiates Doreen's point with regard to the importance of the United States and the influence of New York, in particular, on the ways in which youth fashion becomes coded as stylish or not. In response to a query as to peer response to a different dress style that he adopted Gerald suggested:

> **Gerald:** People just like looked at me. Like my friends say things, that's wicked and stuff, but people never really come up to me and say anything. Because they didn't know, like for all they know, it could be like something new from like New York. So they wouldn't have just come up to me and started "dissing" it like, "Ah that's dry," and the next thing you know they turn on TV and like Method Man is wearing it or something. So they don't say anything.

As well, U.S. style shapes consumption patterns and availability of certain consumer items in Edmonton. Frank describes this tension between demand and consumption:

> **Frank:** Well recently, everybody was asking at Champs for FUBU, 'cuz it's always in like *The Source,* you know what *The Source* is? . . . All the latest clothes are adver-tised in *The Source* usually. So then people would see it and then they would ask for it here. And Champs started getting it 'cuz all the Champs in like the U.S. have them already.
> **J:** What's Champs?
> **Frank:** That's like a sports store, like shoes and stuff.

Style was also read intertextually in relation to peers. One could be considered outdated by the extent to which others had access to a similar dress style. Being styl-ish is a complex maneuver requiring knowledge of both the local and the global or, more specifically, the U.S. fashion market. Again, Doreen's narrative indicates that time and timing were important in terms of maintaining a sense of being fashion-able. So if one had an outfit that reflected a new style, then it was best to reinforce that sense of the "exclusiveness" and its consequent scarcity value by wearing that outfit to indicate a sense of the difference and the unobtainable. The following nar-rative shows how to shop and maintain a sense of the unique that evokes a sense of desire in the "other."

> **Doreen:** Know what you have to do? You have to go in like totally different stores and buy one shirt there and pants there, then you bring it all together, and you match it up. Because if you go and you buy a whole outfit, like you know, Stitches in West Ed-monton Mall. If you go in there every guy, everybody in this whole entire school, like goes and shops at Stitches, so you have your South Pole, you have your Mecca, and

all that stuff. Everybody has it, and you can't buy like an outfit in there without see-ing like six or seven girls. You see how big this school is? Like fifty girls might have that outfit. And when you go out to the clubs or whatever, when we have like Teen Nights or something, man, you see like more than ten, twenty girls wearing your clothes. Oh, you can't go to those places. Like you should go and buy something at one store, and then you walk to the other one so nobody can have what you have.

Thus, being fashionable was dependent upon maintaining a distinctive sense of self, while not being totally outside the "norms" of dress style. However, to be unique was not necessarily stylish, as Gerald's narrative suggests:

**Gerald:** If I like it, if I like the way they are dressing, I'll dress like them. If I don't, then I won't. Plus you can see things like when you are shopping and stuff. If you see something like no one else has it. You don't want to get it. I am not saying like I see what everyone dresses like, like I want to be like everyone. But just like sort of like it's like guidelines kind of. Like I wouldn't like, everyone how they wear jeans, I wouldn't go and wear like spandex pants and try to start my new style or something. Like I'll still wear the jeans, but try to get something that no one else has.

Or as Langston, who perceives himself as stylish, indicates, fear of straying beyond the "norm" acts as a form of social control on others:

**Langston:** Like it's the kind of thing. You see people wear it. Like you saw people wear it on TV. But it's like people don't have the. . . . This is what I think. Like people are scared to come up and do it themselves. And when someone does it, it's like okay, it's accepted. So you go ahead and do it.

So adoption of style also represents a relation of power between different geopoliti-cal areas as well as between peers.

As the commodification of hip-hop has increased during the latter part of the twentieth century and the twenty-first century, so has the cost of maintaining such a style. The narratives outline how keeping "in style" is an expensive business for the students. Many of the clothes associated with more recent hip-hop style are part of a growth in consumerism within youth culture. This growth[4] can be linked to white designers' development and mainstreaming of hip-hop-related style. R. Jemal Ste-phens (1996) argues that after initially ignoring hip-hop

established white designers expressed an interest in hip-hop clothing. These designers include Tommy Hilfiger, Polo, Guess, Girbaud, Nautica, Versace, and Marc Bucha-nan. . . . Many now use rappers in their advertisements for leather jackets and jeans. In the shoe wear market, white designers that initially rejected opportunities to market and promote their products in *The Source* have jumped on the bandwagon as well. (p. 200)

Phyllis outlines how a designer label increases the cost of being stylish:

> **Phyllis:** Oh yeah. If I was to get this shirt without the Nike check or anything on it, I probably could have got it for $20, but this one is like I got it on sale for $45, and its actual price was $100.

This process of commodification is based on the cultural economy of taste, but the decision to purchase is based on cultural value. Storey (1996) regards the latter as indicative that: "consumption, in this sense is an active, creative and productive process, concerned with pleasure, identity and the production of meaning" (p. 198).

With the expense of maintaining a hip-hop-related dress style comes the necessity to increase economic resources. For some students, part-time jobs or parents were used to finance such patterns of consumption:

> **Melvin:** I had, actually, no serious job. But like a paper job. Like delivering for the [Journal], and I used to make money off that. And then I did flyers, and my parents would buy me stuff for like special [occasions] like my birthday or Christmas or something.

Or Langston:

> **Langston:** My mum, she gives me clothes. And she gives me money. I do get a job, well not really job, do this for somebody, do that for somebody.

The lack of direct access to economic resources alluded to by Langston meant that for financially dependent students, parents become important in mediating the student's ability to consume dress styles related to hip-hop. For one student, parents buying his clothes meant that he was unable to fully subscribe to and subject himself to a hip-hop style:

> **Omar:** It used to be, like I used to dress to be able to like say like I am part of the hip-hop crowd.
> **J:** So what did you dress like when you were part of the hip-hop group?
> **Omar:** I tried. I tried. It didn't work out. //Didn't it?// I can go on, like my mom buys my stuff. She even bought my stuff back then. She wasn't, she wasn't really into that [hip-hop style] right. So I tried but never like, I had like some tight jeans in grade 7, and I felt uncomfortable wearing that stuff. Not because of the way it looked, but it just felt uncomfortable. So, as I grew older, I got more money to buy for myself, and I started to like buy jeans like that were more comfortably fitting. But I was still thinking of what other people would think I look like.

Omar's narrative makes clear that for some students, consumption of hip-hop style was often partial rather than full. His narrative also alludes to the importance of style in terms of generating a sense of acceptance by peers. As such, the narratives reinforce how style is as much for public consumption as for private pleasure.

## *Performing Style*

Public spaces such as school, clubs, and social events were the locus for articulating identity through dress style. As the students indicate, male dress style is constantly undergoing changes. Omar identifies the ways in which the school provides a site that reflects those changes:

> **Omar:** It's kind of changing. It used to be big, big, big clothes and sneakers and the hat and what not. But now it's kinda changing into like the, what-you-call-it, the preppy styles. Or whatever. I wouldn't say it's changed to that. But like there are some people who are like experimenting or whatever you want to call it. Like with the boots, the rolled- up jeans, and like the dress shirt and all like that.
>
> **J:** Rolled up jeans?
>
> **Omar:** Oh, like not rolled up. Like you know, like, instead of where'd I see it?
>
> **J:** Turned up at the bottom, and the dress shirt.
>
> **Omar:** There are some people who will come to school. I know black people who will come to school dressed like that. It's just, it's just anything that's kind of different.

Or, as Phyllis identified, socio-economic status was now much more evident in youth style:

> **Phyllis:** Like for some of the guys here. Before it was like the lower and baggier you could wear your pants, the "cooler" you were. Like the more boxers you were show-ing, it was the better. Now, it's the nicer clothes you wear, the better you are. Like if you are wearing a Polo or the Gucci or the Tommy Hilfiger, then you are alright. Like baggier clothes, like people are coming out of that now.

Interestingly, the explanation for this change in dress style was attributed to changes in youth culture in general, and rapper P. Diddy's influence, in particular, as style among the males moved towards a more "smooth" look:

> **Melvin:** Actually, that's true. If you walk down the hallway right now, you could see like [Will] standing on one side of the hall. And he'd be like all like his nice preppy type shirt and like his jacket and his glasses.

Langston, who saw P. Diddy as representing "smooth" dress style contrasted his own dress style as "dressing rough." In his narratives he identifies how the term operates to describe dress style:

**Langston:** "Rough." It's just an expression. Rough, I look good; I look rough. I could be dressed in a suit, and I'll think I look rough. Just as long as you look good. But there is also the other part of saying you look rough. You know when you classify yourself in contrary to say, the way a prep dresses. You say I look rough; he is a prep. Just a difference because you are dressed in different clothes. Like they wear nice button-up shirts, and I am wearing a T-shirt. Or I am wearing a big sweater with a zip down, or he is wearing a hat, I am wearing a bandanna, or I am wearing a stocking. He is wearing boots, and I am wearing runners. He is wearing loose fitting jeans. I am wearing baggy jeans.

At times, this presentation of self through style at school becomes intertwined with issues of motivation as well as connotation of a type of academic self. In particular, a certain style of dress identifies an individual as "cool" or not.

**Langston:** Like, obviously people who aren't cool don't care, or else they would try and be cool and they'd be "cool." And everyone would just be cool, I guess. But sometimes I can see like people who just totally don't care if they are cool or not. They just care about like going to school. Doing their best. Going home, doing their homework, studying, don't care what they look like. They don't care what they do after school. Just care about that [schoolwork]. So like I can see how they think. But I don't think I can ever think like that. Sometimes I wish I did, but like I couldn't just change and start thinking like that. Sometimes I wished that was the only way like I was ever brought up—to think like that. But it's not so.

The cool identity referred to is contrasted with and often used to differentiate oneself from geeks or nerds who were constructed as "just caring about school" rather than what they look like. For Melvin, this process of differentiation began early in his school life:

**Melvin:** Junior high, when I was in grade 7, I was, I guess you could say I was a little geek. I never thought I was. But I was, you know. I guess it's because I used to like dress differently to everyone else.

Gender was an intervening factor in presentation of dress style. Within the narratives of a few of the female students, there is an indication that style was used to present differing senses of self. This differing presentation of selves indicates that style was used inconsistently as a means to evoke differing meanings in differing contexts. At times, one dressed in a totally different way.

**Phyllis:** Describe my dress style? That's a hard one. I think it just depends on my day. Like sometimes I can be kind of dressy, but yet other days I can be like just grunge, or else I can be right in the middle.

Or as Joy identified, with regard to dressing like women rappers on videos, dressing allows the representation of differing-gendered selves, a mix and match, between "feminine" and "bad girl":

> **Joy:** That's a hard question. It's like some of them dress the same way. Actually, I no-tice [with] what all of my little crew, we, like, one day we will go like kind of like "bad girl style," and then another day we will go kind of like "nice and feminine," whatever. [laugh] Like kind of dressed up, we always "mix and match" like that. I think it's kind of similar [to singers] but just different clothes. But we are like what they [women rappers] are wearing too.

The ability to produce a sense of self through dress style is, however, conditioned by prevailing normative standards. As Denzil indicates, if women wear what they want and show off their bodies then:

> **Denzil:** That's fine. But then they shouldn't complain about guys staring at them or hitting on them or anything like that because basically they are asking for it. If they dress like that to get attention, then they are going to get attention.

Another student's narrative indicates an awareness of such normative discourses that shape style. She identifies how desire to imitate the dress of the women repre-sented on music videos is constrained by gender expectations rather than being "open." A young woman indicates how she is subjected to expectations of gender and femininity:

> **Doreen:** On TV you see the girls in those videos have like shorts and all that stuff. You know the Spice Girls? //Yeah// You know the black spice girl, you know how she wears those [laugh] long, long, dresses, and they have like the biggest slit coming up. Boots with hot pants and everything? //Oh yeah// I remember I used to be like, "Oh that's nice, I want them." But I am like,"Oh no you don't." But I am just saying I want them, but I don't think he'd like [mind me wearing] them. But I know when I got it; I am that type of person if I get something tight. And I go to a party, I'm like, "I shouldn't have worn this" and Paul's like "Why not?" I go, "You should know. I feel so weird about my body."

Doreen's narrative reveals the tension between collective norms and individual de-sire: norms that are reinforced by the expectation of the male gaze and meanings that are produced therein. It is a disciplining of the self, what Foucault (1988) would identify as "technologies of the self," a process that

> permits individuals to effect by their own means to, with the help of others, a certain number of operations on their own bodies and souls, thoughts, conduct and way of

being, so as to transform themselves in order to attain a certain state of happiness, purity, wisdom, perfection or immorality. (p. 18)

In some narratives, dress style within the school was also identified with particular racialized groups. The narratives indicate that students from specific ethnic/racialized groups could be identified through certain ways of dressing.

> **Phyllis:** If you are going by like races, I guess you could say a white kid usually, the average white kid that you see around, wears like the perfect fit jeans. I don't know, they just dress different from us. Like they don't wear the big baggy pants as the black kids do. Then you have the Orientals, who wear their hair short and they have two bangs coming down off the side of their face, and they all dye their hair like different colours all the time.

For one student, not only is there a racialized link between clothing and identity, but the very ways of presenting the body through style heighten a form of black masculinity that other males cannot achieve. In response to a question on the existence of black style, she affirms the links between black style and designer label as well as the ways in which clothing can construct and reinforce desire:

> **Doreen:** Okay. Well. As for the guys, it's like the nice, like Fila or Nike runners. Or like they've got the boots, right? But for some reason Oriental guys dress one certain way, right? But when the black guys wear that style, it makes it look totally better. Anything a black guy wears, they make it look better, for some reason. I don't know what it is. And I think black guys look so good in white jeans. I don't know. They just look good. Like everything they wear. Like, they've got like their baggy jeans; they have cord; they've got their Nike; they got their Fila, Adidas. No, black guys don't wear Adidas, come to think of it. Not many of them do. Adidas is like kinda for natives.

This construction and contouring of desire were not confined to females, but as the narrative of one young man indicates, dress style was an integral part of attracting the female gaze:

> **Melvin:** I used to dress up in all the latest fads. I'd like be one of Tommys, [Hilfiger] all this stuff. But now I just like, I just throw on whatever. I don't even care. I don't even have any one to impress any more.
> **J:** So who were you impressing before then?
> **Melvin:** Well, it was pretty much like pursuing girls.
> **J:** Oh really? That's your main focus of dressing?
> **Melvin:** Oh yeah! [laugh]. You got to like look good, or else the girls are just going to be like, oh they'll be like "Forget about him." So then I was like strutting my stuff. So I could like show the girls. But then, I don't know, pretty much now I feel that I am married, so I can just like "chill." Go round with my belly hanging out.

This student's narratives construct style as something related to age and development. For him, getting older was marked by less emphasis on consumption of designer labels—a position which might well be influenced by his long-term relationship with his girlfriend and a decrease in the desire for the female gaze.

For young blacks, males and females, the way hair is shaped and styled may be seen as both an individual expression of the self and as the embodiment of society's norms, conventions, and expectations (Mercer, 1994, p. 100). The following student narrative iterates the ways in which adoption of a specific hairstyle can act as a signifier for other meanings not always intended. In this case, the signifier is translated and slides into a sign of "coolness" that draws upon codes and meanings evoked by the rap group Onyx:

> 'Cuz I had my whole head "Fro." And like everyone [at school] said that I looked like a geek, and I was like maybe I should just cut it down short. 'Cuz I didn't want to like look like anything. No, no, [that's wrong]. I started, like, I cut it short, right? And I keep like the top a little bit higher. And I wanted him to trim down like the sides and the back. And then by accident he shaved a bald spot, right? So I, then like I shaved off the sides and the back and then, I don't know. I was all of a sudden cool. Every one liked the style. "So cool." I was just walking around. I was like "Hey!" Then, like I shaved off my hair because, I don't know, that was the thing going through too. I think it was the time of Onyx. The rap group. And they were all bald, and they were like the big thing. And then, so I like shaved off my hair.

For another student, it was his father who, using a gendered discourse, was most influential in determining his hairstyle—a style that cohered with presentation of a mainstream masculine self:

> **J:** Your dad, then, thinks that you should look more conservative?
> **Denzil:** Yeah. He doesn't like, well, he doesn't want me to worry a lot about my hair. He thinks that's kind of, like "girls worry about their hair," he says. "Only girls worry about their hair" [gruff deep voice]. "Only girls do this and only girls do that." And so he said "Your hair grows this way easiest; so do it like this." And I have always had it like that. He made me do it like that, so I keep it like that.

Another student felt hair was a way of creating different styles and presenting a different sense of self:

> **Langston:** Yeah. I had braids, really long braids. Like when I pulled it down, it used to stretch that long. The thing is that like I grew my hair in the first place, to try something different with my hair. 'Cuz I had been cutting it all my life. It's like I grew it, had tiny braids all over my head. I used to have cornrows. I used to style the cornrows. Instead of going all the way back, I could have them go forward. Sometimes I had designs in my head from corn rows. After a while it just got boring, so I cut it off.

These students' comments concur with Dick Hebdige's postulation that style is not just the expression of class location, it is a signifying system, communicating both cultural identity and cultural difference. Youth subcultures communicate their distance identity and their cultural difference from and in opposition to peer, parent, and dominant cultures through a politics of style (Storey, 1996, p. 120). This politics of style is evident in the following narrative, as the student identifies the ways in which dress style is very much about representation. It is not an incoherent practice. It is something to be worked at. As well, he identifies how adherence to a specific style is no longer part of his repertoire:

**Melvin:**   Previously? I was like, I have like actually a certain amount of clothes that I use for the weekend. And like I wouldn't wear them during the week. It would be something that I'd come out with at the weekend. And like sometimes, too, I'd like go out and buy something to like go to some party or something. Like if it was something big, I'd go out and get something. But like otherwise, pretty much, I have like a certain set of clothes that I wouldn't wear . . . like these would be my Friday pants. And I'd have a Friday shirt, unless I'd already done gone to like some party with the same people on Friday before, so that I've got to like change to my Saturday stuff.

Although dress style is often presented as innocent of power, it is anything but. Certain rules about style were evident in the narratives. As indicated by Doreen above, style has various meanings attached by peer groups. The wearing of fashion had unwritten rules. Not anyone could wear anything, anywhere. The discussion of "style" in the sense of fashion and clothes is an important part of identification with being, and presenting of one's self as, black. It is a way of marking and differentiating the body that is constructed through an interconnected series of hierarchical systems of race, class, gender, sexuality, and religion.

## Summary

This chapter has examined the ways in which hip-hop magazines are consumed by the students and the ways in which these consumption patterns help to develop a sense of style. Location is important to being stylish and in enabling access to certain styles. However, Edmonton's geographic location makes being stylish problematic. As one student indicated, Edmonton is "dry." Desire for U.S. products is generated through the magazines the students read and music videos that are played on programs such as *RapCity*. Two main hip-hop magazines are read, *The Source* and *Vibe*. School is thus an important site for displaying one's dress style and producing social meanings. In analyzing the growth in production of mass designer fashions such as Tommy Hilfiger, it is evident that specific discourses and ideologies are operating in and on consumption patterns. Coded within the students' narratives on dress style is a linking with rap and periodization. P. Diddy is perceived as a "playa" because he raps about his money and women rather than "keeping it real" and rapping about experiences in the "hood." His dress style is seen as a reflection of his non-identification with the hood. This coding of dress style through music was translated to the school site and was further used to categorize peers. Also evident is the way that the descriptors "cool" and "nerds" are based partly on dress style that then gets coded with other discursive practices to produce specific school identities.

*The Source* is identified as a male space for young men to access the "real" knowledge on rap. This conception of real knowledge becomes anchored in U.S. rappers and, consequently, operates as a code to delegitimate Canadian rappers' claim to authenticity.

The next chapter, "Urban Legend," illustrates the ways in which discourses and ideologies are given symbolic meaning during everyday experiences. By examining the way that discourses work, we should be able to gain a greater understanding of how the tension between structure and agency plays out in the students' lives.

# CHAPTER 6

# Urban Legend

*Thanks to Adobe Photoshop and similar image-processing technologies, skin tones
can be more easily manipulated than the indelibly marked musculatures that
sell the sweated and branded products of Tommy Hilfiger, Calvin Klein,
Timberland, and Guess in the glossy pages of overground publications like* Vibe
*and* The Source *that trade widely in aspects of black culture but are not
primarily addressed to any black reading public.*

GILROY, 2000, p. 23

## Introduction

In the previous chapter the selected narratives explored the ways in which identities are produced through consumption and production of certain styles. This chapter illustrates through three concrete examples the ways in which discourses of style become saturated with black-identified meaning. The narratives identify quite clearly how media are "resources to think with," and how the students use style as a signifier to connote meanings in other areas of their lives. What is evident in the narratives are the ways in which discourses struggle with each other to produce "truth effects." This production of truth does not refer to a truth in the absolute sense but rather a discursive formation sustaining a truth (Jensen, 2002). Three main themes emerge in the narratives: a racialized urban legend related to style, division of urban space based on style; and the ways in which black identity, through style becomes identified as "acting." Further, highlighting these themes illustrates the ways that identity is both symbolic and social and shows how "the struggle to assert different identities has material effects and consequences" (Woodward, 1997, p. 10). These discourses of style produce material consequences in terms of youth consumption and in terms of relations of power. As with Foucault the narratives examine how things work "at the level of on-going subjugation at the level of those continuous and uninterrupted processes which subject our bodies, govern our gestures, dictate our behaviors, etc." (Foucault, 1980, p. 97). Intertextuality is evident throughout the three highlighted themes especially through the ways in which meanings with regard to identities are produced in relation to existing Black Nationalist discourses. The chapter highlights how discourses are not just language but do produce meanings within a relation consisting of other discourses.

## *Urban Legend*

One of the most important aspects of mediazation is the extension of information and knowledge to individuals and communities who because of geography, time, or distance would not have had access previously. Mediated interaction means that first-hand, face-to-face experience is not as readily available to verify and validate experiences. In light of the latter the following section highlights how an "urban legend" discourse affects students' ability to relate to certain black-identified subject positions. Leonard Stern, in an Edmonton *Journal* article, defines urban legends as "those astonishing, amusing, and sometimes scary stories that are told and retold around the world, the individual details of which may vary depending on local circumstances—the one constant element being that the stories are passed off as true" (Stern, 2000). Such a "legend" was evident in the "Tommy Hilfiger is a Racist" stories that emerged from the narratives of the students. Such a story provides an interesting example of the ways in which discourses of the "real" and the "unreal" can collide. Although the story has been challenged and identified as inaccurate, nonetheless, through racialized and economic discourses, the story produces certain social effects, via subjectivities. What the latter would seem to reinforce is that "discourses are true in so far as they are accepted, so that people act as if they were true. Discourses can be understood only in relation to other discourses and their truth or falsity cannot be proved by reference to an outside" (Woodward, 1997, p. 253).

The discourses at work reveal an ideological tension between a subject position that supports "blackness" and a positioning of one's self as "stylish." The purpose of the ensuing discussion is not to verify or dispute the students' narratives but rather to look at the ways in which the students come to accept, or not, the discourses surrounding the "legend" and also how they link such discourses to other discourses in order to identify and position themselves as specific black subjects. In many ways, the discursive practices evoked by the legend illustrate the power of discourse and the ways in which discourses have material effects as, at times, the edges of "reality" and e-mail-generated "cyber-reality" become blurred. The narratives reveal what O'Sullivan et al. (1994) describe as "ideological struggle between discourses": between (legitimated, naturalized) black consciousness and (emergent, marginalized) laissez-faire attitude. Students' awareness of these emergent discourses of consumption exists alongside traces of the previous discourses. So the narratives, in highlighting this urban legend, illustrate the ways in which discourses slip and slide.

This specific urban legend is interesting because it is based on comments that Hilfiger allegedly made on the *Oprah Winfrey Show*. According to the legend, Hilfiger's racist remark was that, "Blacks and Asians don't look good in my clothes." Despite the fact that it is possible to verify that the comment was never made, its continued currency is a testimony to the power of such legends to operate as "truth" and to produce consequent effects. The narratives reveal the ways in which this legend draws on discourses of dress style and consumerism as well as a politicized identification with being black.

Within Eulyn's narrative below, the pleasure of dressing in Tommy Hilfiger is subsumed to perceptions of herself as black. Her actions illustrate what Smith (1988) identifies as the "simultaneous operation of agency and subjugation" (p. 132). She perceives herself as free from the ideology of consumerism while at the same time accepting and subjecting herself to the ideology of black consciousness:

J: Have you ever worn Tommy Hilfiger? //nuh huh// How come?

Eulyn: Well, I always say, Tommy Hil, Tommy is for "wiggers." Because he is a racist. So [pause] I wouldn't wear his stuff.

J: So what did you think when you heard that, and what happened after that?

Eulyn: Well, I just thought, well, obviously, if he thinks that way, well, then you know. I am not going to spend my money to support him.

J: Did you used to buy his clothes before that?

Eulyn: Some of them.

J: So you made a conscious decision. Did you talk about it as a group, as friends?

Eulyn: Yeah. Some of them are just ignorant. They just think, "Well, oh no, he didn't say that." Or "they took it out of context or something."

J: So not everyone said "Oh, I am not buying his clothes he is a racist."

Eulyn: And they will say "Oh, it's so nice though."

For Eulyn, as her narratives make clear, production of herself as consciously black makes wearing this specific brand of designer clothes unacceptable. Her peers, in contrast, are portrayed as either ignorant of such "truth" or are compromised by their desire for style.

For Etta, the "truth" of the legend was legitimated by reference to her friends who claim to have seen the program in question:

Etta: No. First of all, basically, it's too expensive. Second of all, I've heard a lot of things about him. Very bad. //Have you?// Oh yeah. When he was on Oprah, he said that black people don't look good in his clothes. //Oh right// Did you see that show?

//No // I never saw that show, but I actually heard like a lot of people like [Gloria] and that saw it, so I believe them. Things like that I don't understand. I think it's almost stupid of people to buy his clothes after that.

The result for Etta is that available economic resources, reinforced by a politicized identification with blackness, dictate that Hilfiger's clothes are not for her.

Another student cites economic factors to account for his action and reinforces them with racialized meanings:

**Denzil:** I don't wear Tommy Hilfiger stuff. It's too expensive, and he is kind of a racist too. So I heard. So, I can't afford it, so I am not going to wear it anyway.

For another student, the availability of economic resources was not as important a constraint on his purchase of clothing as the ostensibly racist comment in response to a question on buying Tommy Hilfiger style:

**Frank:** Not any more. I used to.
**J:** Did you? And what made you stop?
**Frank:** When I found out like what he said about black people, I switched over to Nautica.
**J:** To where? //Nautica// So you switched over deliberately? // Yeah// You thought of that, and thought, "I am not wearing that?"
**Frank:** Yeah, lots of people have switched over, actually.

Economic resources did not limit Frank, unlike both Etta and Denzil. His narrative indicates the ways in which socio-economic circumstances and class location can contour racialized understandings. While Etta and Denzil drew primarily on an economic discourse supported by Black Nationalist discourse to support their rejection of Hilfiger designs, Frank was able to abandon Hilfiger and move onto a similar high-status designer (Nautica) without loss of status. He could be consciously black and stylish. This class location affects the way in which youth are subjected to and become subjects of discourses of style.

Phyllis's narrative indicates that the urban legend has produced material effects, making Hilfiger clothes a less-desirable consumer item than other designer labels:

**J:** That's very expensive. Is there much in terms of people stealing clothes?
**Phyllis:** Used to be. With Tommy Hilfiger it was really bad. A lot of people were stealing Tommy Hilfiger. Because their shirts were going for like; $200, $150. And even though it was like a T-shirt, it was like 150 bucks. And it was like, "I'll just steal it." And now nobody really cares because Tommy Hilfiger is losing so much business. Especially since that whole thing when he said, "Well, I don't like 'niggers' and 'chinks'

and this and that." He lost so much business, and then he had to make a public apology, and all his prices went down because so many people stopped buying.

The following narratives reveal how, when discourses collide, the positioning in terms of subjectivity is unpredictable. Unlike other narratives above, this student's orientations to the discourse move between positions identified as individual and collective. In response to a direct question on the issue of Tommy Hilfiger, the following narrative emerged:

**J:** Did you hear about the controversy with Tommy Hilfiger and comments he made about Chinese and blacks wearing his clothes?

**Melvin:** Like how he is racist or whatever? //Yeah// I heard that, but like I also saw that somewhere written that like he was happy that black people were wearing his clothes because, like I forget, some nonsense. I didn't pay much attention to it. But, yeah, I heard about all that.

**J:** Did it affect you and wearing his clothes or buying it? // No// Tell me why not?

**Melvin:** There is always something going on. Like Tommy Hil is a racist. Snapple is owned by the KKK. Same with like, what kind of shoes? Doc Martens were like some like they were Nazi skinheads or something. People ran that and like, I forget, Nike has got its story about how they paid people like two cents a year. Whatever. I don't even know. It doesn't affect me either which way. Like I'm sure, well, everybody has got to get paid somehow, whoever they are. I find those racist guys quite interesting anyways, like all the Klan people. Like on Jerry [Springer], too, they are all interesting. And if they've got to make a dollar by doing something in order to make their dollar. . . . I don't support their view, but I can support their clothes. I am sure //Really?// they are saying "Hey, black people cannot buy this you know, yah de dah de." If black people are going to sport their gear and look good in it then hey! Then we might as well make you mad, instead of like steering away from it.

For this student, consideration of style outweighed other ideological considerations. The ability to display a fashionable self evoked a sense of pleasure that could be turned back upon itself. It could be represented as a challenge and resistance to Hilfiger's perceived racism. Using a discourse of consumerism as a point of resistance, Tommy Hilfiger's views are negated by further consumption and increase in sales for Hilfiger. This student, using consumerism as resistance, was able to consume without subscribing to the ideological orientations attached to Hilfiger. This narrative, unlike others, highlights the contested nature of the urban legend. Interestingly, it is not the "truth" of the legend that he draws on to legitimate his position. Rather, he presents himself as resisting Hilfiger's racism.

As his narrative continues, it is obvious that at times, dress style is able to override alignment with a Black Nationalist discourse, as individual desire outweighs the collective black consciousness:

**Melvin:** Yeah. I'll sport his gear. I have no problem with that. So like if I met the man, Tommy Hilfiger, and he is like "Yeah, I don't want you wearing my clothes, because you are black," and he starts calling me names and all this, then I would knock him out. And that would be the end of the story. But otherwise, I know I'm never going to meet him. And like I do want to look nice every once and while. So I'll wear his clothes.

Another student identified the ways in which the boycott on Tommy Hilfiger's clothes was short lived and how discourses surrounding the boycott could reposition students as resisting racist meanings while still consuming Hilfiger style:

**Phyllis:** Oh yeah, everybody talked about it. Everybody stopped wearing Tommy Hilfiger for awhile. And then everybody like thought, everybody thought about it and they're like, "Why would I stop wearing it. If I like it I am going to wear it anyway. So they bought it and they thought well, if he came to Edmonton—oh well, he is going to get pissed off. Too bad kind of thing. And then he ended up coming back to make a public apology. So everyone was kind a like well, okay, whatever.

**J:** So did you believe his public apology?

**Phyllis:** No. No. Even though he has got oriental and black models and all this stuff, whatever. You can't just change just because your line of clothing stops selling. Your mind just doesn't go, "Oh."

For some, the urban legend was drawn on to reinforce existing tastes:

**Langston:** Some people don't care. Like I don't really care. It's just that I don't like Tommy Hilfiger. And it just give me more reason not to.

Langston's narratives indicate that discourses often operate with and through other discourses that shape the relations of power. Similarly, Wayne below, in using two discourses, draws on a normative discourse of religion in order to position himself as against consumerism—Hilfiger included. For Wayne, Hilfiger's clothes were perceived as symbolic of consumerism and "worldly goods" and, as such, incongruent with a sense of a religious self. As he sees the situation, Hilfiger is part of consumerism, which is part of a craving for worldly goods, in opposition to a spiritual craving:

**Wayne:** I don't have any Tommy Hilfiger. I am not the kind of person that goes for name brand. I just go for casual wear. No name brands. Still good clothes, you know. It's just the Nike check that makes the price so high. And like there's some Nike shoes like for 200 whatever, whatever dollars. And you can take 200 whatever, whatever, dollars and buy at least four shoes. So tell me, which one is better?

## North/South—East/West: "We're Not Really Like the Rest"

This section examines the ways in which the students use style and draw on regime of representation mediated through youth culture to code urban space. This coding is based on discourses of socioeconomic status. Student discourses weave a relational classificatory system through which meaning becomes constructed. One such example concerned the issue of urban space and emerged in the use of the spatial metaphor "North/South." In particular I want to highlight Chris Barker's point that, "though material objects and social practices exist outside of language, they are given meaning and brought in to view by language and are thus discursively formed" (1999, p. 26).

Geographic location in Edmonton emerges in the narratives as an important signifier of difference, a difference that fragments conceptions of a unified black collectivity. I have drawn on the following theme to highlight the ways in which one cannot think in terms of a homogenous black group and to identify the ways in which media culture plays a role in helping to classify fellow blacks as "different from." What the discourse reveals is the binaries Northside and Southside, in which each category is defined in relation to its difference from the "other." The comments illustrate the ways in which racialized subjugation cannot be viewed only in binary terms. Subjugation operates within racialized groups. This understanding also indicates that power is not just top down and one-dimensional but is more complex and reminiscent of Foucault's understanding of the micropolitics of power (Foucault, 1980).

As well, style and fashion become linked with the ways in which we come to give meaning to specific situations. The narratives suggest that the students draw on media images and youth culture in order to make sense and mark off an "other" who, in many ways, looks like themselves. For Kathryn Woodward (1997):

> This marking of difference takes place both through the *symbolic* systems of representation and through forms of *social* exclusion. Identity then is not the opposite of but *depends on* difference. In social relations, this form of symbolic and social difference is established, at least in part through the operation of what are called classificatory systems. A classificatory system applies a principle of difference to a population in such a way as to be able to divide them and all their characteristics into at least two opposing groups; us/them self /other. Each culture has its own way of classifying the world—by means of classificatory system culture gives us the means by which to make sense of the world. (p. 28)

The following section reveals how some of the students create a binary between differing areas of the city, using media culture and dress style to symbolize difference. These narratives reveal what can be identified as a discursive formation, since in many ways they "refer to the same object, share the same style and . . . support a strategy . . . a common institutional, administrative or political drift" (cited in Hall, 1997, p. 45). Further, if we analyze these narratives as discourse, rather than to prove their "truth," we can instead examine when and how the discourses are mobilized and used during social interaction. As discourses, they illustrate how "every discourse is part of a discursive complex; it is locked in an intricate web of practices, bearing in mind that every practice is by definition both discursive and material" (Henriques et al., 1984, p. 106).

The students' comments indicate that urban space is clearly demarcated through the descriptors "Northside," "Southside," and "Westend." Although Westend is mentioned it is the Northside and Southside that are presented as binary, and the Northside that is classified most negatively:

**J:** Oh really! There's a distinction?

**Eulyn:** The Westend is like the soft side of the city. Then you have Southside, which is like in between. And then the Northside is just like "the hood."

Joy's narrative links the Northside with the number of black people living there as well as an exotification of the males, resulting in an ambivalence that generates an appeal of the "other."

**Joy:** On the Northside it seems like there are more black people, but I am not quite sure about that. But I think so. The people don't . . . it seems more like there are better-looking guys down there. It's like, "Yeah, let's go to the Northside!" [conspiritory] But then, also, like some of those black guys down there are slack too. They are like nasty. So, I don't know, but it's still like the Northside! [whispered] He is a Northside guy. "Whoa." That means he is fine, or something. So I don't know. It's funny, it's so funny how these things—I don't even know how it originated from, but it just happened like that. And usually people from the Northside think they are all bad. They think they are all tough and whatever. So I don't know.

Throughout the narratives there was a degree of coherence in terms of geographic alignment and the descriptors Northside and Southside. Specific schools were seen as part of communities included in these geographic areas:

**J:** You mentioned Northside and Southside. That's come up a lot. In terms of these interviews, what would you say was the Northside?

**Melvin:** Pretty much Newtown. 'Cuz that's where like, I don't know, most of the black guys that whoever, like Newtown and Stadium, like they were like, 'cuz a lot of black people that like used to do whatever like came from around there.

While binarism is evident in the production of Northside and Southside differences, at times maintaining binaries become problematic as experiences intervene in the production of discourse. A student who identifies a dichotomous north and south distinction then has to specify and narrow the area in order to include family and friends and to avoid cognitive dissonance. Other factors, such as social compositions, are drawn on to make even finer distinctions within the geographic areas.

> **Etta:** But mostly I am thinking Newtown area. 'Cuz like if you are talking about like Meadowdale, Towerbrooks, where my mum's friends live, and their kids, that's different. Because it's a different kind of atmosphere. It's kind of like a Crystalclear different kind of neighbourhood. And it's not a black neighbourhood. It's just whatever. How would you put it? Even though it's the Northside, I don't really consider that. I'm just thinking Newtown.

For another student who mixed regularly with youths who lived in other areas of the city, the marking of and differentiation between such urban space seemed irrelevant. Thus, for Omar, experiences of different areas of the city and his friendships that extend beyond his own bounded geographic area of the Southside prevent him from seeing the two sides of the city as binary opposites. Having friends on both sides of the city and being able to cross boundaries enabled him to problematize the North /South dichotomy:

> **Omar:** 'Cuz like people fight over the stupidest things. Like you're from the Northside, I am from the Southside, you suck. And they will actually almost fight over that just because you live on one side of the city. Me, like I said, I know a lot of people. I know people from the Northside. I know people from the Southside. I know people from the Westend. There are some people in the Southside that don't want to know people from the Northside just because [of where] they live. And like I have slept over at friend's houses on the Northside. I've slept over at friends' houses in the Westend and the Southside. So for me, when it gets to that type of thing [disputes], I am usually the person, I am either a) the person that'll say "Ya leave it alone" or b) I'll just watch it 'cuz I don't want to get into this. So it's gotten to the point where I look at it sometimes and say, "This is stupid; I am leaving."

The students varied as to the extent to which they thought there was an ongoing dispute, based on symbolic differences, between the north and the south sides of the city. For the following student, the differences between north and south sides of the city were no longer issues of dispute:

> **Mirelle:** That, too, is like before like long ago, that used to be a big thing—Northside, Southside. Now I think it's more calmed down. It's not big no more.

Another student's narratives reveal a different picture:

**Doreen:**  You know, the Northside and Southside have beefs too. Did those guys talk about it? Southside guys and Cherryfields always have problems with the guys in Newtown. For what reason? It's just so dumb.

Some students, even if they saw the dispute as in the past, could still identify specific social descriptions related to dress and style that characterized North/South. My response of incredulity did not deter Melvin from attempting to present a rationale and basis for the differentiation:

**J:**  Come on, Melvin! It's not in the water.
**Melvin:**  No, no. I am serious, actually. 'Cuz it was kind of weird. A lot of them were taller. And on the Northside you have like a whole bunch of like the short guys. It just happened like that. And there is a whole lot of explanation. Plus they dress differently. They talk differently to a certain extent. Like I don't even know how anybody talks any more.
**J:**  So tell me, how did they used to talk?
**Melvin:**  I don't know. They talk differently from the way we talked. I don't know 'cuz I can't remember how I used to talk. 'Cuz my lingo has like changed like so much. They used to use like different words and stuff. It's not so much like how they pronounce things or anything. It's just like there are different words to explain different stuff. And then we'd like use like different words to explain different stuff. It wasn't nothing like too big.

This discussion also reinforces the ways in which speech, argot, and slang are always important in identifying differences from and in reinforcing social boundaries. In this instance, a specific argot—"they speak like that" and "we speak like this"—is identified with a geographic area, reinforcing differences.

For one student who had lived on the Northside, the rivalry was still very much in existence:

**J:**  So what about the rivalry between Northside and Southside?
**Student:**  Childish. Little kids. Like, no seriously like, when we got here, we didn't have a problem with Southside. One thing that I notice is that they do a lot of things different from the way we do. They act different and treat people different. Like they have some very stupid ways of acting. Like just like yesterday when we were talking about the code of dating, blah, blah, blah. Like I come down here. I have a girl friend that lives on the south side. They get mad. Why would you get mad? They are not all there. That's not the way it is. It's not big rivalry or nothing. Like I don't have an outstanding problem with them. It's just that we are different. And they feel so [cocky] about themselves. You get into an argument with them and they say something stupid like, "Well, you come from Northside and Northside is a slum."

This student's narrative highlights the ways in which discourses draw on other dis-courses to produce subjectivity. In this instance gendered discourses are called on to produce young women as objects who have their access to social spaces determined by young men. To "date" across spatially defined borders was to transgress a taboo built on the Northside/Southside distinction. Eulyn's narrative below also illustrates gendered discourses and how they intersect with and give meaning to gender rela-tions. Here, she illustrates how knowledge/power operates to produce a specific sub-ject on whose production certain forms of behavior are enabled or constrained. Liv-ing on the Northside was sufficient explanation of "bad" behavior. Descriptors based on popular hood movies allow access to a language through which communication can take place.

**Eulyn:** He lived on the north side too, so there you go.
**J:** Oh? What does that mean?
**Eulyn:** That's like, the hood—Edmonton's hood. They want to be like the States.

This particular distinction of Northside/Southside draws on the language of hip-hop culture and rap music to explain and develop a classificatory system to account for the differences in dress and to make comparisons. Melvin extends this distinc-tion, alluding to differences in hip-hop culture.

**Melvin:** And like most of the people from the south side had like bald heads. They all had hair. We had bald heads. They would like wear like bigger jackets with like toques and stuff, and we would like wear smaller jackets and like some form of a hat or like a visor. Then like they'd dress darker. We'd dress brighter, this type of thing. It's kind of like we were West [Coast], and they were like East Coast. It's like that.

Here Melvin echoes the distinctions/rivalries drawn in the rap music world during the 1990s between the East Coast and West Coast. Within the United States this distinction draws on other discourses that make "roots" rather than "routes" a pri-mary means of identification and a means of reinforcing a strong sense of affiliation with and loyalty to, the local.

Other discursive practices are associated with this classificatory system of North/South. The narrative of one student indicates that student dress on the Northside has tended to maintain the same "baggy" style, while the Southside boys are "riding the sleeker Puffy train":

**Melvin:** They kind of like stuck to their guns you know. They are still the same. And they like dress the same and do whatever the same. And then like most of the guys from the Southside are like riding the "Puffy Train." And they are the ones that are dressed up like that. Actually that's true. If you walk down the hallway right now, you could see like [Will] standing on one side of the hall. And he'd be like all like his nice preppy-type shirt and like his jacket and his glasses. And I don't know if you saw [Coolio]. Like say [Coolio] he'd be like wearing his baggy pants and his like jacket and his hair braided up.

This reference to "Puffy" draws attention to the hip-hop artist Puff Daddy (P. Diddy) as a trendsetter who is leading a change in dress style, away from the previous "authentic" hip-hop towards a slicker, more commercial representation. There is a view among some, as indicated in Chapter 6, that P. Diddy symbolizes the decline of "authentic" rap. Part of being able to distinguish one's self from "them" is also the formation of a sense of "us." The following example illustrates the way in which gendered discourses come to be used in order to make a distinction. Although the student is reluctant to name the Northside as deficient nonetheless, a sense of deficiency emerges to reinforce "difference" and to bolster the position of the Southside. Here Southside girls are seen as somehow "nicer," easier to get along with:

Etta:  The Southside is pretty good because the girls here like I guess you can see we all kind of like a lot of the same views, but I am not sure you would find that everywhere else in every other school. I think there is a difference between—a lot of people say, well, Northside they say is a rougher side.

Why, when the black population is so small, there should be a need to make a distinction between differing geographic regions of the city and urban space is an interesting question. Although any answer can only be speculative and tentative, it may be that relations of domination are at work. While, on a denotative level, the discussion is about differing geographic areas of the city, at the connotative level, the narratives above draw on signs of socioeconomic status:

Student:  People on the Southside think, just because they live on the Southside, they think they are rich or richer than people on the Northside. But they don't understand that people on the Northside, just because they live on the Northside doesn't mean they are not rich.

The use of specific signifiers that draw on media images is useful in that it produces and reproduces codes that represent socioeconomic status. Exposure to differing forms of media culture enables the students to have access to a common language that exemplifies what Saussure terms "langue." Evidence that it is socioeconomic status that is being displaced can be seen in the ways that the students draw on specific classed signifiers in their earlier narratives. This use of the term "hood" also draws on the code constructed through the hood movies such as *Boyz N the Hood, Sugar Hill, Menace II Society*. The term acts as an anchor (Barthes, 1977) for the preferred meanings that are evoked through its use. Thus when "hood" is applied to a geographic area, the connotative second level of meanings emerges. This coding and anchoring of meaning enables the students to consequently develop a common sense understanding of those designated as Northsiders. So Northsider males come to be viewed, self-evidentially, as "rough."

## *"Acting Black"*

In this section of the chapter, I would like to highlight two dominant discourses within the narratives, the first based on black consciousness movement; the second based on youth culture. Highlighting these discourses illustrates the ways in which the students orient themselves to and within the discourses as well as the ways in which they use the discourses in their everyday lives. What is evident is that black identification is associated with specific discursive practices and is intertextual in nature. The latter is not a new phenomenon and has certainly been consistent since the 1960s discourses on black consciousness.

Since the early twentieth century the black consciousness movement has conceptualized black identity as based on technologies of the self that draw on knowledge of black lived experiences. Etta's narrative on blackness indicates a black identity aligned with this latter sense of consciousness. For her, being black involves a specific presentation of self:

> **Etta:** You mean like how some people view some people, like even if they are black they'll say, "Oh, he doesn't act black" or something like that? Okay, well, I think being black is like being proud of who you are. Proud of who your people are too. Proud of your culture. You are not ashamed of being black. Basically that's all, I think.

Etta's narrative identifies two differing discourses on being black. In one sense, blackness is based on physical appearance. In another sense, blackness is not just phenotype but also a state of consciousness. One is either proud or ashamed of being black. In the latter discourse it would be possible for one to be defined as black by physical appearance but then to be consequently identified, by behavior, as not "acting black." Being black involves meeting certain behavioral expectations that position an individual as an "authentic black." This distinction between consciousness, or a lack thereof, is evident in the Black Nationalist discourse of the 1920s and 1960s. Mercer (1994) argues that these discourses of Black Nationalism, such as Marcus Garvey's "always acknowledge that racism works by encouraging the devaluation of blackness by black subjects and that a recentering sense of pride was a prerequisite for a politics of resistance and construction" (p. 103).

Style, as a representation of a black identity, depends on evoking disclosures of authenticity. These discourses of authenticity and consciousness were evident in students' discussions of black consciousness style and were evoked most powerfully over the narratives of hair. For three of the young women, the issue of performing an authentic black self arose from a discussion with a mutual male acquaintance. For them, the ways in which they wear their hair does not in itself imply a particular identification with a specific black self:

**Eulyn:** I don't know. But he said one time that all black girls sell out to their own race, because we straighten our hair or we wear braids, and [he] mean to say that we are not happy with the way we are, so we want to look white. 'Cuz that's attractive or something.

**J:** So what do you think of that?

**Eulyn:** I don't think that's true.

**J:** Do you not? What would you see as a "sellout"?

**Eulyn:** Um, sellout, um . . .

**J:** Or is there no such thing for you?

**Eulyn:** No, there is such a thing. Maybe someone like a black person who didn't really know who they are. So they go like say to the white race or something. Put us down and stuff like that. You know. Because they are not really [black].

Such narratives reveal that historical traces remain of an earlier 1960s' discourse that links presentation of hair with a consciousness of being black. In the 1960s, Black Nationalism drew on earlier formulations such as Garvey's and linked them to Franz Fanon's work (1967) and "his systematic framework for political analysis of racial hegemonies at the level of black subjectivity" (Mercer, 1994, p. 103). Within this discourse on black identity, care of hair became symbolic, socially and politically, and straightened hair was seen as a reflection of "psychic inferiorization."

Through more recent representations in the media and youth culture in general, hair color has become an open sign/signifier of blackness. The following student's narrative bears the traces of Black Nationalist discourse and suggests that blackness is opposite to "whiteness." As such, blonde hair is seen as outside the norm of what one might identify as black:

**Melvin:** Like you can straighten your hair if you want to like. But, like, keep it the colour it is.

**J:** How do you come to that?

**Melvin:** I don't know, it's just like something that's always in my head. Like if I see like, you know, Demolition Man, no, Media Man, how they have like all those kids. And everybody—they all have their bleached blonde hair. I just think it looks stupid. Like no matter, everyone can say "Oh, he looks good with blonde hair," or "She looks good with blonde hair," I'm like, "No." They all look good with black hair, or they all look good with their natural colour hair.

In this instance, the narratives reveal an oppositional reading of the media text. This student closes down an attempt by certain rap artists to open up the signifier "black." This also indicates that there is no passive acceptance of what is represented within media culture. Discourse of authenticity and discourses of plurality collide within the discursive space of style and fashion.

"Acting black" was not always related to a sense of pride. For some it was a product of youth culture. One student's idea of "acting black" as a young person is identified not so much by what it is as what it is not:

> **Denzil:** It's more just talking. I don't know it's just like. If you act black, most of the white people are going to think you are stupid. Especially adults. They think he is just, "He doesn't know what he is talking about." So you have to act somewhat mature in that sense. Yeah, mature, basically. That's what I think is not acting black. For a kid. For an adolescent, I don't know. I haven't experienced acting black as an adult yet, so I don't know [laugh].

Denzil's narrative identifies "acting black" as being negatively assessed by white adults. Acting black is seen as a performance, as not acting "natural." The following narrative explicitly distinguishes acting "black" from acting "natural"

> **J:** This young man then, is he one of these, who sees himself as a North American in the "hood?"
> **Eulyn:** Well, that's how he portrays himself. He mightn't want to come across like that but . . . .
> **J:** So tell me some of the ways that you could just look and say, "Yeah, He is trying to be in the hood."
> **Eulyn:** I don't know, it's just you know they don't act themselves. They are not just natural really. 'Cuz people in the States—it's natural for them to be like that because they grow up in that environment. But there's nothing that drastic here.

Eulyn's understanding of black identity is one that is related to hood films. As well, she alludes to geographic location as important in terms of acting black. The specific representation of blackness that she identifies is based on experiences in the United States. Such a sense of blackness is not necessarily dependent upon a consciousness of self or a sense of pride.

Since this sense of blackness is based on experiences in the United States, living in Canada is problematic in terms of identification. There is a sense of geographically bounded blackness. As several narratives in Chapters 2 and 3 indicate, black youth in Canada were perceived as yearning to be black Americans. Joy also alludes to the way in which some youths in Canada align themselves with the experiences in American inner cities portrayed in many of the hood films:

**Joy:**  You see some of the kids up here; they want to have a ghetto and stuff. But the people down there, if they had a chance to get out of there, they'd go. They don't want to be in that kind of environment.

Another student comments on a male friend in Edmonton who had adopted this identification with the U.S. inner city:

**Student:**  Yeah. You are like, "Come on, you know you are living in Edmonton. Why are you trying to go on [laugh]? You know Edmonton is dry. So leave it alone." Like, I hate to hear those guys. Like I remember this one guy, like my friend, [Vincent] he is like, "Oh yeah man, we shot this guy the other day." I am like, "What movie are you watching?" Like I told him. Like whatever. It seems like they read that magazine *[The Source]* and they come back and they're, "You know what happened to me, me, me." I am like, "Whatever, shut up."

**J:**  So how would someone who is imitating that, someone like this Vincent, how would they behave?

**Student:**  Like "Yeah man, and I capped him this way and he boxed me that way and we got in this big fight man, and after that we smoked a spliff." I am like, whatever. Like they are so dull.

For this student there is a direct link between media representations and the identity adopted by her friend. Etta makes a similar observation:

**Etta:**  Mind you, I know Canada is different than the States. But people here still do that. //Do they?// Yeah. Not like the way—they don't have the ghetto and everything like that. They imitate, and they try to imitate the States. It's not as much as the way they dress. But they try to act rough or whatever.

In these discourses, acting black is linked to constructions of an authentic black youth identity that is "rooted" in the United States. Several students discuss the way in which young black males, in particular, identify with representations of blackness on music videos, or films. Some see this direct identification with U.S. images as problematic. For them, Canadian "location" and the socioeconomic circumstances diminish the ability to be "authentic." The following student sees public exposure to U.S. rap music videos as resulting in a cross-border affiliation that is not necessarily beneficial to African Canadians. Here the suggestion is that for some youths, "thinking" and "being" become conflated as they watch and then act like the images that they view:

**Denzil:**  The black community here. They act like we see on MTV. We see rap videos and we go, "Oh, we should act like that." I don't see why. Those guys act like that because they live in the States, and that's what it's like in the States. But here it's different.

For Denzil, being black was a product of experiences within specific geographic location. Further, video representations are held accountable for the ways in which certain black males behaved. This video-based representation of "acting black" is rooted in a U.S. "location" and is not consistent with the Canadian reality.

Although the student narratives generally attributed "acting black" and the negative effects of watching music videos primarily to males, a similar analysis of consumption and production was used to explain the sexually explicit behavior of one young woman:

> **Melvin:** She just like started like getting like, same thing. She started listening to rap. Started dressing like she was one of those girls on the rap video, and now she is all over the city. She is like, man, she is crazy.

The narratives also indicate that the ability to act black well enough to be accepted, as "one of us," requires certain signifiers, one of which is a dark skin. Wearing the right clothes, speaking with a specific inflection, or argot, and "walking the walk" are not enough to make a legitimate claim to being black. This raises the question of whether those classified as "white" can act black. The students often discussed non-black students who tried to "act black." In such cases, students spoke of their white friends who attempted to perform blackness as lacking a "true" self and attempting to align themselves with blacks in order to gain a sense of self. Black phenotype was an important part of being able to perform a black identity. For students who were not of African descent, it was perceived as problematic to take on a black identity. Denzil's comments illustrate this discourse that students who attempted to take on a black identity via dress, speech, and walk were trying to "fill a lack" in their lives:

> **Denzil:** He has no personality whatsoever. He is a manifestation of everyone else's ideas, everyone else's feelings, everyone else's emotions, everyone else's opinions. He has no personality. No opinion of his own.
> **J:** So he acts black to try to take one.
> **Denzil:** Yeah. He acts black 'cuz he thinks its "cool."

Gerald, identifies the problems of non-blacks taking on a black identity as represented by media culture:

> **Gerald:** Like he would talk like he was black.
> **J:** Oh, I see, and that's why you thought it wasn't. So what was it about it that made you think, "That's just fake," or "he is putting it on?"
> **Gerald:** That I don't like? //uh huh// 'Cuz he is [Malaysian].
> **J:** So you think that if you are not black, and you are trying to talk black then . . .?

**Gerald:** It's like obvious, like you are trying. I don't even think [Malaysians] liked him. [Malaysian] people like they'd look at him and they would laugh.

Gerald's objection to such identification is based on an understanding of blackness that is biologically essentialist, wherein biology determines behavior and culture. The young Malaysian man was viewed as imitative, not original. Melvin's narrative, below, alludes to a friend of European descent as lacking originality in terms of presentation of self:

**Melvin:** Pretty much. He is not original. It's like everybody who is there, he like takes an idea from them and like slaps it onto himself. Like there used to be a thing where, like with us. . . . You can't get the same clothes as with anyone else right? And like that was the thing that like started to hurt him . . . because like—if someone would get something he would get the same thing. You know. //Oh, right// And then like, and then I forget, we joined up with somebody in the group. And then they are like, "Yeah, well, whatever, don't dress like this and this and that." So then he started like losing his originality and started flying off in a different direction. Well, he never had it, but like, um, he like tried to get it kind of and still like maintain his dressing like the rest of us. And like [so] he could be like accepted. But I don't know. He was kind of losing it.

In some ways, blackness as a performance—a way of acting—was seen as part of the repertoire of styles available to students from Africa and the African diaspora. The narratives highlight that such performances were often equated with black youths, primarily males, who seemed to adopt and make hypervisible the dress style, slang, and walk associated with hip-hop and U.S. youth cultures.

## Summary

The chapter highlights that dress style is not just about wearing clothes in the right combination, but it is also important to the students' identification as blacks. The students' narratives reveal that traces of the 1960s Black Nationalist ideology/discourse are still evident in terms of self-presentation. Contesting such discourses are more recent understandings of blackness that are based on media representations. Ideology—meaning in the service of power (Thompson 1990)—also becomes intertwined with style, which the students use to identify themselves as authentically black. Ideology and style are again evident in terms of the ways in which the narratives come to divide urban space into Northside and Southside in ways that are aligned with style and socioeconomic status. It illustrates the way in which discourses produce specific subjectivity through a plurality of competing discourses and that discourse is not just language—language produces material.

The following chapter reinterprets the students' *doxa*, highlighted in Chapters 2 to 6. Further, I will revisit my cultural studies literature, the historical section on Alberta, and the students' perspectives on school climate with regard to the key concepts identified in Chapter 1, and the sociohistorical analysis of racialization in Canadian society.

# CHAPTER 7

# Borrowed Identities

*Imaginary blackness is being projected outwards, facelessly, as the means to orchestrate a truly global market in leisure products and as the centrepiece of a new, corporately directed version of youth culture centred not on music as and its antediluvian rituals but upon visuality, icons, images.*

GILROY, 2000, p. 270

## Introduction

The earlier chapters of this study focus on what Thompson (1990) identifies as symbolic culture. By this he means, "the patterns of meanings embodied in symbolic forms, including actions, utterances and meaningful objects of various kinds, by virtue of which individuals communicate with one another and share their experiences, conceptions and beliefs" (p. 132). Often, the source for this symbolic culture is youth culture. This is a generation of youth that cannot remember a time without televisual images and the consequences of living within an age of electronic media. Thus media culture offers not just sites of pleasure but also a source for what Paul Willis (1990) identifies as symbolic creativity. His use of the term entails:

> [the] extraordinary symbolic creativity of the multitude of ways in which young people use, humanise, decorate and invest meanings within their common and immediate life spaces and social practices—personal styles and choice of clothes; selective and active use of music, TV, magazines; decoration of bedrooms; the rituals of romance and subcultural styles; the style, banter and drama of friendship groups. (p. 6)

It is within this social space of symbolic activity that this chapter attempts to identify the ways in which students receive and appropriate media culture. As Hall observes, media are the key mechanisms for centralizing cultural power, a social process that is achieved via cultural reception and the articulation of ideology into social formation. In terms of explaining or accounting for relations of domination, my conceptual use of ideology is a cautious one in light of recent poststructuralist re-theorization and critiques of ideology. Thus in this study ideology is not viewed as gen-erated directly through the economic relations of production; instead ideology is re-garded as a formation "in which systems of ideas are employed in ways which attempt to justify or rationalise forms of domination and make them seem natural and eternal" (Layder 1994, p. 106). And while more recent theorizing around media reception and consumption would eschew the concept of ideology for discourse, this study tries to avoid such problematic dualism. Thus linking the two concepts offers the opportunity to analyze not just ideology, which produces effects in the name of specific powerful positioning, but also the process of that production through discourse analysis (Purvis & Hunt, 1993). In this instance one can regard ideology as effect while discourses can be regarded as process; a link, which allows for the use of discourse as a means of ex-plaining how power works through the students (Purvis & Hunt, 1993).

## Diasporan Blackness and Borrowed Identities

Although, as indicated in Chapters 2 and 3, the students construct a sense of transna-tional diasporan blackness, this sense of blackness is one that is influenced by under-standings of symbolic forms constructed primarily via youth culture in the United States. Relations of domination are evident in the ways in which the United States comes to represent a sense of blackness within the lives of the students. Such a plac-ing of African-American cultural formation within the Canadian context means that in some ways the African-American discourses of blackness seem to dominate in an almost hegemonic sense wherein Canadian identity is often interpreted in relation to its U.S. counterpart. This phenomenon is not new; Andre Alexis (1995), in his arti-cle "Borrowed Blackness," has alluded to the complex relationship and importance of the United States in the lives of African Canadians. For him black American identity is portrayed as a universal identity for all blacks. He argues further that:

> Canada is often invisible in American writing, black Canada even more so, and it seems
> to me that black Canadians react to that invisibility in at least two ways. One way is to
> assume that we *are* all included in definitions of "New World Africa" reality, that Can-
> ada is America (but *pianissimo*) and that bell hooks and Derrick Bell are speaking about
> (louder) versions of our experiences. The other way is by trying to sing, dance or write
> Canada for ourselves, to define our own terrain and situation. (p. 17, original emphasis)

Looking specifically at Toronto, Alexis argues that intellectually there is a strong alignment with the United States and that blacks are conceptualized by mainstream Canadians as a recent phenomenon from the United States which has crept North or emigrated from Africa. This tension in terms of the projection of U.S. experiences onto Canada is also evident in discussions of Canadian literary criticism. As George Elliott Clarke (1996) reveals:

> denials of what I term African Canadianite illuminate the dynamic dilemma of African Canadian culture. Euro-Canadian critics consider it as Other, while African American (and Caribbean) critics read it—unabashedly—as extensions of their own. To complicate matters further, African Canadians utilise African-American texts and historical cultural icons to define their own experiences (a fact which can seduce the unwary in to believing that no uniquely African Canadian perspective exists). (p. 57)

This belief that no uniquely African-Canadian experiences exist can be seen in the ways in which students orient themselves to an African-Canadian identity. For some students, the lack of recognition of a historical presence of blackness within Canada reinforces the sense of blackness as "Other." Even for those students whose ancestors are Canadian it is difficult to identify any symbolic representation within Canadian society with which they can align themselves. Thus for some students Canadian identity is perceived as problematic, not readily available, and thus we can surmise official citizenship does not automatically lead to recognition of self or acceptance by others as "Canadian."

Theorist Benedict Anderson argues that, rather than being innate, such identities are imagined through specific public symbols that are constructed in relation to the nation, and that as such it is more than a political entity it also produces meanings, a system of cultural representation (Hall, 1991, p. 292). In a similar vein Barker (1999), argues that:

> National identities are a constitutive representation of shared experiences and history told through stories, literature, popular culture and of course television. . . . Such narratives emphasise the traditions and continuity of the nation as being "in the nature of things," though they may be "invented" traditions including the foundational myth of collective origins. (p. 68)

Barker's description of a myth of collective origins seems evident in terms of how the youths position themselves in relation to, or within, a specific discourse on national identity. For students, such as Etta and Doreen in Chapter 2, identification with a specific nationality is constructed through discourses on historical origins and "roots" rather than discourses that emphasize routes. As Henry Giroux (1996) argues such myths are not innocent and often operate through popular memory to link culture and citizenship:

> National identity has all too often been forged within popular memory as a discourse that too neatly links nations, culture, and citizenship in a seamless and unproblematic

unity. Invoking claims to the past in which the politics of remembering and forgetting work powerfully to legitimate a notion of national belonging that "constructs the nation as an ethnically homogenous object. (p. 189)

The ways that the students identify, or not, with a specific national identity is related to context as well as the availability of symbolic representations with which they can identify. Thus, identification with Jamaica or Trinidad varies according to the racialized identity of the questioner as well as the geographic context of the social exchange. While the latter fluidity in identification might subscribe to Hall's evocation that "identities are about becoming" such variability in identification does not imply a totally decentered sense of self. I think it can be implied that while "post modern politics of temporary alliances, partial identities, is attractive as against the dyed-in-the-wool prejudice and exclusions of xenophobia, racism and sexism; alliances and affinities mark some degree of ongoing identity and commitment, however provisional" (Andermahr, Lovell & Wolkowitz, 1997, p. 125). These provisional alliances and affinities among the students, like identification, were also dependent upon context so that although at times their identification as black was paramount, at other times, a national identity related to geographic region would emerge as a qualifier of their blackness. Often these national identities emerge at times when a relation of dominance is most evident. For example, in Chapter 2, the ways in which some young women whose families in islands other than Jamaica indicated a closer alignment with differing genres of Caribbean music to make a distinction between themselves and Jamaicans. Thus these young women's identification with genres such as soca and calypso, as opposed to reggae, indicated a production of difference from Jamaica. The narratives indicate that this tension between Jamaica and other smaller Caribbean islands is attributed, as one Jamaican student suggested, to the idea that "our community is popular—it's more well known." This dominance of Jamaican identity in Canada is based on media construction and hypervisibility of Jamaicans, the size of population in relation to other islands, as well as the popularization of reggae, in various musical forms, since the 1970s. Paradoxically in terms of Canadian society, the hypervisibility of Jamaicans is related primarily to their criminalization through the media in Toronto and elsewhere. Henry and Tator's (2000)[1] study "Racist Discourses in Canada's English Print Media" argues that:

> The case study of the racialization of crime reveals the complex vocabulary of crime-related language that includes phrases like "cultural deviance, Jamaican or Black crime." The press creates a sense of moral panic in which isolated cases of violence are represented as an indication of a profound societal crisis that imperils the nation. (p. iv)

This process of criminalization through the media articulates with regimes of representation discussed in this study to construct another layer in racialization.

This relation of dominance is not just between students with Caribbean ancestry; further intra-black distinctions are also evident within the data as students identify how the use of jokes displaces tensions between the different national groups. Such tensions seem to be based on the common sense understandings of Africa and the Caribbean constructed through discourses in wider society. Many of these discourses construct Africa, in particular, as "backward" and a "nation" lacking in technology and consumer goods. Within a few students' narratives, youth culture is drawn on in order to code jokes and contour meanings around discussions of "Africa" and "development." The latter process is illustrated in Chapter 2, where one student identifies how access to consumer goods such as the Nike brand is equated with modernity and thus links continental development to a North American norm and context. In contrast to the latter position, Africa is posited as lacking in consumer goods, a "lack" which is consequently used to position it as "not modern." Such an understanding of the African continent in some ways reflects the existing relations of dominance within society, regardless of the students' identification as black. The latter understanding also identifies that there is no automatic alignment between black identity and Africa. It would therefore be difficult to align the students consistently with what Paul Gilroy (1995) calls:

> a diasporan consciousness, in which identity is focussed less on equalising, proto-democratic force of common territory and more on the social dynamics of remembrance and commemoration defined by a strong sense of the dangers involved in the forgetting the location of origin and the process of dispersal. (p. 318)

There is no consistent discourse of historical memory that is dominant across all the narratives. For some students such as Etta and Denzil there is a struggle to excavate this memory through school curricula, while for others such as Doreen, we need to "get over it."

Afrocentrics such as Molefi Kete Asante (1989) argue, "regardless of our various complexions and degrees of consciousness we are, by virtue of commitments, history, and convictions, an African people" (p. 27). While Afrocentric discourses would produce all the students as African and with a strong identification with Africa, in actuality, many students' narratives illustrate identity production that has undergone a process of "translation" (Bhabha, 1994). Their identity is more hybrid than fixed historically. These discourses of translation were evident in three examples of students' narratives in Chapter 2. First, for the students of Caribbean ancestry, a return to the past was a return to the Caribbean. There is little or no sense of a return to Africa as the spiritual home of blacks. For example, Wayne, in Chapter 2, recognizes that he has a familial connection with Africa but he perceives no tangible cultural links that would position him as African. Interestingly, when read intertextually, Jamaica, his last port of call, is a society within which public recognition of

African roots has always been contested. As a colony of Britain, Jamaica was a primary site for the dissemination and reproduction of racist discourses on Africa. Racialization and production of the "other" was active throughout all segments of society and permeated dominant discourses of knowledge. Jan Pieterse (1992), in analyzing these discourses, illustrates his case with reference to Edward Long, a nineteenth-century scientific "authority" on African slaves. Long's basic argument was that:

> European and black do not belong to the same species. Black children like animals matured more rapidly than whites; mulattos in his view were infertile—a belief widely held at that time . . . . Long divided the genus homo into three categories: Europeans and other humans, blacks, and orangutans. (p. 41)

It is hardly surprising that discursive formations concerning the hierarchy of races should also be active within slave and colonized societies. Subjugation of an African presence was, historically, a part of the dominant discourse among Jamaicans of African descent. This negation of an African ancestry was consistently maintained until the 1960s, with the growth and rise of the Black Power movement in the United States and the consequent growth in acceptance of Rastafarians in the 1970s through popularity of the music and personality of Bob Marley. Stuart Hall's article "Cultural Identity and Cinematic Representation" identifies how Jamaica has only more recently claimed a sense of blackness. In his childhood this was not evident. As he recalls, "although almost everyone around me was some shade of brown or black (Africa "Speaks"!), I never once heard a single person refer to themselves or others as, in some way, as having been at some time in the past, African" (1996, p. 216). While the latter discourse illustrates the production of African peoples as "other" and "different from" those of us in the Caribbean, it also has to be recognized that such discourses were at times contested through counterdiscourses such as Garveyism, which was dominant from the 1920s and 1930s onwards.

Second, and perhaps not surprisingly, for those students born in Africa or whose family arrived recently from Africa, identification with Africa was more readily accepted. However, this identification was hybridized and, as with other students of the diaspora, strongly accented with hip-hop culture. This is not surprising in that such identification offers the possibility of an immediate sense of community and belonging (Ibrahim, 2000; Forman, 2001). These students with close familial links to the African continent seem not to use music or dress style as a source of identification with countries in Africa. However, it also cannot be read that they were totally assimilated into Canadian society, since they may well draw on other sources and resources, not evident through the narratives, to give meaning to an identification with Africa.

Third, a number of the students were of mixed heritage but self-defined as black.

For these students, family visits to Africa did not bring automatic acceptance. They were recognized as "diasporan" and other than African; cultural markers such as language and color revealed that they were "translated" Africans (Bhabha, 1994). Thus the production of the descriptor African was not ahistorical and consistent across time and space.

Hall's conception of black identity as operating along vectors of sameness and difference coheres with the ways in which the students constructed their identities. These intragroup differences were not evident at all times but tended to emerge during social situations that highlight a tension between individual identity and group identity. Although this identification of a black/national self through different music consumption patterns was primarily among the young women, I would urge caution in attributing this difference as due only to gender, since girls who were non-Jamaican but associated with the Caribbean were over-represented in the sample.

While the student narratives constructed blacks as a group with a plurality of identities, they also indicated that "black music" was a common source of identification. The descriptor "black music" is itself, however, highly problematic. As Keith Negus (1996) argues:

> It is out of . . . struggles, arising from unequal relations of economic and cultural power, that black music has been made. Black music has become an important category because of conditions of oppression, segregation and ghettoisation and due to the way that a particular population has had to live and make meaning within and across "racialized boundaries" (Anthias and Yuval-Davis, 1992). While there is racism, social segregation and economic inequality, the term "black music" will continue to have resonance as a signifier of a culture created out of these experiences. (p. 112)

Negus's comments, interestingly, undermine many biologically based "essentialist" claims to purity, in terms of music creation while also questioning a direct association between skin color and musical genre. This problematization is also illustrated in student narratives, which draw on discourses of purity, while revealing identification with a plurality of black-identified musical genres such as r&b, rap, reggae, soca, and calypso. As forms of music created primarily by people who identify themselves as black, it might be more accurate to use a plural descriptor for black music, thus emphasizing its heterogeneous rather than homogenous construction. The similarities that exist within these musical forms are social as much as stylistic, since the musical genres are generated through differing social and lived black experiences. Where the musical genres identified by the students cross and intersect, such cultural crossings can be attributed to a movement of humans through a process of migration and immigration. This is evident in the musical choices identified by the students, where musical genres such as rap and reggae are cultural formations that draw on areas of a Black Atlantic (Gilroy, 1993). An understanding

of black-identified music as purely static and fixed within a geographic region becomes problematic when one notes the actual ways in which musical genres draw on
a variety of Black Atlantic influences. Much-acclaimed Jamaican dancehall singer
Beenie Man, who has managed to successfully transfer his skills to the United States,
remarks on these diasporan links between musical genres represented as Jamaican
and musical genres represented as American:

> I say hip-hop is American dancehall . . . Busta Rhymes dem is Jamaican. Canibus is Ja-
> maican. Slick Rick is Jamaican; Biggie Smalls is Jamaican. You're talking about some of
> the roughest rappers in the business who is Jamaican. So catch the link from there. It's
> just the same ting; it's the same vibe. (Beenie Man, cited in *The Source*, No 108, Sep-
> tember, 1998)

Such postulations as to the hybrid nature of music can also be seen in Nelson
George's analysis of the origins of rap music; being identified as a pure African-
American creation negates the plurality of its construction. While accepting this
hybrid rather than any singular source of black music formation, it should also be
noted that there is an element of what Gilroy identifies as the "changing same" of
culture. This "changing same" involves:

> the paradox of ethnic sameness and heterogeneity. This is the paradox that the recog-
> nition of a shared culture and history (rather than biological or "racial" essence) com-
> bines with a sense of the deep divergences and differences encompassed by the term
> "black." (Hall, 1990, p. 223)

There are also similarities in terms of marginalization of black experiences that
cross national borders. This is, perhaps, why the students consistently identified music
as a source of unification in that often music is also a dominant discourse through
which black lived experiences intersect the white-dominated public sphere. However,
there is no inherent transcendental essence to black music that remains the same over
time. As Negus notes, the social conditions of black experience provides a source for
musical developments. Conditions of oppression, segregation, ghettoization, and the
way that a particular population has had to live and make meaning within and across
racialized boundaries are important components of musical development. Gilroy
(1995) also notes the ways in which music is identified as indicating the essence of
blackness, yet as a cultural form it expresses hybridity rather than uniformity:

> It is also in music that the most intense legacy of the African past is concentrated and
> though the significance of that legacy is open to dispute, the link itself is impossible to
> refute. It is important, then, that the area of cultural production, which is most evi-
> dently identified with racial authenticity and Black particularity, is also the most mut-
> able and adaptive form. (p. 25)

It should also be noted that there was no real attempt among the students to represent themselves as distinctly Canadian through musical choices, even for those who were aware of the relations of power and dominance between the United States and Canada. The flow of dominance from the United States in music production, via rap and r&b, was interrupted only by reggae, a product of Jamaica, which is embedded with similar signs and codes as rap and has had more media exposure than other musical formations associated with the Caribbean region. Although the students from North America and the Caribbean are part of an African diaspora, there is little recognition of, knowledge of, or musical identification with the continent. In the long run such a lack of connection may undermine the youths' ability to view music as constructed in a social formation.

Overall, the students' identities can be viewed as hybrid, in that they position themselves in a variety of ways and draw on the diaspora as well as national formations as sources for a black identity. It can be argued that they weave a complex cloth of identity. Their identities encompass cultural responses ranging from assimilation, through forms of separation, to hybrids that stabilize and blur cultural boundaries. However, as Barker (1999) notes in Chapter 2, such cultural hybridity does not represent the "erasure of boundaries, and we need to be sensitive to both cultural differences and to forms of identification that involve recognition of similarities" (p. 70).

## Racialized Regime of Representation

In this section the data will be interpreted with regard to Stuart Hall's (1997) phrase "regime of representation." Here, we move on to examine youth culture to ascertain the ways in which blackness is represented across a "regime" constructed through magazines, music videos, and rap music. Such construction has implications for identity formation and contours relations of power and dominance between the United States and Canada. The examination illustrates the ways in which a focus on individual consumption can illuminate areas of economic contestation and hegemony.

The students indicate that music is a common source of identification. If one looks across the various media forms, one can identify what Hall (1997) describes as a "racialized regime of representation." Television music videos and music magazines mediate style, images, and representations of hip-hop culture and blackness between the music industry and its consumers. This process of mediation is

> facilitated by the development of digital storage techniques and satellites, telecommunication technologies are also playing an increasingly important role in mediating popular music by enabling phone-line musical competition between artists, computer-networked dialogues among fans, and the production of "interactive" musical material by musicians. (Negus, 1996, p. 68)

At this historical conjuncture these mediums percolate knowledge and experiences that come to form part of a storehouse of ideas. Concepts can then be drawn on in terms of meaning making and representations of self and others. Opening up Canadian borders to U.S.-dominated images extends the meaning-making repertoire that the students have at their behest. Thompson's concept of mediazation is evident in the ways in which the students' narratives identify how information and culture are transported across borders via various media forms. These media forms have enabled a general development and flow of images. In the case of blacks, this exposure has increased the accessibility of black images to a much wider audience than in previous eras. Unlike earlier black-inspired musical forms such as jazz or blues, rap as part of the hip-hop family is a child of the electronic and televisual age and is accessible to a much wider audience. In support of the latter, and by way of comparison Nelson George (1998) argues that in the United States

> compared to the exposure white entertainers like Glen Campbell, Sonny and Cher, or Tony Orlando could achieve, black music was shown only briefly and often in a very culturally hostile environment. Videos, in contrast, are repeated endlessly and usually presented by hosts who feel kinship to the culture. The images, just like the music, have a just-off-the-street immediacy that excites kids in Iowa and Tokyo just as much as those in South Central Los Angeles. (p. 102)

This digital linking of geographic areas provides a common space within which specific cultural codes can be produced, reproduced, and drawn on. As John Storey (1996) suggests:

> what makes meaning production possible are the shared cultural codes upon which both the producers and consumers of an image are able to draw. Connotations are not simply produced by the makers of the image, but are activated from an already existing and shared cultural repertoire and at the same time adds to it. (p. 92)

One of the effects of these waves of hip-hop culture emanating from the United States., via satellite, cable, or magazines is that African-American youth have become identified with "authentic" hip-hop and rap. This coding is contoured in two ways. First, in comparison with those in the United States, the students lack consistent exposure to Canadian rap via magazines, music videos, and rap music. Second, the construction of "authenticity" occurs around U.S.-based media culture, thus increasing the desire for U.S. produced goods. The narratives of the students support the position that access to Canadian rappers is primarily via cable channels. Both RapCity[2] and XtenDaMix[3] were aired on the Canadian-owned MuchMusic station and have a mandate to "give Canadian urban artists much-needed exposure." Nonetheless, the videos shown construct the meanings of rap via the airplay and visibility given to African-American rap groups and rappers. With regard to the construction of discourses of "authenticity," meaning operates via a system of representation that is constructed and then fixed by a code that sets up the "correlation between our conceptual system and our language" (Hall, 1997, p. 21). In the case under discussion, codes developed around concepts of "geographic location" and "experiences" are used in order to fix such meanings around hip-hop and rap. As Hall (1997) suggests, with reference to children becoming cultural subjects:

> they learn the system and conventions of representation, the codes of their language and culture, which equip them with cultural "know-how" enabling them to function as culturally competent subjects. . . . They unconsciously internalise the codes which allow them to express certain concepts and ideas through their system of representation—writing, speech, gesture, visualisation, and so on—and to interpret ideas which are communicated to them using the same systems. (p. 22)

Hip-hop based upon African-American experiences reinforces the relations of dominance between U.S.-generated rap and its Canadian version. As implied in the following comments by Master T, former vee-jay and producer of *RapCity* and *Xten-DaMix*, "Canadian artists have learned their craft and they are stepping to the plate. . . . I get e-mails from Ohio requesting *Rascalz*.[4] This is cool—America's watching!" (Hayashi-Tennant, 1999). Master T's comment demonstrates that discourses of rap construct and reinforce the presentation of the United States as a source of authentic rap. Validation and the worth of Canadian rap are determined by an external source (i.e. the United States). This need for recognition and external validation results in further marginalization of Canadian rappers and a consequent undermining of their ability to position themselves in relation to the U.S. rappers as "authentic."[5] Even though the Canadian rappers of African descent might rap about their experiences in Toronto or Vancouver, such experiences are coded through discourse and discursive practices as "softer" than the authentic representations that emerge from the U.S.-based production studios.[6] This sense of the authentic also comes into play if Canadian rappers try to imitate U.S. rappers. Ivan Berry, a Toronto-based expert on the rap scene, argues that for Canadian rappers to be successful abroad, they have to be uniquely Canadian. He continues, "why would any American label release a Canadian signed artist if it's the same type of sh** they could go around the corner and sign in America" (Matthews, 1998).

This positioning of Canada, economically and socially, in relation to the United States can also be seen in the narratives of the students in Chapters 3 and 4, where they identify with magazines that "present deep knowledge" and align themselves with discourses of "true" or commercial rap. Here we can also view the ways in which discursive practices operate through desire to produce material economic effects. It is a situation akin to Lacanian psychology wherein ". . . the infant . . . desires and identifies with that which it does not have in the image of the other" (Easthope

& McGowan, 1992, p. 68). To undermine and contest this relation of economic dominance, some Canadian rappers have formed independent record labels, such as Treehouse Records, and Knee Deep Records, but these cannot compete with larger American corporations. Adam Matthews (1998) notes that "in the last few years Sony, BMG and Virgin have created full-fledged urban departments, but there are no urban departments with the authority to sign artists. These departments have been put in place to market and promote American records" (p. 71). For example, Canadian firms earn about 90 percent of their revenue from selling Canadian-content recordings, while 88 percent of the revenues of foreign-controlled firms comes from selling recordings made from imported masters. Foreign firms have five times the revenue, eighteen times the profit, ten times the long-term assets, and sixteen times the contributed surplus and retained earnings of Canadian-controlled firms (Task Force 1996, cited in Shuker, 2001, pp. 73–74).

While the regime of representation offers the black students a resource through which to identify, it also provides fertile grounds for other racialized groups to develop an "understanding" of blackness based upon racialized stereotypes. The students learn codes as part of their culture—a specific youth culture that is contoured through regimes of representation. As indicated in Chapters 3 through 6, meaning is produced through regimes of representation mediated by magazines, music, and television music videos. These media representations enable students to code and construct common understandings. They provide a language through which meaning is produced. Although not discussed in detail in Chapter 3, reality television crime programs such as *Cops* or the news programs, local and North American, also play a part in constructing common conceptual codes. Himani Bannerji (1995) identifies such a process of construction as active in Toronto newspapers:

> One only needs a periodic look at the *Toronto Sun*, for example, or the television, to see what images and assumptions are circulated by the popular media among masses of people both black and white. Stereotypes range from "yellow peril" to "black (now Asian) criminality," and are cultural lenses through which communities are viewed and introduced to each other literally via media. Mis- or disinformation crowd the news and other television programmes, while the fashion industry, sports and music equate black people with the body and the natural gift for rhythm, and the Chinese with an innate propensity to do well in mathematics. (p. 155)

This regime of representation is available as a source for constructing images and knowledge of blackness, not just for black youth but also, just as importantly, for the wider society. The production of knowledge through these racialized regimes operates in nuanced and ambiguous ways. First, this construction of black identity as hypermasculine is surrounded with ambivalence, since youths also suggest that through a regime of representation, it connotes both fear and desire among their peers. Such a desire for mediated blackness was evident in the discourses on acting black by white peers. Similarly the connotation of fear was played out through the ready identification of black youth as a threatening presence in public spaces.

Second, it is noticeable across these racialized regimes of representation that it is black males who are at the centre of identity production. This is evident not only in hood films, and "booty/playa" films that are constructed from a male heterosexual perspective but also in gangsta rap, the mass media, and mainstream black leadership. U.S. black leaders such as Louis Farrakhan commonly cast the problems of the inner city as problems of male authority and discipline, problems that can be corrected via assertion of patriarchal relations (Kelley, 1994, p. 217). Reinforcing this dominant patriarchal discourse is the way in which women's experiences are marginalized in much of the youth culture that the students consume. As well, gangsta rap's lyrics often devalue and demean women. In accounting for the latter, Tricia Rose (1994) suggests "many men are hostile towards women because the fulfilment of male heterosexual desire is significantly checked by women's capacity for sexual rejection or manipulation of men" (p. 172). On the other hand, Kobena Mercer (1994) sees this hostility as related to constructions of masculinity and the dominance of black male experiences. He argues that "the master-codes of a race-relations narrative . . . depend on gender polarisation and the denigration of black women in order to emblematise black male experiences as "representative of black experiences as a whole" (p. 167).

While the young men's narratives were not overtly misogynist in content, their discourses did attempt to legitimate rather than condemn such gangsta rap lyrics. Drawing on the codes and discourses of "reality" constructed across and through regimes of representation they argue that the lyrics describe "real" women who have cheated on personal friends or used them in order to gain material goods. This understanding of real is highly problematic. The following focus group discussion illustrates this process through one young man's recollection of his negative experiences with a young woman who initiated a relationship. His everyday experiences are linked with rap lyrics to produce a discourse of verification:

> **Student 1:** There was something wrong with that girl. She asked me out; she acted all interested, and I turned round and she was gone. I wasn't chasing her or nothing.
> **Student 2:** Whoa! deep [clicking finger].
> **Student 1:** She was with Jake and he taped her. Taped her? And black girls are wondering why guys won't go out with them [sarcastically].
> **Student 3:** Its not just black girls.
> **Student 1:** It's not true, but that's what you think about. Same as girls think black guys are just into. . . .

Rappers themselves use such discourses of legitimation, as illustrated by the following response of rapper Eightball to a charge of promoting misogyny in his lyrics:

Well, those critics who say that need to go with us one night. That would explain everything. I mean, how many times do we have to say that we ain't talking about all women. . . . Man you go to the club today, there are women out there—and make sure you put this in here—there is a group of women out there that will do anything to a nigga in the limelight, and that's who we are talkin' 'bout. You really have to be there to understand it man. All that sh** that we talk about, it's a group of women out there who make those statements true. (Braxton, 1998, pp. 89–90)

A corollary to the strong construction of black identity as male within youth culture is an emphasis on heterosexuality as a norm. This construction and reinforcement of relations of dominance through a regime of representation take place primarily via rap, dancehall reggae, and the films that the students watch (see Chapters 3 to 6). However, media are not the only sites where discourses of heterosexuality are normalized. Religious discourses reinforce this construction of lesbians and homosexuals as outside the "norm" of society, as is illustrated by the students' reactions to films such as *Set It Off* (refer to Chapter 4). Even within the limited school discourses that produce same-sex relations as among a plurality of relationships competing discourses are evoked to challenge such production of sexualities as within the norm:

> **Student:** Last year when I was in my CALM[7] class, like the teacher said we have like a choice: "Disagree" here, we have "Agree" here, and "Not so sure" here. And the teacher asked that question like, "If a bunch of gay children were just migrating to here, and were all coming to this school, would we accept them into the school?" And I tell you 95 percent of the class went to agree.
> **J:** That they would accept them in the class?
> **Student:** Yeah, 95 percent. That was a [laugh] oh, and like let me see how many—like just a few went to disagree. Not a few, about four of us. And about ten or so went to "not so sure." It was really surprising, man. So, it's just like they will accept anything. It's really bad.

It might be argued that as blacks who might have experienced the hurt caused by use of a derogatory term such as "nigger," these school youth would be more attuned to homophobic slurs such as "faggot." This was not the case. As illustrated by the conversation in the following male focus group, acknowledging the inappropriate use of racial epithets does not mean the direct transfer of such recognition to other derogatory terms such as "faggot."

> **Student 1:** One of my English teachers, Ms. B., she actually asked me, how did I feel when people call me a nigger. In a classroom! So I am like it doesn't really affect me, but I don't like people to call me that. Then she said "Why do you call people faggot and gay?" ('Cuz I was making fun of some gay person in the class). Right. So then I am like, well, there is a big difference between nigger and gay. Then she said some-

thing like "Nigger." Now, don't you feel bad. That's like the same as somebody going gay or faggot. There's big difference with that word. She tries to compare that word together. You can't do that.

**Student 2:** You should cut her down, man. Put her in her place.

**J:** What do you feel about use of that word nigger?

**Student 3:** Big difference between fag and nigger. Fag, you can be any race because you are weird. Call a guy nigger, I look it up in the dictionary, it means something that gets in the way of progress, that's what nigger means. To call some one that, it's way more than calling someone gay. Most time you call some one gay, you don't mean it. You don't know if a person is gay. They might talk like a girl, walk like a girl, but you don't know. Then you can guess.

**Student 2:** I can joke around with a friend and I can say, "Oh, you are gay," and we will laugh about it. Can joke around with the same friend and say "You nigger," we'll laugh about it. When it's offensive is when the person means it. Like someone could call me gay and mean it, and it wouldn't offend me much because I know I am not gay. If someone calls me nigger and means it, that's a different story, that's a bigger insult. Being called gay doesn't mean anything. There are people out there who are gay, but I don't think there is anyone out there that's a nigger.

**J:** What if that person doesn't want to be called gay?

**Student 3:** You can't choose not to be black, but you can choose not to be gay.

This discussion illustrates how problematic it is to see relations of oppression as equivalent in terms of their construction and representation. Some cultural theorists would imply that to teach about oppression in general is an effective strategy to transform students' levels of consciousness about social justice. However, the narratives highlight the ways in which the students' racialized and sexualized discourses intersect each other. Their discourses make a simple "one fits all" solution of oppression highly problematic and unlikely to be effective. When the latter is examined in relation to some of the narratives that discuss the film *Set It Off,* one is able to see that such discourses do not operate in isolation. In this case, students call on religious belief in conjunction with youth culture to construct gays and lesbians as "other" and thus produce/reproduce themselves as heterosexual. The students would seem to be more open to acknowledging oppression when it relates directly to their sense of self. This entrenchment of "othering" is hardly surprising with regard to sexuality, if one concurs with social theorists such as Lacan who postulate that the "other" is necessary in order to bring one's subjectivity into being. Thus the more one can maintain a distinction from the other—the more the fiction of a secure and solid identity is maintained.

Such production of meaning is not homogenous when the students put the media representations to work during the process of identity construction. We find that the discourse of style can be used not only to present specific social and individual identities but also to produce collective identities such as those illustrated in the north

/south demarcation of urban space (Chapter 6). It is evident that hood movies, rap music, and magazines provide the language used by the students in this demarcation of urban space. Coded to their own specific location, the discursive formation that is produced relates to socioeconomic status as well as urban space, a production based on "us" and "them." In analyzing the sense of blackness that the students garner through a regime of representation, one finds that it is heavily contoured through African-American experiences, since that is the source of much of the music videos, films, and types of music to which the students listen. It is an identity that is produced intertextually in relation to African-American identities as well as other diasporan identities and subjectivities. This dominance of the United States in terms of the students' consumption of dress style, magazines, and music video would seem to indicate a sense of "borrowed blackness," a borrowed black identity formation that is not directly derived from within the borders of Canada. If one views blackness as multiple identities and about "routes" as much as "roots" (Gilroy, 1995), then this research illustrates the ways in which blackness is a contested discourse within the Albertan/Canadian context.

The construction of this borrowing, from a dominant U.S. culture can be viewed not just as intertextual but also as hegemonic, as a relation of power, in that:

> The dominant culture is able to "frame" the ways in which subordinate groups live and respond to their own cultural system and lived experiences; in other words, the dominant culture is able to manufacture dreams and desires for both dominant and subordinate groups by supplying "terms of reference" (i.e., images, visions, stories ideals) against which all individuals are expected to live their lives. (McLaren, 1994, p. 183)

While historically African-Canadian identity has consistently been formed in relation to African-American identity and while the two identities have much in common in terms of experiences of exclusion and racism, there are also differences in terms of national and historical formation. As the dominant partner within the relationship, African-American identities have stood as the quintessential example of black identities. Hence, the youths in the study can quite accurately claim that what limited inclusion of black lived experiences there is within the Alberta curriculum tends to highlight African-American experiences through discussions of slavery and civil rights leaders and movement. There is an erasure of African-Canadian experiences within the Canadian mosaic. So it is that the students are not able, within the space constructed by the official curriculum, to access information on the human rights struggles by the Brotherhood of Sleeping Car Porters, who, in conjunction with the other African-Canadian activists and Jewish and labor groups in Ontario, fought to extend human rights to issues of employment and immigration (Mathieu, 2001; Lambertson, 2001; Calliste, 1987; Grizzle, 1998).

## *Summary*

This chapter has interpreted and reinterpreted the students' *doxa*, opinions, and beliefs as reproduced in the narratives. It highlights the theme of "borrowed blackness" to illustrate the ways in which African-American youth identity has become the universal in terms of blackness and as such reinforces a process of borrowing. This borrowing is further contoured by the specific historical juncture of globalized capitalism as well as the various ways in which desire is constructed. The representation of blackness constructed through youth culture is hegemonic and interacts with the dominant discourses of the American media. The theme of borrowed identities is evident in terms of the discourses of consumption through which these students position themselves as desiring specific U.S.-based youth culture. It should also be noted that although magazines and music videos heightened the students' desire for U.S. dress style, consumption was not uniform across all students. Instead, the students' desire for U.S.-derived style was often constrained by economics as well as geographic location. These constraints also act as enablers in the ways in which style becomes important in terms of its "use value" in a social context. It is at this point of the argument that one can see most clearly the ways in which the school acts as a stage upon which the students get to play out and use dress style in order to position themselves within discourses of consumption and identity. Being able to purchase and wear many of these hard-to-access styles enhances social status, as style becomes commodity. The ability of a student to access style before anyone else increases the cultural and social value of a specific item of clothing as well as its " use value." In terms of style, larger, more cosmopolitan centers such as Toronto are perceived as much less "dry" when compared to Edmonton.

At times the students can be seen as passive consumers without self-critique of their actions, especially in the ways in which some black males adopt and take on the dress style, walk, street slang, and argot of African-American youths as represented through rap and hip-hop. These representations are garnered through a "regime of representation" (Hall, 1997) and based on a specific form of hypermasculinity, coded through dress, talk, and walk. However, the emergence and use of the term "acting black" seems to be a way of "challenging" this passive sense of "borrowed blackness" and making a distinction from those who adopt this stereotypical representation of blackness. The phrase calls into question the idea that such representations might be homogenized through a discourse of "authentic" blackness. There are also degrees to the acceptance of this performance of blackness. Males can wear hip-hop clothes without being challenged as acting, but if one also has the walk and, especially, the argot, then it is more likely that one will be identified as acting. As well, the overall emphasis on the black male body in sports and style has in some ways contoured the understanding of blackness to emphasize blackness as style at the expense of former political/nationalist discourses of blackness as based on knowledge and shared experience. The latter is akin to Gilroy's (2000) conception of "stylish solidarity" (see Chapter 8). In terms of school, the students indicate that peers categorized as non-black regard blackness with ambivalence; as a sign it can evoke both fear and desire.

Another interesting way in which youth culture, through music, television, and music videos, is used to make identification in the students' lives is through the Northside/Southside binary. Although not all students subscribed to this dualism and translation of geographic place into social space, the discourse was acknowledged by most as either being active in the past or still active, to some extent, in the present. Using style and codes that draw on the hood genre, the students, in their individual interviews, consistently described the same area of the city as being designated as Edmonton's hood. The narratives construct a distinction based, to some extent, upon socioeconomic status in conjunction with style. This use of the term "hood" draws on codes constructed through hood movies such as *Boyz N the Hood*, *Sugar Hill*, and *Menace II Society*. The term "hood" acts as an anchor (Barthes, 1977) for the preferred meanings that are evoked through its use. The latter is also of interest because it shows that although the narratives attempt to construct black identity as having a sense of sameness, these same discourses act back upon themselves, through highlighting the concept of "acting black."

The next chapter will continue to examine the students' *doxa*, but this time through the concept of "stylish solidarity." The chapter ascertains the extent to which the students have a sense of blackness coded through dress style and consequently what this might mean for future black identification within the diaspora.

# CHAPTER 8

# Stylish Solidarity

*Ritualized sexual play of various kinds and an erotic delight in the body supply the new
means of bonding this new freedom and black life. What was once abject life becomes
nothing more than life-style among other, less exotic options.*
GILROY, 2000, p. 185

## Introduction

This chapter identifies three themes through which the students struggle to
give meaning to their lives. The three themes are: "Slangs, Slurs, and Development of a Public Sphere," "Stylish Solidarity," and "Knowledge and Experience." First, youth culture as a communicative resource indicates the ways in
which the students use slang and slurs to develop an argot, a common culture that is
produced/reproduced in a public sphere. Second, "stylish solidarity" draws on Gilroy
(2000) to illustrate the ways in which black youth culture has become identified
with the body and style. A sense of collectivity is based on style rather than on a
more direct, politicized understanding. Third, knowledge and experience indicate
the intertextual nature of the way in which meaning gets translated from one social
situation to another. All three themes indicate the intersubjective basis of assigning
meaning to social situations. They draw on a variety of identifications and differen-
tiations that the students make during their lives. Some of these themes highlight
black identification, while others highlight gender, sexuality, and age.

The students portray themselves as active recipients of media culture and meaning making. "Meaning in this context is not something which is given or which can
be taken for granted. It is manufactured out of historically shifting systems of codes,
conventions and signs" (Strinati, 1995, p. 110). They do not subscribe totally to
Adorno's fears of the mass stupification of society in the interests of what he identified as the "culture industries." Gordon (1980) argues that Foucault's theorization

suggests domination works not so much through "ideological mystification" as through its ability to define a certain field of empirical truth (p. 237).

## Slang, Slurs, and Development of a Public Sphere

The narratives suggest that youth culture provides a language that operates through slang and slurs. This language is articulated among and between the students within what can be described as a "public sphere." For Thompson (1990), a public sphere is a place:

> in which issues [are] debated and positions challenged. It was in the cleared space of the public sphere that the discourse of ideologies appeared, constituting organized systems of beliefs which offered coherent interpretation of social and political phenomena. (p. 80)

This public sphere provides a space for the contestation and production of empirical truths or "regimes of truth." For these students, the school acts as a site for the exchange of language and meaning within the public sphere. More specifically, theorists such as Mark Neal have identified a black sphere operating within white-dominated society. Often this sphere is constructed through music dissemination and acts as a counter sphere to other dominant white public spheres. For Neal and to some extent Paul Gilroy in his earlier work *The Black Atlantic*:

> the black popular music tradition has served as a primary vehicle for communally derived critiques of African American experience, and that the quality and breadth of such critiques are wholly related to the quality of life in the black public sphere. (Neal, 1999, p. xi)

Television, magazines, and music provide a language, verbal and nonverbal, through which students communicate. This language of communication enables one to engage in public discourse—to talk. Throughout the narratives, the students use phrases and metaphors, slang, and idioms derived from media culture to communicate with peers; phrases such as "being a playa," "playa-hating," "hoochie," "Adam and Eve not Adam and Steve." Status can be gained from being able to engage with and wield such terms in general day-to-day conversation within peer groups. Media provide common experiences that extend beyond the local to become local/global. Television programs, music videos, and music magazines act as a communicative resource for school-based discussions among the students and their peers. Media provide a source of content for social interaction, reinforcing the need for students to continue to watch the program so that they will "have something to talk about." The ability to join in the conversation of such a media-constructed community enables the positioning of oneself within an actual community of peers. Cultural theorist Paddy Scannel argues that:

> broadcasting has brought the private into the public, re-socialising the public domain, making it a space in which talk for talk's sake, talk for enjoyment, talk as a sociable activity has its place alongside talk that is informative, that is getting its message across, that is trying to persuade [ . . . ]. [These] sociable forms of interaction sustain a world that is, if not more rational in a formal and theoretical sense, altogether more reasonable. (1990, pp. 20–21)

This public sphere provides a space where gender, race, class, and other key social relations are connected and reproduced via talk. Media offer powerful sources for the presentation and representation of images that increase the cultural repertoire available to students. However, as Gilroy (1995) argues, it also has to be recognized that this source of representation and the symbolic does not mean an automatic identification. Gilroy's postulation is evident throughout the students' narratives as they consume and produce meanings through what he identifies as "black popular culture." Willis (1990) would seem to concur with Gilroy's summation as to the importance of popular/youth culture for purposes of identification as well as providing a public sphere. As he sees it:

> Popular music can be a conversational resource. The knowledge of lyrics, dress styles and genres is often used as the coins of exchange in casual talk. By listening to music together and using it as a background to their lives, by expressing affiliation to particular taste groups, popular music becomes one of the principal means by which young people define themselves. (Willis, 1990)

Construction of this public sphere through youth culture is not unproblematic, however, since the youth culture that is consumed through the process of mediazation is one that draws heavily on American rather than Canadian experiences. Thus, the students are exposed to a broadening of the public sphere that is contoured by discourses and experiences garnered in the United States. It is evident that magazines also construct discourses that are active in the public sphere. In terms of the commodification debate discussed in Chapter 3 we can note how the rapper in the hip-hop magazine *Rap Pages* constructs similar discourses to those exposed through the youth's narratives. The following extract from *Rap Pages* illustrates the ongoing contestation surrounding discourses of commodification discourses that echo the sentiments of the students:

> Ali isn't too thrilled with the current state of affairs in Hip-Hop, and he doesn't hold his tongue about it either. "As far as Hip-Hop is concerned, it's about love for my car, for me getting ahead at all costs, to whatever extent. If it's at the expense of another

brother, then whatever. That's not good. We're supposed to be together in what ever it is our endeavours are, and not stepping on the next human being. It's just a lot of egos, a lot of arrogance in the music." (Abdul-Lateef, 1998, p. 78)

Throughout the students' narratives there is some evidence to support Jakobson's postulation that meaning is constructed through the fundamental modes of metaphors and metonyms. Such language allows classification and differentiation from others by making parts represent the whole syntagmatically (metonymy) and drawing attention to similarities as well as differences (metaphor) to make one group stand in place of another. These tropes relate primarily to sexuality as well as gender relations and may well allow students to talk around and about topics that might otherwise be taboo within space traditionally constructed as public. In listening and reading the narratives, it becomes obvious that hip-hop/youth culture uses a specific language as part of the hip-hop discourse and that the ability of the students to use this language allows them to present themselves within or in relation to subject positions. As part of accessing a style, communication, via argot, enables the formation of a group identity and the creation of boundaries between "them" and "us." Ibrahim (2000) has noted in his research with a group of Franco-Ontarian youths recently arrived from continental Africa how important accessing Black Stylized English (BSE) is in being able to perform a black identity and gain a sense of belonging. As Ibrahim explains it, this BSE:

> refers to ways of speaking that do not depend on full mastery of the language [of Black English] it banks on ritual; expressions such as whassup, whadup, whassup my Nigger, yo, yo home boy, which are performed habitually and recurrently in rap. (2000, p. 119)

Within this Edmonton-based study, the students most recently from Africa did adopt hip-hop dress styles popular in North American youth culture. They were also familiar with the slang and slurs of BSE. However, the extent to which they used slang and slurs varied during daily interaction. Many of the students used variations of BSE, and this may well reflect the way in which style was weighted most heavily in terms of representing blackness. While use of BSE could cause one to seem stylish, so, in contrast not using slang could produce one as mature. The following student identifies the way in which people talk with what he identifies as an "accent." In the following narrative I ascertain what he means by having an accent:

**J:** "Wha's up, man?"
**Student:** Yeah, that! Everyone already talks sort of like that. I don't know why. Like here the demographic is kinda like black is cool. To be acting black is to act "cool."
**J:** Is it?

As he continues, he makes a distinction between those who act black and those who do not:

**Student:** But like also Langston, he is a respectable guy. He doesn't have to act like anything.

**J:** He acts like himself you think?

**Student:** I like that. I respect that about him. He's a good [neat] guy.

The narrative highlights the way in which the ability to use this argot is important in "performing" blackness and also in placing one within the student-driven school hierarchy of styles. Argot and slang are complex constructs in that while their purpose is to maintain and mark distinction, this is often achieved by a delicate balance between change and continuity in use. One illustration of the changing nature of the language among some of the students occurred during a focus group interview in which one young man was constantly using the rap-inspired phrase "pimping ain't easy" during his first interview and by the second, had changed to another more gangsta-inspired phrase. While the argot used by the students enables communication, it was also a medium that was constantly changing. The ability to be up to date with the latest argot represented one's self as stylish. The media, especially that related to hip-hop culture, enable not just a common reference point for discussion but also a specific language for the students to communicate with each other: a language that changes according to developments within media culture and, to some extent, geographic location. The following student describes a visit to the United States, where he found that meaning was communicated using different slang and with that change of location came a redefinition of argot as "normal English":

**Student:** Like they use words like "Off the hook."

**J:** What does that mean?

**Student:** That means like "that's cool" or that's "cronk."

**J:** "Cronk?" What does that mean?

**Student:** That's "cool" too, but referring to like shoes "those are cronk." Or then they'd be like "that's tight." That's like the same thing as "cronk." They say like "mug" um, "those mugs are tight,"// And they'd be talking about shoes? They call them "roaches." Like "give me some "roaches." They use all kinds of different words.

At times, hip-hop-enhanced argot was inflected according to national formation. Thus "batty boy," a phrase used in Jamaica to describe homosexuals, was understood and occasionally used by black students from in North America or continental Africa. In response to a query from me as to the use of "batty man," the following student indicated:

**Student:** Here? //Yeah// They say batty boy a lot. //Oh batty boy?// Batty men, batty riders, batty everything.

**J:** Oh that's interesting. And they use it, and then because it's used, you then pick it up?

**Student:** Yeah. You start then understanding what it is or like, "Hey what's that mean?"

**J:** So do you ever use it?

**Student:** No. I've said batty boy before, but I really don't. Actually I am like laughing, mimicking it or something. I don't really be meaning it when I be saying it, 'cuz I really don't know how to use that word in a phrase. (individual interview)

By communicating in the public sphere, students are, to some extent, fixing the codes between linguistic and conceptual systems (Hall, 1997, p. 22). The incidental use and reference to youth culture and media to contextualize and give meaning to and understanding of the everyday can be found in the ways in which the students' everyday narratives draw on youth culture to increase understanding and the depth of communication. For example, in the following narrative describing someone "preppy" as being like "Carleton off of *Fresh Prince*" enables "anchoring" of meaning even if temporary:

**Student:** Whitewashed I've heard, but never towards me. There was one kid that went here, everyone called whitewashed. He wore the perfect fit jeans, like the not baggy and not tight. They . . . just, sit on him you know. And he wore like the fancy dress shirts . . . kind of like those guys you see on TV that go "Buffet." Like Carlton off of Fresh Prince. He was kind of like that. He was like one of the only ones that ever was called whitewashed.

Or production of the ideal father:

**J:** So what would a Canadian father act like do you think?

**Student:** Like talk to their kids more . . . about life, like take their kids out to like movies, like, I don't know. Like you see on TV! They take the kids to baseball games, and all that kind of stuff. Play with their kids and just be like friends. Try and be a friend with their kids instead of like master.

One example of the ways that gender relations are played out in the lives and culture of the students was through the phrase "being a player." The term, derived from films and music, symbolizes one potential set of gender relations. Although it is a new phrase, its roots can be traced within other eras of popular culture. One student argues that "playa" was a replacement for 1970s inflected phrase "mack." The words change but the meaning doesn't fully change; it becomes recoded through discourses that are dominant during that particular period of youth culture. Among the students "playa" is related not just to the conduct of gender relations but is also linked via the issue of commodification to Sean (P. Diddy) Combs and his public display of wealth and women. Some male students traced the origins of the term to the United States, indicating its constructed nature by alluding to the existence of rules and taboos in playing the game. In the gendered discourse directly below, one rule that reinforces patriarchal relations, and male bonding is clearly articulated in the phrase "bros befo' hoes." Further, the following focus group indicates the way in which gender relations get played out through the symbolic coding of the phrase "playa":

**Student 1:** It's like a game.
**Student 2:** It's like what kind of mind games you could play with them. If you can go out with two girls at the same time so that you can play them.
**J:** Where does it come from?
**Student 3:** I think some movie.
**Student 4:** So people just use it.
**J:** Do you know any girls who are players?
**Student 1:** A girl can't be a player. If it's a girl, it's a slut. A girl, she ain't going to admit it.
**J:** It's similar?
**Student 3:** It's the same thing; it's not similar. Everything a black man does, he tries to make it look good. A drug dealer calls himself a gangsta. A pimp don't say he is a pimp. They say, "I am a big boy."
**Student 2:** I'm not. I ain't no player.
**J:** If you discovered that someone was playing your friend, what would you do?
**Student 1:** "Bro's before hoes." (male focus group)

This use of media to enhance talk within the public sphere is not just applicable to black youths and hip-hop. Similar use of the media as a channel of communicating was made by youths in Marie Gillespie's (1995) study of Punjabi youth in London. She notes that such meshing of the televisual media and everyday language provides "one of the most tangible examples of the way that the discourses of TV and everyday life are intermeshed is when jingles, catch phrases and humorous storylines of favourite ads are incorporated into everyday speech" (p. 178).

Although not obvious, reception and appropriation of media language—the process of making one's own something that is new—was often filtered through discourses of blackness. These discourses come into being in the public sphere. The students' narratives indicate that reception is filtered through and in relation to what can best be identified as an ongoing Black Nationalist discourse. Stokely Carmichael,[1] as one of the leaders of the Black Power/consciousness movement, and civil rights activist Charles Hamilton indicate that:

we aim to define and encourage a new consciousness among black people which will make it possible to proceed towards those answers and those solutions. This consciousness . . .

might be called a sense of peoplehood: pride, rather than shame, in blackness and an attitude of brotherly communal responsibility among black people for one another. (1967, p. 12)

Some students who position themselves and others as consciously black highlight a discourse of black consciousness based on pride rather than shame. This classification is most evident in the narratives and discourses concerning the urban legend that links Tommy Hilfiger with racist statements and the commodification of hip-hop style. Hilfiger can be seen as an extreme case of how the idea of mass designer fashion operates:

> Mass designer fashion is a specific formation within the industry; it is not equivalent to traditional haute couture (which is often dependent upon highly-skilled artisanal means of production and which is still somewhat outside the circuits of globalizing capital that nurtures the mass clothing industry). (Smith, 1999, p. 3)

Mass designer fashion illustrates the present-day concern with image/style rather than just the production of a consumer item. At times, concern with style collides with concern about consumption as in Chapters 5 and 6, where students discuss the ideological implication of wearing Hilfiger clothes. In the latter example, mass consumption collides with issues of black entrepreneurship.

The discussion on Tommy Hilfiger indicates the ways in which consumption becomes implicated in issues of ideology in the name of power. This equation of blackness with consumption of brand name, and more, specifically, Hilfiger style, is often accomplished through representations of style in magazines and music videos. Paul Smith (1999) indicates that:

> Having been frequently donated Hilfiger outfits for use in performances and, more importantly, in their music videos, rappers have functioned as conduits of approval and authorization—authenticity, perhaps—for this white business attempting to sell what are essentially white styles to black consumers. (Smith, p. 6)

Smith, in analyzing the anti-Hilfiger Internet sites, argues that "the most common strand of objection to Hilfiger . . . appears to be an objection to the very principle of black patronage of white business" (Smith, 1999, p. 7). This similar coding of the Hilfiger debate in the U.S. Internet sites illustrates the ways in which constructions of the meaning of blackness become local/global. While Internet and word of mouth affect formation of discourse, music also acts as a means of conveying meanings of the Hilfiger urban legend. Hilfiger's mass designer fashions can also be seen as a move towards regulation of subcultural identities in the north, as they market and contour the tastes and desires of this group of youths. In the following narrative, the student illustrates how rap musicians also play a role in constructing the discourse on Tommy Hilfiger, while linking the debate to discourses of black entrepreneurship:

**Student:** He talks about everything, black people, his one song, "Black and White." He says, "Why is Tommy Hilfiger discriminating on us?" But I understand it because black people don't buy black-owned clothes. Then he goes off and he talks 'bout how they killed Martin Luther King and all kinds of stuff like that.

Youth culture is based on patterns of consumption through which certain identities are projected or cut. It is evident from the narratives that the students are engaged in a process of discourse production as well as consumption. In terms of Hilfiger, Smith (1999) argues that:

> Similarly when black kids wear TOM logo as signs not just of fashionability but even of racial authenticity, they are doing more than just establishing a cultural identity and communality; equally, they are placing themselves in a particular relation to political-economic circuits for which the possibility of their consuming in this way is one of capital's central desiderata, or even imperatives, at this juncture when capital is dreaming of globalizing itself. (Smith, p. 7)

## Stylish Solidarity

While the above narrative suggests that youth culture provides a common language through slang and slurs, the students also access discourses that offer a critique of the commodification of rap/hip-hop and youth style. Thompson (1990) argues that symbolic forms constituted as commodities "can be bought and sold on a market for a price." Further, he argues that often this process assigns different degrees of symbolic value to those who produce them or receive them. In this way, he argues, conflict of symbolic valuation can occur according to context and social asymmetries. Linked to commodification is the way in which, for some of the students, style has become a sense of black solidarity. What Paul Gilroy (2000) identifies as "stylish solidarity":

> Blackness emerges as more behavioral, dare I say cultural? It can be announced by indicative sexual habits and other bodily gestures. Under some circumstances it can even be acquired in simple economic processes. Identity as sameness and solidarity is definitely not being essentialized here. Items can be purchased that lend an eloquent uniformity to the mute body on a temporary, accidental basis. This is not an internal journey after all but a journey to the mall. (p. 268)

One of the most consistent discourses that can be traced in the youth-generated public sphere occupied by the students concerns commercialization and commodification of black youth culture. Youth culture, as indicated earlier, has become in some ways synonymous with hip-hop culture and black youth culture. As such, regimes of representations, via magazines and music videos, have constructed the body as the center of hip-hop discourses via an all-important emphasis on how the body is positioned and decorated. In accounting for this emphasis on the body, Armond White (1995), the rap critic, argues "since whites can't cut it vocally in hip-hop, where the texture of African American speech is as musical an element as the samples, the visual image is all important." Canadian cultural theorist Rinaldo Walcott (1997) intimates that this emphasis on blackness has been ongoing rather than just related to white consumption of hip-hop:

> culturally, black youth have demonstrated a real concern with the body and its performance. Their use of the body echoes the various ways in which black cultural practices have always treated bodies as a canvas upon which historical and contemporary social relations may be signified, inscribed and rewritten. (p. 64)

Whatever the dynamics of this specific phenomenon, it nonetheless draws on other discourses within society that privilege the body as a site of theoretical focus as well as a site of control (Foucault, 1980). Chris Weedon (1987) argues that:

> discourses are ways of constituting knowledge, together with the social practices, forms of subjectivity and power relations, which inhere in such knowledges, and the relations between them. Discourses are more than ways of thinking and producing meaning. They constitute the "nature" of the body, unconscious and conscious mind and emotional life of the subjects which they seek to govern. (p. 108)

Throughout the data chapters, a variety of contesting discourses are evident in the students' narratives. These discourses are constructed through descriptors such as "authentic" rap music vs. mainstream rap music: old-school[2] vs. new-school rap; *laissez-faire* consumption vs. black-identified consumption. That these discourses should be competing is not surprising if one notes Easthope and McGowan's (1992) comment that "within any given social and historical moment a variety of discourses exist and compete for control of subjectivity. The subject thus becomes the site of a discursive battle for the meaning of their identity" (p. 69). That the students have a variety of ways in which to understand and give meaning to the production and consumption of youth culture is evident within the narratives. Critical theorists such as Adorno, from the Frankfurt School, assume that the role of "culture industries" is to keep the masses ignorant so that they do not recognize their "true" economic conditions of oppression. However, the students indicate an awareness of a situation that is neither simple nor clear cut. These students are aware, as black youths, that black-identified cultural forms such as rap have been commodified and that in an earlier era of black consciousness, consumption of white products was perceived as undermining black economic activity.

The youth are able to draw on these various discourses in order to contest an ideology of commodification (Chapters 3 to 7). This ability of the students to contest discourses undermines any claims of passive consumption. Instead, the students' narratives position them as being both active and passive in their choices and consumption. So practices of consumption that the students engage in during everyday life seem to act back upon and thus come to shape, discourses, just as the discourses themselves shape practices. The ability of the students to use contesting and competing discourses cannot bring about immediate change, but it does offer a way to interrupt meaning that might lead to different consumption patterns. As to whether a different pattern of consumption leads to social change is a debatable, if not problematic, question. Examples from other areas of social life indicate that using consumption patterns to bring about change has mixed results. While boycotting South African goods may have worked to some extent in the fight against apartheid, everyday recycling has yet to make a difference to the depletion of the ozone layer. However, these students do develop a black consciousness, even if filtered through a youth culture based around issues of consumption. This consciousness, although not politicized at the moment, has the potential to be channelled into other avenues of social change. It also illustrates that, as Gramsci argues, it is on the level of culture that ideology is often fought. It can be suggested that:

> in the light of receiving media messages and seeking to understand them, of relating them and sharing them with others, individuals remould the boundaries of experience and reuse their understandings of the world and themselves. They are not passively absorbing what is presented to them, but are actively, sometimes critically, engaged in a continuing process of self-formation and self-understanding, a process of which the reception and appropriation of media messages is today an integral part. (Thompson, 1990, p. 10)

However, it should also be noted that while some students drew on discourses that linked a sense of consciousness with support for black-owned businesses, such actions were articulated within a framework of capitalism. Using an argument that fits within a framework of relations of representation, it is assumed that changes can be brought about for blacks if they, too, are allowed into the "free market" of capitalism. In actuality, the issues surrounding blackness in the United States will not be changed solely by a support for black capitalism, because issues of economic distribution will still be evident within the uneven and unequal development of capitalism.

This process of "self-formation and self-understanding" identified by Thompson is most evident in the narratives concerning the conscious support of black community control of capital through specific patterns of consumption. In such consumption, some students draw on existing Black Nationalist/consciousness discourses supportive of black community self-sufficiency to position themselves as consciously black. In positioning themselves in relation to the Tommy Hilfiger urban legend and in relation to P. Diddy's genre of "new school" music, the students say something about themselves and their identification as black.

This process of identification via dress style has become heightened in an age when the body has become paramount:

> **J:** So your job will be [in the media] // Yeah// So what about your style of dress then? Do you see yourself still wearing the same stuff when you are [working at the media]?
> **Student:** Oh no, no. I'd be dressed up in the sweetest suits, wicked suits. I'd just be lounging there in my suits, man. And then my hair wouldn't be like it is. I'm planning on shaving my hair low sometime. Like even maintaining a nice appearance.

It is evident that there is no one style of dress to which all students adhere. As with musical choices, the media personalities that they identify with vary from the "smooth" of Will Smith through P. Diddy to the "rough" of Method Man. It is this coming together of cultural icons and musicians with consumption of style that heightens the nature of commodification that is underway in this process (refer to Chapters 6 and 7). The body image gives a certain potency to identifications that are made, and, therefore, identification should be regarded as a "cut of identity" that is momentary, and based on a process of "becoming" as well as "being." This reliance on style and body as representative of blackness, what Gilroy identifies as "stylish solidarity," is an important discourse in the lives of the students. For the males interviewed in the focus group, athletic ability was perceived as both a positive aspect of blackness and an object of female desire. Such an understanding bears the historical trace of dualism and viewing black males in terms of body and physicality rather than the mind and intellect. In this context, the phrase "acting black" connotes both stylish solidarity and physicality. This phrase is polysemic—capable of signifying multiple meanings—and describes the assumption of a media-generated black identity that includes dress, walk, and talk. This specific black youth identity has, through mediazation, become coded as authentic blackness. It also allows black males to continue to be regarded ambivalently by their white peers with desire and fear. Marc Speigler alludes to this in discussing the memoirs of "white" author William Wimsatt:

> The attraction, he says, is part admiration, part fascination, and part fear. "A lot of white kids suspect they wouldn't make it through what inner-city blacks do, so there's an embedded admiration that's almost visceral," Wimsatt says. "Fear is one of our strongest impulses, and poor black men are the greatest embodiment of that fear." (1996, p. 127)

However, for some of the students, the ability to define such identification as "acting," positions the descriptor as an important signifier that gives recognition to heterogeneity of black identity. The latter also allows for the possibility of developing a way of being black within Canadian society that could be different from, yet related to, the United States. The use of the phrase, "acting black" questions the dominance of U.S.-generated images of blackness as universal and problematizes the representations of such identities. While such a problematization might not lead to direct change, it does provide a breaking of the binary between blackness as color and blackness as "image." It allows for the emergence of questions such as what is *not* "acting black?," i.e., a debate on the meaning of blackness across geographic locations.

Although hip-hop culture is identified primarily with blackness, with commodification, it has come to be seen by some cultural theorists as a "multicultural" style that many who are racialized as whites have accepted and adopted. As one student described the social interaction at school:

**Student:** Yeah, everybody tries to act black around here.
**J:** Really!
**Student:** Even a white guy in the hall. "Wha's up?" Not "What's up?" or "how you are doing?" To act black is to be cool. And that's a big part in this country, at least in this community. And we know it [he laughs].

Some critics regard this ready adoption of black-identified style as an indication of the growing tolerance of hip-hop nation and blackness. However, the ability of non-blacks to "act black" through dress and style is seen as problematic by some black students and indicative of a psychological lack in their white peers. Such an analysis is similar to that of cultural critics, such as bell hooks (1994) and Yvonne Bynoe (2000). Bynoe is sceptical of the ability of hip-hop to transcend racialized experiences. She regards the lure of rap for a white audience as similar to that of Norman Mailer's 1957 construction of a "white Negro" who "drifted out at night looking for action with a black man's code to fit their facts." She thus argues that:

For whites brought up in suburbia or in affluent, homogenous urban neighbourhoods, the biggest, nastiest, lustiest, most uninhibited edge they can find in their nearly all-white experience is dressing "black," talking "black," and walking "black": even as their "black" is a distorted MTV version. (Bynoe, 2000)

So it would seem that while hip-hop offers a social space for dialogue on blackness, it is a dialogue that is mediated through stereotypes of that blackness.

Issues concerning stylish solidarity and commodification, like those of the above discussion of "acting black," bring into question the role of ideology in relation to agency and structure. Are the cultural industries determining the students' consumption and consequent identification that they make through those consumption patterns? Research on audiences and their reception in general of media lies at the heart of much cultural studies discussion and is linked to the concept of ideology. As indicated in Chapter 1, ideology can be conceived of as one of the ways in which the meanings mobilized by symbolic forms serve to establish and sustain relations of domination (Thompson, 1990, p. 7). This interpretation of ideology differs from those theorists who would position themselves as on the political economy wing of social theory. Turner, in an admittedly simplistic tone, identifies this difference in orientation to ideology as one whereby, for political economist, the "function of ideology is instrumental—to misrepresent the 'real,' and to mask any political struggle; for cultural studies, ideology is the very site of struggle"(1992, p. 197). Rather than adopting an either/or positioning with regard to this dualism, McRobbie (1994) argues for a return to neo-Gramscian theory. Use of such a framework would allow recognition of the

> dialectic between the processes of production and activities of consumption. The consumer always confronts a text or practice in its material existence as a result of determinate conditions of production. But in the same way, the text or practice is confronted by a consumer who in effect produces in use the range of possible meaning(s), which cannot just be read off from the materiality of the text or practice, or the means or relations of its production. (Storey, 1996, p. 5)

Thus discourses of blackness as political consciousness emerge through much of the students' narratives. "Keeping it real" and "keeping it true" are the phrases that identify this discourse. Thus "keeping it real" is used to identify one with one's social background and one's "roots." In the case of hip-hop, "roots" are identified closely with one's neighborhood. This linking back to the hood is reinforced by various codes within music videos that position rappers as tied to, or linked with, the neighborhood they grew up in. Contesting and competing with this discourse of "keeping it real" is another discourse that constructs rap as primarily a product for sale to the larger non-black public. For some of the students, this positioning of rap as commercial is aligned with rapper P. Diddy, who, as the section on rap as commodity (in Chapters 3 and 4) indicates, is perceived as having very few rhymes, using recycled beats and rapping only about his money and women. This descriptor of P. Diddy exemplifies a person that is viewed as opposite to and different from someone who is "keeping it real." As well, constructions of "keeping real" are also based on being able to draw on one's concrete experiences of living in the hood. What is interesting about the latter constructions is that although commodification of black experiences is contested through a discourse of commercialism, these same students are colluding with commercial enterprises whereby the experiences that are on sale through "keeping it real" are representations of poverty. In some ways "keeping it real" rap sells the experiences of the poor so that individuals can become economically advantaged and thus leave the hood. It is, in some ways, as Doreen identifies (in Chapter 5), an indication of rappers "making it." But at the same time it is an individual success—the rest of the brothers are back in the hood. There was no discussion within student narratives of the responsibility of rappers to plow back money into the community, whose experiences they are selling.

Stylish solidarity becomes linked to issues of black authenticity and representation through the personae of various rappers. The ability of rappers to take on the role of "authentic black," knowledgeable in black experiences, has increased with the commodification of rap and its ability to represent itself as the universal in black experiences rather than the particular. This coding of rappers as "knowledgeable," as "telling it like it is," has enabled them to be coded as "authorities on life in the "hood." This linking can be seen in the much-used descriptor "raptivist," i.e., an activist rapper. In the United States the importance of the raptivist has grown in a period when, relationally, other political activists have become muted within the media. For some youths, the rappers have become coded as equivalent to past social activists. Nelson George (1998) would disagree with this statement. For him, hip-hop is not a political movement in the usual sense. The advocates don't elect public officials. It doesn't present a systematic (or even original) critique of white supremacy (p. 154). Recently this issue has come to the forefront of the rap community in the United States. High-profile individuals such as Russell Simmonds have been organizing.

Within Canada, this discourse is constructed through a lens filtered by national formation, since rappers, Canadian or U.S., are not represented through media as embodying authentic African-Canadian experiences. They cannot come to represent the universal in black experiences. Thus, they cannot speak on behalf of the black population in Canada. The latter reflects the socio-economic and political formation of the African-Canadian community where settlement has occurred over a lengthy period of time and consists of groups from differing geographic origins.

Also significant in the latter scenario is the way that "keeping it real" is an important aspect of maintaining a sense of legitimacy. However, this legitimacy involves more of a sense of memory rather than any specific action to be undertaken. It bifurcates thought and action, body and mind. As well, in an almost parasitic relationship, the rappers are dependent upon the lived experiences of poverty and violence in the hood in order to define themselves and escape that world. These competing discourses around rap within the student group interviewed are also, not surprisingly, to be found in magazines read by many of the students. Thus Max Glazer (1998) in *The Source* indicates not just the rationale of commodification but also the longevity

> Ever since the corporate forces got their hands on this Bronx, NY-based rap music thing, artists, fans and the industry alike (especially those residing in the East Coast) have struggled to define what's beneficial to hip-hop culture and what's detrimental. (p. 152)

What is surprising however, is that magazines that are a part of that commodification process should espouse such critique. This critique of commodification finds an alignment with earlier discourses drawing on the Carmichael and Hamilton's (1967) definition of black power and the need for not only pride and consciousness in order to perform blackness but also self-determination:

Black people must lead and run their own organisations. Only black people can convey the revolutionary idea—and it is a revolutionary idea—that black people are able to do things themselves. Only they can create in the community an aroused and continuing black consciousness that will provide the basis for political strength. (p. 60)

Through these competing discourses and discursive practices, the students can align themselves and others with subject positions such as "black" or "not black enough." Although not yet evident among the students, these discourses on blackness are getting played out through the consumption of styles. Several narratives in Chapter 6 noted the ways in which some students are moving away from the "traditional" baggier styles of hip-hop towards the more fitted, preppy look. Nelson George (1998) also notes the link between preppy clothing and more recent hip-hop-derived style. In particular, he argues that:

Hilfiger found that the kids wanted his logos larger, more plentiful, and more colorful. Hilfiger accommodated them and this evolving style became known in the fashion biz as "urban prep," a way of dressing that took prep-school clothes and stretched them to fit the loose, baggy feel of '90s teen garb. (p. 162)

This recoding of blacks as dressing preppy is interesting in light of the binarism that also exists within some students' narratives on this subject. As with the descriptor "alternative," students often coded preppy connotatively with whiteness and opposite to existing understandings of what a black identity means (Kelly, 1998). This may well be the next site of contestation. Will those who adopt the "preppy" style be coded as "white-wanna-be's?" Coded within this discourse on style is the contouring of space, where the Northside is positioned as dressing in the more traditional "authentic" black style, and the Southside will be constructed as dressing like "pretty boy" P. Daddy.

Thus, to reinforce the main point of this chapter, although the students are influenced by African-American styles, it is not a passive reception but often involves appropriation filtered through wider societal discourses on blackness and the ability to define and construct a certain field of knowledge as truth. It is noticeable, in terms of black collectivity, the way that black identity has become embodied as stylish solidarity among youths rather than political consciousness as in earlier eras of Black Consciousness/Nationalists such as espoused by Marcus Garvey, Frantz Fanon, or Stokely Carmichael (Kwame Ture). While the link between black identity and commodification is heightened during this specific historical conjuncture, it is not a new articulation. Mark Neal has noted:

The commodification of "Soul" had a particularly compelling impact on African American popular expression, in that political resistance was often parlayed as an element of style. This is not to suggest that the Afro hairdo or the Dashiki was as politically meaningful as sit-ins or mass rallies, but that many of the icons of black social move-ment were invested with some vestige of oppositional expression. Nevertheless the mass commodification of Soul reduced Blackness to a commodity that could be bought and sold—and this is important—without the cultural and social markers that have de-fined Blackness. (1997, p. 117)

## Knowledge and Experience

As stated in the last sections on slang and slurs and stylish solidarity, discourses are produced and reproduced within a public sphere. This next section highlights again the phrase "keeping it real" to indicate its intertextual nature—its ability to evoke meanings through being read in relation to other media and knowledge sites such as schools. As well, this section highlights how the relationship between knowledge and experience gets coded through the phrase "keeping it real." This phrase can be viewed as homological in that it reveals the relationship between the particular cul-tural choices of the group of students and how these choices are used to construct the social meaning of the group. Such appropriation is enabled and worked through within the public sphere of the everyday, in schools, workplaces, and homes.

"Keeping it real" returns again as a phrase that crosses over from the realm of rap music and is brought into use in order to legitimate violent representations in films such as *Boyz N the Hood*, wherein the use of violence legitimates the film as realistic. In particular, this coding of social relations as "reality" allows the emergence of rep-resentations that under other circumstances would be challenged as ethically un-sound. An example is seen in the students' view that *The Jerry Springer Show* pro-vides a public language that is similar to that constructed through youth culture. The following student narrative indicates the way in which the program is used as a resource for bringing gendered relations into the public sphere:

Student:  At school all the time people talk about Jerry Springer:
J:  Do they? //yeah// What do they say?
Student:  "Did you see Springer yesterday?" "Did you see them beat that girl?" or "clap that girl," stuff like that.

It is a realism to which students relate and are interpellated even though viewing the show is sometimes infused with guilt as much as pleasure:

Student:  Okay. Jerry, I must admit I am ashamed to honestly say so. Sometimes I do watch it. It's a really bad show. He is like totally demoralized. But I can't help it. It's like kind of addictive sometimes. People are so stupid. But it's funny, it's really funny. Because, well maybe some of them are faking it, but you can tell that some of them are not faking it. And they are so dumb.

The strong confessional mode of the program is seen as offering an insight into the "real world" and the ways in which gender dynamics are often problematic in everyday life. Jerry Springer himself argues that the show is not scripted:

> I want the show to be real. I think it is much more effective, entertaining, and compelling if the viewer is sitting at home watching and going, "Wow, these folks are real. It's amazing!" If it's fake, then we might as well do a soap opera where everyone's a good actor and they're all drop dead gorgeous. (Springer & Morton 1998, p. 106)

Jerry Springer's allusion to soap operas relative to his own show is evident in the comments of a student who sees reality as problematic rather than smooth. For the following student, soap operas and sitcoms are based on real situations. But the way that the actors behave within those TV-constructed formats is often "unproblematic" and, therefore, not "real."

**Student:** The only one I can handle is maybe like *Family Matters*. That's only 'cuz Steve [Erkle?]—my mum likes him. She thinks he is funny. That's like the only thing. I find them too fake. Like they put out real situations. Like I understand. But they don't do things that actual people would do. Like times when they say "Oh geez," it would be "Oh shit," you know. And it's like, uum (pause); No. . . .

**J:** So that's how you think they would make it real by using language. What other ways would make it more real for you?

**Student:** People don't. They don't react the same way as normal people would. Like one time I was watching *Family Matters*. And Laura got a gun pulled on her, and her jacket taken away by three of the biggest bullies in school. Like someone is going to stand there and say, " No, I am not giving you my jacket."

**J:** So they wouldn't talk about it you don't think? // No! // So where does your understanding of that come from then?

**Student:** Just from my (pause) past experiences, people who I have talked to before. Umm, like being a bully myself.

As well, the student normalizes this construction of social reality in order to legitimate her own position as acceptable.

In general, the students' reception of the *Jerry Springer* program is akin to Ien Ang's conception of three possible subject positions in relation to reception of the TV soap *Dallas*. For Ang (1985), these subject positions consisted of fans, ironical viewers, and those who strongly dislike the program. Produced in relation to and through a discourse on the "ideology of mass culture," the students show a similar positioning. However, as the referent point against which their views were measured the students used a discourse of "reality." Some students positioned themselves akin to Ang's conception of "ironical viewers." For such students, *Springer* is a comedy to be laughed at—"pleasure without guilt"—whereas to be a fan, to like the program without irony, is to be positioned as duped. The origin of these types of "reality pro-grams" has been attributed to a variety of sources, including the MTV *Real World* program in the 1970s. Armond White (1995) suggests that the original *Real World* gimmick is based on the 1973 public television series:

> "An American Family"—a continuing series that peeked in on a white middle-class American home. Shot on film rather than video, "An American Family" offered docu-mentary drama revealing the parents' marital breakdown, a son's admitted homosexu-ality. As if countering the sitcom mythological view of American domestic life, "An American Family" depended on the shock of real life and unscripted behaviour but it was a smug TV coup. Cinema verite technique was used without admitting the degree of intervention by the video crew. (White, p. 395)

With regard to television, discourses of the "real" and the "not real" are deployed in order to construct specific meanings from the plethora of "reality programs" that in-vade the students' everyday lives. It is not just *Jerry Springer* that operates through this code of reality—other TV programs such as the hit shows of 2000, *Survivor,* and *Who Wants to Be a Millionaire* are constructed through similar codings. This justifica-tion of the outlandish in the name of reality and its challenge of what is socially ac-ceptable within the public sphere and in society is also evident in discussions above into the use of misogynist language in hardcore and gangsta rap. This point is rein-forced by Ernest Allen Jr.'s (1996) comment that, "gangster rappers tend to assert that what they describe is 'like it is,' claiming that they are simply articulating atti-tudes as they exist within African American communities" (p. 189). Yvonne Bynoe (2000), in challenging rappers' use of "telling it like it is," argues that:

> at this point in time, rap music and Hip hop culture has become corporate entertain-ment, whereby many Black rap artists get paid not for speaking their individual truth but for performing the roles of "gangsta," "pimp" and "ho" for the enjoyment of white audiences. (p. 3)

Bynoe's comment highlights the tension and relations of dominance within the rela-tionship between the performer and audience and further alludes to an element of voyeurism that places whites as subjects and black rappers as objects to be consumed.

In terms of gender relations, it is interesting that in the film *Set It Off,* which challenges the hyper-masculinity of the "hood films," its lack of realism is presented as a factor in not accepting it as plausible. Bearing in mind gender relations and dominance in society, Daniel Chandler (1998) advocates caution in trying to iden-tify social realism. For him:

> what counts as "realistic" modes of representation are both historically and culturally variable. The depiction of "reality" even in iconic signs involves variable codes, which

have to be learned, yet which with experience, come to be taken-for-granted as transparent and obvious. (p. 1)

*Set It Off* also provided an opportunity for taboo subjects such as sexuality to come into the public sphere and to be talked about. The issue of lesbianism within the film is a taboo for some students. For many of the students, identification with a fundamentalist religious/moral subject position contests any representation of lesbians as acceptable. Here it is interesting to note the ways that discourses and ideology do not run in a straight line. Whereas on issues of dress, dancing for pleasure, and profanity, religious discourses often contest discourses produced within and around youth culture on the topic of sexualities, forms of youth culture, such as reggae and rap, also cohere with religious discourses in positioning heterosexuality as the norm. Thus the understanding of realism that the students use is a common sense one. O'Sullivan et al., suggest that "often [it] refers merely to the extent to which representational details resemble or concur with the knowledge of the object (which may be an emotion, theme, or idea as well as a thing) that we have already" (O'Sullivan et al., 1994, p. 257). Often the theme of realism operates intertextually as it weaves within and between the narratives concerning films, television programs, music, and identity in an attempt to locate differing media texts as "real" or "not real." It is interesting that the real is so important in an age when one encounters so many experiences that can no longer be validated and coded in conventional ways of defining reality. The construction of blackness that takes place through regimes of representations is based upon specific forms of masculinity that subsume and deny the experiences of women or gays. In undermining this coding of black masculinity with violence, bell hooks (1996) argues that hood films such as *Menace II Society* "offers itself to us as 'black culture,' yet what the film actually interrogates within its own narrative is that these black boys have learned how to do this shit not from black culture but from watching white gangster movies." She continues:

> The film points out that the whole myth of the gangster—as it is being played out in rap and in movies—is not some Afrocentric or black-defined myth, it's the public myth that's in our imaginations from movies and television. (p. 116)

At times, linking of gangster movies with gangster rappers is evident. For the following student, this association between gangster rap and white gangster movie was not lost:

**Student:** One thing, rappers are entertainers, just like you watch a movie, gangsta rap is like a story, say someone like Nas Foxy and JZ it's called The Forum [?], and on the album it's all about drug deal and killing. But one thing you notice, every song is a story. They don't do that in real life. It's a story of how they beat the cops. They don't do that in real life. It's just entertaining. It's like going out to watch *Donnie Brasco*. (focus group, males)

This section has described the ways in which definitions of the real are of importance in reception of media and in making meaning in everyday life.

Having examined the way in which the construction and identification of reality have enabled relations of domination to be maintained, we can look more directly at how this construction of reality affects understandings of school. As indicated above, the students access not just pleasure but also knowledge and understandings through hip-hop and youth culture. These forms of knowledge and understandings are often placed in relation to school-legitimated knowledge to give a sense of meaning to their school lives.

Using the phrase "keeping it real," as a starting point of analysis, it is evident that some students, especially males, place school knowledge in a binary to everyday knowledge garnered through direct experiences. The importance of the latter is to be found in the comment that "the quality of discourse about schooling is contingent upon how schooling is understood, the ways in which the multifarious meanings schooling has for diverse people are formed and modified over time" (p. 7).

During the discussion, the students positioned themselves as having knowledge garnered through everyday experiences, a knowledge they argued, that was viewed as illegitimate when placed in relation to school-legitimated knowledge. In the following narrative, the students illustrate how they place learning through experiences in relation to school knowledge. For them, you don't have to go to Harvard to produce poetry:

**Student 1:** I saw this guy [on TV] and this guy was supposed to be the biggest drug dealer in Washington who was in jail, and this was someone who hasn't been to high school. And the way this guy talked, he blew me away, he was brilliant.

**Student 2:** People who are harassed most by the cops on a daily basis, they begin to know how things work for themselves and how to get around certain questions.

**Student 3:** It's like Tupac. Most people who went to Harvard will be like blah blah, I can write this, and Tupac knows [how to write poetry].

The students transfer this discourse of the "real" and learning through experience to the school site in order to construct an understanding of the purpose of schooling and their place within it. For some of the students, particularly males in the focus group, school knowledge was positioned as binary opposite to knowledge gained through experiences. They see a split between emotional and rational; experience and books, real and abstract, and life and school. The ability to construct such binarism allows these males to position school learning as "other" with regard to their lives and to developing an understanding of self.

This mediation of reception of school activities through constructions of rap-generated reality is also evident in what the students read. Autobiography and biographies were popular among the students who indicated that they read very few books unless requested to do so for a class assignment:

> **J:** So what would you choose to read?
> **Student 1:** I don't read as much as the next person. Biographies, Jimmy Hendrix or Malcolm X.
> **J:** How come?
> **Student 2:** Because they made a change.
> **Student 3:** I like young adult, some adventures. Well I am still reading this book about Martin Luther King Jr.

It is also noticeable how the biographies and autobiographies mentioned concerned the lives of African Americans. This may well indicate that the students have a level of racialized consciousness not always apparent within other areas of their narratives.

The response to school was to some extent gendered, and the young women, while not expressing the same degree of alienation between the curriculum and life experiences, nonetheless coded their perceptions of pedagogy in a similar vein. They attributed their boredom to teacher style and pedagogy as much as the actual curriculum. For them, teachers, who were bored themselves, laid back, or just waiting to retire, often made no attempt to engage the students. Interestingly, the students identified as "fun," one teacher who was interested in the ways in which the student's lives outside school intersect their identification as students. As the focus group described this "fun" teacher:

> **Student 1:** He always answers your question—he makes it fun.
> **Student 2:** He gives you all the information, stuff like that.
> **Student 1:** He knows how it is to be a student. He relates to us. He'll say, "I know you guys are going to be bored doing this. Let's take a break point."
> **Student 2:** We wanted to know about the teachers' strike. Some teachers are like "It's none of your business." But it affects us all. And he knows that, so that's why.
> **Student 1:** He tells us everything. (focus group, girls)

In line with issues of individual freedom, contoured through relations of power between adult and youths, some students also see knowledge as imposed—just words, with no transmission of emotions. By constructing school knowledge as denuded of emotions and actions, these students can then suggest that little is learned about the self. While one can argue that the students' narratives are constructions and part of a wider discourse used by many students to indicate a sense of alienation, nonetheless, these discourses do have material effects that reveal that the students use understandings and meanings acquired in one area of life to translate and give meaning to another area of life. Thus, understandings of what is "real" are affected by the dominance of discourses constructed through popular culture that comes to affect perceptions of how school knowledge is generated. For some males, binarism comes into play, as message rap is coded as allowing one to learn about the self, while the official curriculum is constructed as "doesn't let you learn about yourself." The latter construction of binaries with regard to learning is related not just to pedagogy but also to desire. In particular, we can note Peter McLaren's (1994) comment that experience is an understanding derived from specific interpretation of a certain "engagement with the world of symbols, social practices, and cultural forms" (p. 332). Both music and dress style involve production of meaning as well as a placing of the self within discourses of pleasure. In contrast, the official curriculum, as described by the students, offers little in terms of pleasure or placing of the self. Thus, the curriculum as a form of representation is seen as distant, lifeless, predictable, not really what the "real" world is about. So one can postulate that if the student constructs school knowledge as not having much to offer in terms of understanding the self, then this might well affect students' levels of motivation.

In continuing with the theme of learning about the self through the curriculum, one can also highlight the narratives of the students that construct the official curriculum as teaching little or nothing with regard to an understanding of a black or racialized self. It is an example of how, as Foucault (1980) indicates, "the exercise of power perpetually creates knowledge and, conversely, knowledge constantly induces effects of power" (p. 52). Here the students construct this displacement of the black self from the curriculum as evidence of a relation of dominance constructed between black and white rather than one constructed between adult and youth. This construction of the curriculum as racialized echoes the perspectives of other African-Canadian students in Brown and Kelly (2001). It is not just a matter of inclusion but also representation. Thus, for one student blackness was included in the curriculum but coded negatively:

> **Student:** Usually well for Social Studies. It consists basically of history and economics. With economics you do deal with the whole world. That's not so much on cultures. But most likely, if anything, when they make black people look bad. They'll go and talk 'bout Third World countries so they'll go "Oh, the Caribbean, and Africa and Indian whatever." So that's the only view that people get. That's what I mean to say. So that's all. So there is no whole story. I suppose that like real, real African history you would have to go back really, really far.

The argument used by the students is one based upon what Stuart Hall (1996a) might identify as "relations of representations" as much as exclusion. As Hall explains this process, it is "the contestation of the marginality, the stereotypical quality, and the fetishized nature of images of blacks, by the counter position of a 'positive' imagery" (p. 164).

In a similar way to the mediated black youth culture that the students encounter, the school-legitimated knowledge also centers blackness within the United States or Africa. There is little or no reference to any sense of blackness within the Canadian mosaic, resulting in a reinforcing of the sense of borrowed identities discussed in Chapter 7. One student, whose ancestry is Canadian, articulates how she found out and responded to being part of a historical black presence in Alberta:

> **Student:** I like it; it's neat. Like it's kind of like when I found out that there is like a whole bunch of settlements, black settlements in like Amber Valley and all that. I was like "Whoa, that's pretty. . . ." 'Cuz you don't usually hear about that. You either hear about the States and stuff, different, um, how black people were down there and stuff and of course Africa. But not in Canada [laugh].
> **J:** Do you think it would make a difference if more people knew that there has been a long presence?
> **Student:** I think people would find it interesting, 'cuz I did. I felt kind of proud. I was like "Yeah!" [proud] I think people would find it interesting because you hear about like way long time ago. You hear about the natives. And how white man came and take over, but then also black people settled, perhaps not around that time. But little after but you just never heard about that.

This need for acknowledgment is seen as not just for black students but also as something of which all students should be aware. Within a few of the narratives the students indicated that teaching about blackness is always represented as race specific or ethnic specific. The following student identifies how this coding of knowledge works:

> I have not gone to one social class where we learn about black history. Once actually, in February in junior high. For English class I asked my teacher if we could do something on Black History Month. And the next day she came, we were doing a poetry unit; the next day she comes to school and gives me a whole bunch of suggestions on black poets that I could do my poetry assignment on. //Ah. // But she just gave it to me but I was like. I wanted the whole class to do it. I don't want to be [just] doing [it by] myself. (individual interview)

McCaskell (1995), indicates a similar point in a discussion of the "traditional" curriculum:

> The "greatness" of these works allows them to rise above their ethnic, racial or cultural specificity to deal with "human values" of equal relevance to everyone. Traditional curricula thereby attain the status of the universal, while the work of people of colour, for example, is locked into its ethnic, racial, or cultural curriculum. (p. 262)

So with this equation of the traditional curriculum as the norm, any attempt to request a change in reference point or emphasis is always read in relation to this constructed norm and is thus most likely to be constructed as outside the norm. As well, underlying the teacher's action is an assumption that knowledge and experiences of peoples of African descent are only appropriate for black students. Such a positioning is reminiscent of the ways in which whiteness works to produce itself as the norm against which all others are measured.

Again, the students view schools as reinforcing this sense of hegemonic blackness discussed above. Often the representations of blackness that are included within the school curriculum are heavily weighted towards African-American experiences. African-Canadian experiences are often negated, thus reinforcing the hegemonic dominance of African-American identity to that of African Canadian. This hegemonic process is identified by McLaren (1994) as one in which "the dominant culture tries to "fix" the meaning of signs, symbols, and representations to provide a "common" worldview, disguising relations of power and privilege through the organs of mass media and state apparatus such as schools, government institutions and state bureaucracies" (p. 183).

## Summary

Using the themes of youth culture as a communicative resource, stylish solidarity, and the link between education and experience, this chapter examined how meanings and relations of dominance get produced and reproduced through students' talk. Youth culture provides a common language through which the students are able to create symbolic referents that can then be used in the representation of a variety of social relations based on race, class, gender, sexuality, and religion. Through this common language the students are able to construct a sense of blackness and also develop what Stanley Fish identifies as an "interpretative community." As part of accessing student talk, the chapter draws on the focus group discussions in order to illustrate the ways in which discourses operate intersubjectively and to indicate the times and ways in which youth agree or disagree with each other or the interviewer. As indicated by the narratives and the work of Hall (1996 a & b), hooks (1990), and Diawara (1996), the meaning of blackness is never fixed. So these students make use of youth culture to develop symbolic codes that when worked through existing discourses on gender, class, and religion serve to both unify and fragment a sense of blackness. While some of the students have a political consciousness of being black, this consciousness is often in tension with discourses based on what Gilroy calls "stylish solidarity." "Keeping it real" is an important signifier in youth culture, and this phrase is used to code not just music reception but is also transferred to give meaning in other areas of their lives such as schooling. Overall analysis of the students does not subscribe fully to a cultural populist position where meaning and pleasure are everything, neither do the students subscribe to a political economy that positions them as victims of reproduction. Reception of media often involves contestation as well as contradiction.

Thus, in this chapter, the students' narratives portray them as active rather than passive recipients of media culture; with much of this activity taking place within a framework of globalized capitalism. In many ways, meaning is manufactured out of systems of codes, conventions, and signs, rather than via direct transmission. The findings do not support an "either/or" process of meaning making, whereby the students either subscribe fully to a thesis of cultural domination or to one that positions them as resisting the influence of media.

# CHAPTER 9

# Bringing It Back Home

*What is at issue here is the recognition of the extraordinary diversity of subjective
positions, social experiences and cultural identities which compose the category
"black," that is the recognition that "black" is essentially a politically and culturally
constructed category, which cannot be grounded in a set of fixed transcultural or
transcendental racial categories and which therefore has no guarantees in Nature.*

HALL, 1988, p. 28

## Introduction

This chapter reviews the issues discussed earlier through a cultural studies framework that highlights the implications and possibilities of some of the issues identified. In particular, the chapter examines the implications of the ways in which culture and power become linked to produce relations of dominance. The study has indicated the importance of youth culture and mediazation in terms of how youth identify with blackness and how they consequently come to understand their sense of self in the world. This understanding of self is contoured by a specific historical conjuncture, where youth culture is heavily saturated with representations of blackness that have become a viable economic commodity. Thus, issues of black identification consistently collide with youth culture in order to produce various symbolic codes through which these students give meaning to their experiences. Through what can be identified as discourses—through language (verbal and non-verbal), a racialized regime of representations, and social interaction—the students make use of these space-distanced media to develop a cultural formation. Such a formation, while specific to the students' own social location, nonetheless reflects and reinforces a globalized capitalist economy in terms of its consumerist orientations. Youth culture is very much at the forefront of the intersection of the local and the global.

This final chapter will bring the reader back to some of the themes discussed earlier in the text. It will review the ways in which the cultural intersects the political, how mediazation and identity are interlinked as well as issues around structure and agency. The chapter returns more directly to the school site and identifies ways in which an understanding of Hall's conceptualization of a politics of representation— the way meaning can be struggled over—might be useful within an educational environment.

## Intersections of the Political and Cultural

Historically and in the present day the infiltration of U.S.-based media across Canadian borders has had an effect on Canadian society regionally as well as nationally, socially as well as economically. This proliferation is not new, and if we examine the flow of U.S. culture in the early 1950s, "nearly 75 percent of the feature films that Canadians watched, 80 percent of the magazines that they read originate south of the border. American music also dominated the radio airwaves" (National Film Board, 2002).

In terms of the Canadian government, various border-maintaining strategies have been consistently applied to the perceived problem of U.S. cultural imperialism starting with an examination of the state of culture in Canada by the 1949 Royal Commission on National Development on the Arts, Letters, and Sciences. Unsurprisingly, the Committee concluded that drastic steps were needed to protect Canadian culture. Thus one of its key recommendations was that the Canada Council be established to dispense funds for the country's writers, artists, musicians, and scholars. The latter was viewed as representing a buffer against U.S. cultural imperialism. In more recent times the Canadian government has continued in the same protectionist vein with the 1968 Broadcasting Act and the 1996 Task Force on the Future of the Canadian Music Industry. The consistent hope has been that such developments would produce a dual effect, so that "while cultural objectives should provide the basis for music industry policy, measures that strengthen the creation, performance, production, distribution and marketing of Canadian music will also generate important economic benefits" (cited in Shuker, 2001, p. 75). Similar discourses are also evident in Europe where the specter of U.S. cultural imperialism is often used to produce and reinforce the binary of good/bad culture. As Morley and Robins view this process:

> The real issues concern European identity in a changing world, and 'America' can be a vehicle for defensively containing, rather than resolving these issues. Change and disruption are projected onto an imaginary America, and in the process, traditional and conservative ideals of European and national identities are reinforced. (1995, p. 80)

Underlying the Canadian government's proposals are assumptions that culture is fixed and remains in a static form that is easily codified and measured. The latter assumptions have led to problems in terms of maintaining boundaries through definitions of what qualifies as Canadian and other than Canadian cultural production. For example the 1968 Broadcasting Act requires that the Canadian Radio and Telecommunications Commission (CRTC) to ensure that each "broadcasting undertaking . . . shall make maximum use, and in no case less that predominant use, of Canadian creative and other resources in the creation and presentation of programming"[1] (Shuker, 2001, p. 75). However anomalies have arisen when Canadian-born artists are designated as non-Canadian because their music is produced outside of Canadian borders. In a similar vein commonsense understanding of Canadian music is often constructed through a strong eurocentric/whiteness lens that leads to further marginalization of genres such as rap. As an example of the ways in which such marginalization affects social relations Rinaldo Walcott describes how:

> In 1999, the Rascalz, a Canadian rap group, performed for the first time in the prime segment of the Juno Awards. The Rascalz had refused their Juno the previous year (1998) in what they termed a protest against the fact the Urban music (the new code for Black music) was not supported enough in the Canadian context despite its saleability. (2000, p. 8)

Such marginalized status within Canadian society thus provides a contested terrain upon which issues of hegemonic control are fought over. So cultural dominance becomes intertwined with economic dominance.

While the latter protectionist and anti-imperialist policies would seem to have had some effect on increasing the ability of mainstream Canadian artists to be heard within Canadian boundaries and to gain success in the United States, in terms of visual images (films and magazines), such policies have been less successful. Further the expansion of U.S. cable companies following saturation of their home market has increased the inability of Canadian policies to stem the flow of U.S.-based lived experiences, images, and representations to Canadians. As Banks argues:

> This expansion exemplifies the natural tendency for the U.S. companies with media interests to expand to other countries after the U.S. market is saturated, relying more on foreign markets for future growth. International operations often account for more than fifty percent of revenues of media conglomerates. (1997, p. 44)

Within the cultural studies literature and, as is evident from the student narratives, the "cultural commodity circulates in different though simultaneous economies"—the financial economy and the cultural economy (Fiske, 1987, p. 311). Virginia Nightingale interprets this as meaning that "in the financial economy the cultural commodity has a monetary value and in the cultural economy its value is measured in 'meanings, pleasures and social identities'" (Nightingale, 1996, p. 56). While Nightingale is on the whole dismissive of Fiske's attempts to view audience consumption as enabling, nonetheless, the highlighting of multiple sites is useful in terms of recognizing the ways in which youth consumption can operate on different sites simultaneously. So it is that through discursive practices youth can use media consumption to produce themselves as "tough" on the cultural terrain, while at the more macroeconomic level their consumption leads to the reinforcement of capitalist imperatives and transnational corporations.

The study illustrates the ways in which cultural politics operates in the everyday to "deploy power to shape identities and subjectivities within a circuit of practices that range from the production and distribution of goods and representations to an ever growing emphasis on regulation and consumption" (Fairclough, 1992). In many ways it is easy to see how hegemonic struggles around the political are being fought on the level of the cultural (Gramsci, 1971). Thus the ways in which the students' choices in consumption readily align with dominant neo-conservative discourses on choice and free-market economics are ideologically significant. As an ideology that attempts to fix meaning in the service of power, neo-conservatism links the symbolic to the everyday through the highlighting of concepts such as "choice." Such linking of choice with consumption reinforces and enables the production of discourses that support a free market, a market that is globalized and international rather than contained within the national borders of Canada (Klein, 2000). While it is not implied that the U.S. industry has deliberately targeted Canadian youth in order to undermine economic sovereignty, nonetheless, such consumption patterns and discursive practices as displayed by the students' narratives do not bode well for maintaining future protectionist economic border policies.

## Mediazation and Identity

Mediated culture can be viewed as a resource that youth draw on to make sense and produce knowledge of their everyday experiences. This production of knowledge, of knowledgeable subjects, becomes further implicated in the production of discourses as truth effects and, consequently, a will to power. Michel Foucault describes such a process of knowledge production as one where:

> The division between true and false is neither arbitrary nor modifiable, nor institutional, nor violent. Putting the question in different terms, however—asking what has been, what still is, throughout our discourse, this will to truth which has survived throughout so many centuries of our history; or if we ask what is, in its very general form, the kind of division governing our will to knowledge—then we may well discern

something like a system of exclusion (historical, modifiable, institutionally constraining) in the process of development. (Foucault, 1970, p. 233)

The narratives indicate that knowledge of the "cultural" is useful in understanding how students make sense of school and schooling. "It is precisely on the terrain of culture that identities are produced, and values learned, histories legitimated, and knowledge appropriated" (Giroux, 1997, p. 59).

The youths can be viewed as drawing on various media-saturated discourses that are socially shaped but also socially shaping in terms of identities, social relations, and systems of knowledge. These three latter aspects are evident in the ways in which the students produce and construct discourses in a public sphere. In particular, the discourses to which the students subject themselves, however temporary, become a means of "breaking the boundaries" between private and public space. This breaking of boundaries is akin to what Fairclough (1995, p. 55) describes as "conversationalizing" discourses. For him they have the potential to trivialize complex issues as well as the potential to open up discourses of cultural democracy. In this study the public sphere is contested and ambiguous in terms of cultural democracy. This ambiguity as to the democratic potential of an opening up of the public sphere also illustrates the ways in which the distinctions between private and public spheres are in tension and often slip and slide across each other.

Two main understandings of blackness are struggled over in the youths' discourse. The first refers to that understanding of blackness that is driven by the media. The second understanding draws on historically consistent discourses of black consciousness and black nationalism. Also implicated in the discussion are issues of nationalism in general and questions as to whether and how a sense of blackness can be imagined within the descriptor "Candian." Can sources of identification be found within the Canadian state borders, thus decreasing external influences on identity formation? This question is not new but has been explored in a variety of ways by African-Canadian authors such as Alexis (1995), Nourbese Philip (1992), Walcott (1997), Brand (1997) and Clarke (2000). For Clarke, the tension lies in

the question of the relationship between blackness and Canadianness; indeed, whether there can be a relationship between these identities, even for that matter, whether a fusion (as opposed to the usual confusion) can be negotiated between the Scylla of one and the Charybdis of the other. (Clarke, 2000, p. 8)

These often-competing senses of blackness illustrate the ways in which Black Nationalism operates as a dominant political discourse attempting to unify the "black community." This attempt to construct a sense of community through a singular discourse is inherently problematic especially in light of Manning Marable's observation that Black Nationalism is not a "monolith political ideology but a spectrum of cultural, economic, and political positions which are grounded in the dynamics of black resistance to race and class domination in the United States and indeed throughout the diaspora" (1992, p. 2). This study suggests that blackness is something that is produced and, therefore, has to be worked at. This sense of black subjectivities and identities as having to be worked at problematizes the definition of community and the problematic nature of any community mobilization that might get translated into political action and strategies. There is no automatic unity leading to political action; alliances have to be developed and built. Further, such understandings are also strongly contested through discourses that draw on affiliations to specific geographic regions.

Afrocentric theorists such as Asante (2001) would postulate that blackness, and a close identification with Africa should be a given for the students under discussion. As he argues in a critique of Gilroy's recent book *Between Camps* (2000), any attempt to recognize stubborn difference brought about through history and experiences should be ignored in light of a wider given unity. Asante's caution is that:

> such false separations, particularly in the context of White racial hierarchy and domination, is nothing than a White definition of Blackness. I reject such a notion as an attempt to isolate Africans in the Americas from their brothers and sisters on the continent. (2001, p. 847)

What Asante does not allow for is a process of "translation" (Bhabha, 1994)—an intervention of culture and history. These school youths recognize a historical link to Africa but make no direct claims of present-day association. On the level of common sense understandings, they identify themselves homogenously as black, but when analysis of their discourse is undertaken, it is evident that they position themselves within a variety of subjectivities and identities. Their understandings of blackness within a Canadian social context are hybrid rather than unified; a hybridity that recognizes the heterogeneity of blackness is alluded to in Chapters 2, 7, and 8.

Consequently, the lived experiences of these students undermine any straightforward biological and essentialist discourse that would bind blackness as "sameness." The importance of viewing identity as complex and problematic rather than fixed and unified is evident in the data generated. Within these same discussions, understandings of blackness would seem to align with what Hall (1996a) identifies as the "end of the innocent black subject." However, caution should be taken, for while recognition is not automatic among the youths, neither is there total fluidity akin to some advocates of postmodern ideas. Within the narratives generated, identities can be viewed as "cuts" in a moment of subjectivity, with each cut leaving a trace; a scar that reinforces a lingering memory when touched, a memory that then becomes part of the discourses through which continuing production of subjectivity takes place.

Such an epistemological break in an understanding of black subjectivities reveals how "the end of the essential black subject also entails a recognition that the central issue of race always appear historically in articulation, in a formation, with other categories and divisions and are constantly crossed and recrossed" (Hall, 1996a, p. 444). Further, what emerges within this analysis of identity formation is the way in which discourses of blackness struggle to produce themselves as a "regime of truth," a "real" authentic blackness. These identifications articulate with U.S. media representations to dominate the ways in which black subjectivity gets produced and reproduced among African-Canadian youth.

~ ~ ~ ~ ~

However, while such hybridity might be more in keeping with the postulations of Hall, Gilroy, hooks, and others rather than Afrocentrics, it also underlines the difficulties of forming a united political front or an automatic sense of community based on the descriptor "black." Although these students position themselves within a dominant discourse of blackness, they also draw on other discourses during their social interaction and production of black identities. It is noticeable how other identities (e.g., religious, gendered) at times, intersect their sense of blackness to produce a complexity that is not always accounted for by the traditional psychological literature on black identity (Aboud, 1981; Clarke & Clarke, 1939).

Black youth subjectivities are constituted in discourses through the images that circulate in society. The institutional effects of such discourses operate to govern and produce certain subjects. Foucault's insights into power knowledge can be useful here, in particular, his postulation that "power is exercised to produce and to police individual subjects through the production of detailed knowledge." In this instance the detailed knowledge under discussion operates through representations across magazines, music, and films that act as racialized regimes of representation. These regimes highlight specific forms of black hypermasculinity and toughness, toughness played out specifically through gangsta movies, gangsta rap and everyday life at times. Erased from the lexicon of black identities are women, gays, and lesbians. As well, these regimes draw on other aspects of, youth culture, namely sport—and basketball in particular. Thus even the attitudes and bodies of sports personalities become part of this construction of black males as tough, a toughness that overemphasizes their bodies in relation to their mind, thus reinforcing earlier forms of mind-body dualism. The meteoric rise of African-American basketball superstars such as Michael Jordon, Shaquille O'Neal, and Allen Iverson, all in differing ways become part of a discourse that reproduces an alignment among being physically extraordinary, exotic, and black. Identification with the body is thus heightened through various spheres of youth culture, not just media. Gilroy (2000) argues that:

Here the move towards biopolitics is best understood as an outgrowth of the pattern identified as "identity politics" in earlier periods by a number of writers. It is a mood in which the person is defined as the body and in which certain exemplary bodies at various times during the 1990s . . . could become impacted instantiations of community. (p. 185)

How do we account for the taking on of these identities by African-Canadian youth? One way would be to examine more closely how multinational and transnational corporations produce, through media, the desire to consume. Louis Althusser's concept of interpellation might also be useful here in that for some students the desire to identify with media productions is so intense that it is akin to a process of "hailing." Also of import in terms of hailing are the effects of peer pressure and the ways in which intersubjectiviy operates, especially when one takes into account the ways in which young black males gain a degree of recognition and status for being "bad" boys. Read intertextually, this desire for recognition is heightened in relation to the lack of recognition in other areas of youths' lives. However, it also has to be recognized that their interpellation as subjects within any single discourse can never be final and once and for all. As Easthope & McGowan (1992) argue, "the contradictions brought about by the plurality of discursive fields ensures that the individual is constantly subjected to a range of possible meanings, and is therefore an unstable site of constructions and reconstructions which often overlap" (p. 69).

## Schooling and Media

In terms of schooling, the study indicates the importance of linking cultural studies with an analysis of youth culture, and a consequent explication of the implication of cultural politics on such studies. As one of the foremost theorists in this area, Henry Giroux (1996) attributes cultural studies' reluctance to isolate the study of schooling from youth culture as a contributory factor in its openness "to the theoretical possibilities for understanding education as a political, pedagogical practice that unfolds in a wide range of shifting and overlapping sites of learning" (p. 15). It is this range of overlapping and shifting sites of learning that is evident in the students' narratives both in terms of the formal curriculum and the informal curriculum. Further, school can be viewed as a site for the "expanding of the possibility of politics and critical agency to the very institutions that work to shut down notions of critical consciousness" (Giroux, 2000, p. 356).

It is evident that the school site acts as a place of learning, a place where knowledge is exchanged and transferred wherein the students meet and learn from each other. Within the school site, two main forms of knowledge proliferate and are disseminated. What students learn is not necessarily what is stated in the formal curriculum but rather the informal curriculum that draws on student experiences within the school environment. The significance of this informal learning is heightened when placed in relation to the dominance of U.S. media culture and its ability to proliferate discourses and knowledge on blackness across geographic borders through mediazation, and representations (Thompson, 1990). These U.S.-based images refer in particular to black youth culture, a specific stage of black youth identity formation. Many students recognized that their adoption of a media-generated black identity is something that would change as they moved from adolescence to adulthood, in other words, that identity was not static or fixed once and for all. Further, acceptance of this dominance of African-American culture as a primary site for informal learning varies from one student to another, since students also have available within their cultural repertoire access to parents/caregivers as a source of knowledge about other forms of black experiences. These familial (and national) backgrounds are another source through which the students develop symbolic meanings. For some, the links between their national heritages are strengthened through cultural formations associated with specific Caribbean islands and countries.

In terms of gaining knowledge about the diaspora, the students themselves, in their everyday interaction at school, provide an informal resource for learning about others of African descent. By identifying with the unifying category of "black," the students have the opportunity to interact with other black students whose heritage lies within the continent of Africa and its diaspora and to learn, in however limited a manner, about differences and similarities within the diaspora. For example, students with a family background only in North America or the continent of Africa are learning patois terms that are used in the Caribbean.[2] This transfer of knowledge between the students is not automatic or unproblematic in that while patois can act as a site for broadening a sense of collectivity, it can also act to constrain collectivity through its heavy use in musical genres such as dancehall reggae. The step-team (refer to Chapter 2) also provides a similar site for learning about diasporan blackness as similar but different.

As part of this informal learning about blackness and its differing representations within the diaspora, coming together in high schools provides a way of "coming out" of claiming a sense of blackness. To understand what is going on for these students, I use the phrase "coming out" in terms of taking on and identification with blackness. With the emergence of a dominant discourse in high schools, there has to be an accounting by students as to how they place themselves in relation to, or within, such discourses. There is also a tension in representation evident in this process of being similar but different. This was illustrated during a school-organized cultural event that encouraged representation of cultures. It led to the query: how does one represent a black unity that draws on Africa as well as the diaspora when students' knowledge is limited? For self-identified black students, there was no automatic culture that represents blackness. Rather, there was a situation of "nonsynchrony"

(McCarthy, 1997), whereby identities are never fully aligned in time and space. Under pressure to identify a sense of unity, the students fall back on music and dominant representations constructed and produced through youth culture and media.

Students need to be recognized by teachers as complex beings with multiple intersecting identities rather than one unified identity. This requires more of a focus on the ways in which identities become constructed through discourses of power, gender, race, sexuality, and class. Schools need to provide a dialogic environment in which students can explore dialectic thinking in order to develop critical thinking. By undertaking this, the hegemonic terrain upon which many youth cultures and identities are represented and contested can be exposed and examined. Recognition of plurality allows for working through and across social differences as students come to see that they have more than one identity and, therefore, similarities as well as differences across a range of lived experiences.

~  ~  ~  ~  ~

Among the students of African descent, there is a lack of knowledge about the continent of Africa and its diaspora. Community organizations and schools need to explore and evaluate the necessity of developing curricula that recognizes the variety and complexity of experiences that represent the African diaspora. Such an understanding would reinforce the discourses of diasporan consciousness and could challenge, to some extent, the dominance of what Gilroy (2000) identifies as "stylish solidarity." Cultural workers need to develop a sense of solidarity based on knowledge rather than just body image. Thus recognition of black experiences in the Caribbean and Brazil as well as the United States would enable the development of discourses on black identity that could compete in some minor way with those of media-generated "borrowed identities." It should also be noted that "borrowed blackness" is not necessarily negative, in that most culture is dialogical rather than fixed within state boundaries. Nonetheless, when the process as identified in the study is not dialogical but one-way, other issues of power are played out and serve to reinforce cultural hegemony.

The issues of identity that are raised in the study are pertinent to the classroom teacher, both in terms of curricula and pedagogy. Three main points of intersection with classroom practice emerge. First, the importance of youth culture in the school lives of the students must be recognized. Giroux and Simon (1989), in their groundbreaking article "Popular Culture as a Pedagogy of Pleasure and Meaning," are particularly critical of educators who do not do this.

> Educators who refuse to acknowledge popular culture as a significant basis of knowledge that students actually have and so eliminate the possibility of developing a pedagogy that links school knowledge to the differing subject relations that help to constitute their everyday lives. (1989, p. 3)

Recognition of youth culture within the curriculum would have to be an unstable entity, recognizing the changing emphases of youth culture. While Giroux and Simon's suggestion seems laudable, it is also problematic in a number of ways and may not lead to an adequate critique of these representations. First, students come to school with differing subjectivities and as such might well not regard the inclusion of youth culture within the formal curriculum as necessarily positive since for many there is strong bifurcation between "in-" and "out-of"-school activities. Thus there may well be resistance on the part of some students to teachers trying to cross boundaries in order to reach out to them. In terms of such student resistance, we need to note Jabari Mahiri's (1998) research with the eleventh-grade English classes of two teachers in different urban high schools in the San Francisco Bay area. The research centered on a curricular "intervention" designed to help students become critical consumers of a variety of popular cultural texts, including texts from hip-hop and rap. Mahiri's research illustrates the resistance to the project by some students. As Mahiri indicates:

> These particular students drew distinctions between their "real" lives and life in schools, and they were not initially comfortable with a marriage between the two. For them, schools and traditional curriculums had come to represent the very institutional constraints and socially sanctioned meanings with which some of the critiques and practices of hip hop culture take issue. (p. 4)

Youth culture, as indicated by early Birmingham CCCS theorists such as Hebdige (1979) and Cohen (1973), is often used as an oppositional tool of resistance, resistance to adult authority part of an organized political strategy. It is this construction of difference from adult culture that makes "youth culture" unique. Entry to this cultural terrain would probably have to be dialogical and based upon what Carr and Kemmis (1983) describe as dialectical thinking: "an open and questioning form of thinking which demands reflection back and forth between elements like part and whole, knowledge and action, process and product subject and object" (pp. 36–37). Viewing youth culture per se, not just hip-hop, as a source of pedagogy would allow recognition of the ways in which culture intersects relations of power (race, class, gender, religion, sexuality) within the school environment. Such recognition of youth culture as a terrain of ideological struggle would allow teachers to deal with an ever-changing plethora of youth cultures. As well, the ability to recognize, as Fairclough (1995) indicates, that all texts constitute identities, relationships, and representations would be a useful skill in terms of preparing students to approach their world with a socially critical eye.

Second, in terms of tackling these media-generated representations effectively within the classroom, we can turn to Stuart Hall's (1997) approach of "a politics of representation." Here, the idea is to break apart the naturalized images operating through regimes of representation—to show their constructed nature. Thus by opening up the practices of representation, we can pose the following questions: Where do images come from? Who produces images? How is meaning closed down in the production of image? Who is silenced in the production of an image? Thus it can be argued that interrogation of representations such as "gangsta rappers" could make such stereotypes "uninhabitable and destroy their naturalness."[3]

Third, adoption of a form of analysis that recognizes a politics of representation can be applied to what the students identify as a lack of symbolic representation of African Canadian within the national memory and imagined mosaic. If schools are viewed as sites for the construction of alternative public spheres, then use can be made of a politics of representation in order to re-imagine a more definite positioning of the descriptor "African Canadian." This can be achieved by encouraging students to think critically about the concept of nation and to thus problematize the common sense understandings of concepts such as culture, race, and Canadian. As well, such concepts often intersect each other, thus making any identification complex rather than singular. Willinsky (1999), in his work on the relationship between culture, race, and nation, argues for a postnationalism, at a time when these categories no longer stand for a natural division of humankind. This is a time in which schools convey ideas of Canada as nation based on civil and political arrangements of people who live here rather than, as is the case at present, on ethnic notions dating from the nineteenth century. As Willinsky views it, with postnationalism we should imagine

> a time when these categories are seen as an elaborate means for claiming place and position for establishing an advantage, for policing a boundary. It is about encouraging students to catch sight of how culture, race and nation are used to name the identifiable humanity of a people in ways that more often than not justifies inequalities. (1999, p. 97)

Willinsky's approach is similar to Hall's advocation of an analytical approach based on a politics of representation. It allows for the "opening up" for the denaturalization of the descriptor "Canadian."

What the above represents is a start in the process of the creation of a counter-public sphere (Fraser, 1995) based on the articulation of differing discourses on identities and blackness—in other words, development of alternative discursive resources. A sphere that allows for the development of discourses that could become part of a counter-hegemonic challenge to media-generated representation of blacks. It should be noted that what is being argued for is not a simple replacement of negative images of blacks with positive ones. Since meaning is open to interpretation, adopting such a position of binary reversal would be highly unpredictable in outcome (Hall, 1997).

Further, highlighting the relationship between political economy and production of identity can be used to highlight the unequal ways in which economy can affect the representations that are made available to students. The ability to use such issues within the classroom has the advantage of being able to tap into the students' existing interest and understandings of a situation, no matter how partial. Questions of U.S. commodification can be brought into the public space of the classroom and critically analyzed as it already is evoked within the more ambivalent public/private space of the corridors of schools.

## Agency and Structure

Within the study, a tension emerges around the issue of agency. Proponents of the cultural imperialism thesis "appear to simply assume that exposure to international audiovisual commodities automatically leads to an uncritical acceptance of this material" (Bennet, et al., 1999, p. 205). Are these students dupes of the culture industry, or are they consumers, as cultural populists such as John Fiske indicate, picking and choosing what they desire? This tension between agency and structure, the individual and society, is at the heart of Adorno's work and his critique of the culture industry. While some readings of Adorno and Horkheimer would seem to indicate that people are "dupes" of the culture industry, unable to assert any agency when faced with the ideology of consumption, others argue a less deterministic stance in his work. In reading Simon Jarvis's (1998) interpretation of Adorno and his book *The Culture Industry*, one has to recognize that Adorno's stance was more complex than the position with which he is often aligned. As Jarvis argues:

> If Adorno's theory of the culture industry presented us with dupes on the one hand and conspirators on the other it would indeed be trivial, because the trick would only need to be exposed to be brought to an end. Adorno emphasizes, instead, that "This is the triumph of advertising in the culture industry: the compulsive mimesis of cultural commodities by consumers who at the time see through them." (p. 74)

Thus, if we accept Jarvis's interpretation of Adorno, we would have to admit that it reflects an actuality within this study in that the students' narratives do indicate a sense of being able to see through the media while continuing to consume. Throughout the narratives on consumption, the ways in which the students seem able to critique the relationship between production and consumption yet still consume are striking. It is almost as if, as part of capturing consumers, youth culture allows dissent to be expressed. The narratives indicate the ways in which the culture industry offers alternative discourses through which the students protest and are then consequently co-opted into positions that support consumption. They are provided with a mechanism through which they are able to voice their displeasure while ultimately going on to consume and bolster capitalist production.

These latter discourses that critique yet support consumption can be viewed as ironic consumption—the ways in which we are coerced through discourse production to consume while being all too well aware of the arguments that critique consumerism. It is as though we are left with the desire despite the rational argument. So it is that the common sense binaries emotionality and rationality are bridged through a third positioning—namely, irony. Irony lets us get away—literally and metaphorically—with and from the confusion of identity. Such a subject positioning helps to deal with what psychologists might identify as a sense of cognitive dissonance. It allows us to live out our subordination consciously. This allure of irony is not just evidenced within the abstract theories of postmodernists but also within the empirical and the everyday. The following quote from the zine production *Heimat* illustrates this ironical stance with regard to consumption:

> going to Disney World to drop acid and goof on Mickey isn't revolutionary; going to Disney world in full knowledge of how ridiculous and evil it all is and still having a great innocent time, in some almost unconscious, even psychotic way, is something else altogether. This is what deCerteau describes as "the art of being in-between," and this is the only path of true freedom in today's culture. Let us then be in-between. Let us revel in *Baywatch, Joe Camel*. (cited in Klein 2000, p. 78)

Choice seems to be on offer, yet whatever choice one makes always results in consumption. What is on offer to these students are competing discourses that they can position themselves within or in relation to. The latter highlights that perhaps what is going on is an illustration of the way in which "interpellation" or "hailing" (Althusser, 1971) of these students and positioning as "consumers" are not direct but circumvented through alternative discourses of critique. Theoretically, it might be useful to re-examine the criticism directed against the concept of ideology and to examine ways to link ideology and discourse. If consumption of youth-culture products is undertaken despite the participants' critique, it is difficult to see how such recognition of potential exploitation can be viewed as necessarily empowering, allowing youth to act on their own behalf. As indicated in Chapter 1, ideology is regarded as fixing meaning in the service of power. Thus, while the students do make meaning, as more recent cultural studies theorists such as John Fiske would emphasize, this making of meaning is shaped within an existing framework of power relations—a power relations that would seem to privilege consumerism, consumption, and ultimately capitalism.

Although the students exert a sense of agency with regard to the consumption of media culture, such consumption is not totally within the framework of cultural populism and the "power of the ordinary" (Mukerjee & Schudson, 1991), whereby resistance and voluntarism are perceived in all acts of consumption. Instead it has to be recognized that while the students make meanings that privilege consumption and capitalism with regard to youth culture, these meanings are also shaped within an existing racialized, patriarchal, and heterosexual framework. This shaping of meaning by existing relations of dominance is evident in the ways in which some students responded to issues concerning gender relations and sexual orientation. Further contouring this meaning in line with existing relations of dominance are the students' construction of "reality" that emerges through their consumption of media culture in general and youth culture in particular. The youths' ability to move outside their existing frameworks of common sense understandings is thus seriously constrained by the use of existing experiences to validate differing social "realities." Their construction and use of what they "know" as representative of social "reality" tend to reinforce the existing relations of dominance rather than pose a challenge to the status quo. In terms of explaining the relationship between consumption and agency, Anthony Giddens's (1976) concept of structuration is useful as it attempts to bridge the traditional dualism of agency and structure. Giddens argues that human beings always have the capacity to change their social circumstances even if these are limited by specific social contexts (Layder, 1994).

~ ~ ~ ~ ~

Further, Giddens's comments that modern society is unique in its ability to tie events and activity perceived from a distance in time and space to identity formation that supplants local attachments. Ironically, the distancing of site of production and reception of media reinforces a discourse of desire. It is a desire for what is perceived as lacking to make one authentic and whole in some way. Such a discourse of desire is further strengthened through social relations and as well as the economic dominance and geographic location of the United States. With desire for hip-hop culture constructed and associated so closely with a specific location external to Canadian borders, we can see the implications in terms of reinforcing relations of power and domination. What we have is a desire for elsewhere that is generated through consumption.[4] By purchasing clothes, accessing music, and generating knowledge, youth are able to strive for a sense of authenticity and wholeness external to the self. This production of desire is a complex and layered affair, drawing on existing discourses that link spatial location and economic power. For these youths in the study, this process of differentiating Edmonton from other geographic areas through ready access to U.S.-derived consumer goods results in a relational coding of both Vancouver and Toronto as "not as dry as" Edmonton. This "dryness" is related to the city's inability to directly access certain consumer goods.

Also interesting are the ways in which desire is constructed and articulated with conceptions of authentic and real especially since we are living in an era within which there has been a proliferation of simulated images. This fact reinforces Gilroy's postulation that there is a growing cultural importance of visual thinking, which increasingly influences our conception of truth. So, the present-day dominance of visuality, of image over writing, has had a profound influence over what we take as reliable knowledge (Aronowitz, 2000). This visuality also becomes implicated in a struggle to produce "truth effects," which are achieved through the production of certain types of selves and knowledge.

~ ~ ~ ~ ~

Examining such struggles over truth effects allows us to access the ways in which we are governed by the production and circulation of specific "regimes of truths" which organize the relations between knowledge and action in specific ways and within specific fields. In a similar vein we can link the concept of hegemony to understanding the nuanced ways the struggle for truth effects produces and reinforces a discursive formation that is hegemonic in the sense that power is exercised through consent rather than coercion. As Fairclough (1992) suggests:

> hegemony helps us . . . provid[e] for discourse both a matrix—a way of analysing the social practice within which the discourse belongs in terms of power relations, in terms of whether they reproduce, restructure or challenge existing hegemonies–a way of analysing the social practice within which the discourse belongs in terms of power relations. (p. 95)

Thus such a conceptual framework of analysis that draws on regimes of truth and hegemony allows us to account for any pseudo-resistance to consumerism that the students undertake while also recognizing that they are consenting to their own domination. While some theorists view the concept of hegemony as too class-based (Laclau & Mouffee, 1985), the data generated suggests that for these students, youth culture is a terrain upon which they encounter various discourse and ideologies. As well it would be deterministic to argue that this hegemonic relationship will be once and for all. At some point in the future, these students might well use their identification with blackness in order to challenge consumerism.

## Conclusions

Throughout the study, acknowledgment is given to the process of mediation taking place between individual students and their peers as they discuss and position themselves in relation to various discourses of commodification and consumption. Of import is the way in which the data construct, through youth culture, contesting discourses that enable and constrain certain patterns of consumption. The students' narratives reflect the discourses that challenge the ways in which hip-hop has in recent years become commodified. This commodification of youth culture is not just in relation to hip-hop culture. It is an on-going process that is consistent throughout the youth culture literature, charting the rise and fall of earlier subcultural styles and groups such as "mods," "hippies," and "punks." John Storey reveals such processes of commodification as ones where, "youth subcultures always move from originality and opposition to commercial incorporation and ideological diffusion as the cultural industries eventually succeed in marketing subcultural resistance for general consumption and profit" (Storey, 1996, p. 120). While these discourses of commodification are available to the students for critiquing consumption, few critiqued hip-hop as a cultural form in itself. As well, in examining the hip-hop music magazines such as *The Source, Rap Pages,* and *Vibe,* one finds similar discourses of critique represented with regard to commodification of hip-hop. Perhaps these discourses of critique within youth culture provide a contesting discourse before the consumers construct one for themselves and might, therefore, be regarded as trying to fix meaning in the name of power. As such, one might see an ideology of consumption. Although other explanations might be possible, what is going on can be viewed as hegemonic, i.e., a struggle between differing and existing discourses around consumption and blackness upon a field of black youth culture.

What is purportedly on sale in this process of commodification are the experiences of African Americans. However, as has been indicated through this study, these experiences are mediated and constructed through televisual and auditory images conveyed through the films, television, and music that the students listen to. There are no authentic images that represent an essence of black experience; history, geography, and politics intervene. These images that are consumed by all racialized groups within society are then put to differing uses. For some, adoption of these black-identified behavior patterns, as in street slang such as "whassup," comes to reinforce a desire for a specific form of self-representation. If we regard this desire in an intertextual way, in relation to economic discourses, we can perhaps view the desire for a representation of the self as "rebel" against an economic and social reality that has encouraged youths in general to conform to a social and economic framework that has been identified by theorists as neo-conservative (Harrison & Kachur, 1999; Giroux, 1997; Giroux & Aronowitz 1993). This taking of meaning, is of course, refracted through gender, class, and racialized identity. Thus, the meanings of these televisual and sound images can be seen as offering and operating in differing ways to present the self. Thus it is possible to present one's self as "cool" rather than "nerd" through identification with such images of blackness. It is interesting to note the comments of black students to these "others" who attempt to identify with specific representations of blackness. This questioning of how "others" take on identification makes any liberal multicultural discourse problematic and challenges discourses that would produce rap as consistently libratory and based on a simple sharing of culture.

In this and in my previous research projects student narratives illustrate the importance of religious discourses in the process of identity formation. This is not surprising since the "black" church as an institution has historically provided a site for identity formation and dissemination of black discourses. More students in this research highlight its tension with discourses of youth culture. This tension is evident in terms of the students' consumption of films, music, and television and the ways in which they produce specific religious subjectivities. It is evident in the way in which religious subject positions contest the production of certain school-approved subjectivities. The importance of the latter is further highlighted by the recent inclusion of sexual orientation within the Alberta Teachers' Association "Code of Professional Conduct" (passed 1999). In terms of some of the competing discourses produced by the students with regard to sexualities and religion, it becomes evident that getting students to view such issues as ones of human rights and thus the necessity of adherence to legal requirements might be as much as schools can achieve. This tension also reflects discourses within wider society as to which of these rights has precedence: religion or sexuality? While critical pedagogues would indicate that teaching about race, class, and gender might develop a sense of critical consciousness, some students do not as readily translate recognition of their subjugated positioning in society into empathy with those who are marginalized through sexualities.

These observations indicate a need for more research on the ways in which religious subjectivity intersects with youth culture and construction of school identities. Data generation reveals not just the usual cohort of class, sexuality, gender, and nationality but also religion as important in terms of complicating identity formation. The recognition of the importance of religion is often under-theorized within the cultural studies literature. Cornel West and bell hooks's Breaking Bread (1991) is an exception. Bearing in mind the enabling as well as constraining role that organized religion within the black diaspora and the church has played in the lives of peoples of African descent, it is a surprising omission from the black cultural studies literature. As Neal (1999) points out, not only did the church emerge as one of the most critical institutions for the dissemination of black discourses, it also functions "as a discursive critical arena—a public sphere in which values and issues were aired, debated, and disseminated throughout the larger black community" (p. 7). It is evident that various religious subjectivities are constructed through a positioning that contests a classroom environment that is based upon promotion of equity.

There is also a need to continue with analysis of the relationship between the cultural politics of schooling and identity. The latter type of research assumes even more urgency with recent research findings in the United Kingdom linking black male underachievement with black youth culture (Sewell, cited in Hinsliff & Bight, 2000). By examining the question of cultural choice, one can garner how such choices position "us" and how they tell "us" and "others" who we are not. Such choices sort us into "kind." This sorting of "kinds," this "us" and "them," is evident in the choices that the students make through their reception of media. Culture can thus be seen as a part of that process of sorting, "creating a social space" for ourselves, partly given, partly chosen, in the open-ended formation of our identities.

Perhaps one of the most important questions raised by the study is to what extent is there one ideal black identity and, if it exists, of what does it consist? Such reflections as to what a black identity consists of are important in terms of developing an inclusive school curriculum as well as working across groups in a community setting. At times, theorists have highlighted how conception of "community" as "same" can result in the subjugation of the differences within that descriptor (Hall, 1990; McCarthy, 1997). The students' narratives make evident the ways in which understandings of blackness within this high school are plural, fragmented rather than unified. Thus fragmentation even in the face of the homogenizing influence of the media is based on the "roots" of the students in Africa and the diaspora. Recognition of such plurality, as Elliot Butler Evans (1989) argues in his critique of essentialism, "may very well force us to rethink both the politics of everyday life and the politics of cultural criticism and production" (p. 129).

One can ask the question, "To what extent would one find such a representation of these various student youth identities in another school?" From my research I would argue that one would find many of these "cuts" of identities among black students. However, in terms of the degree of collectivity among black students, there would be variations according to geographic location and school context and the number of students within a high school. As stated above, and in Kelly (1998), when African-Canadian students enter high schools, they are often faced with many more students of African descent than previously encountered in either elementary or junior high. In some ways the process is akin to "coming out," i.e., students have to decide to what extent they identify themselves as black and the significance of this blackness. They have to position themselves within specific black subjectivities. For some students, blackness is based on essentialist understandings of skin color and phenotype. For other students this understanding of blackness is politicized; blackness is consistent with a state of political consciousness. These understandings can be identified as discourses and "regimes of truth."

To conclude I would like to leave you with the voices of three of the students. Through these narratives one can identify the ways in which media culture becomes embedded in the everyday lives of the students and how media culture is a terrain upon which discourses contest each other in a struggle for cultural hegemony. As this student identified, positioning one's self in relation to a discourse and language says something about one's self:

**Student 1:** Okay, me and my people I hang out with, like my—crew. Like, we pretty much listen to rap. And then lines from it stick in our heads. And we use it like all the time. Like the other day when I came in here and I was like talking that line "pimping ain't easy" right? And, um, that's pretty much gone. I stopped using that. I use it every once in a while, like if it's necessary, but it still comes and goes.

Or, to repeat, as one student as "ironic" viewer confessed to the hegemonic hold of the "popular" through desire:

> **Student 2:** Ok. Jerry. I must admit I am ashamed to honestly say so. Sometimes I do watch it. It's a really bad show. He is like totally demoralized. But I can't help it. It's kind of addictive sometimes. People are so stupid. But it's funny, it's really funny. Because, well, maybe some of them are faking it, but you can tell that some of them are not faking it. And they are so dumb.

Or, as another student indicated how consumption can be resisted:

> **Student 3:** I am not the kind of guy who goes for much name-brand stuff.
> **J:** Are you not? How come?
> **Student 3:** Well, I find those worldly stuff. I don't keep my mind on worldly stuff 'cuz I am a Christian.

# Notes

## Chapter 1. Mapping the Terrain

\* J: = Jennifer Kelly // indicates interjection of interviewer with comment or question. All student names are pseudonyms, and names of some residential districts in Edmonton have been changed. Data generation was started in 1998. The title of the book draws on Andre Alexis's concept of "borrowed blackness."

1. Recognition of popular culture as a resource for meaning making and identity production is not a new phenomenon but formed the basis of much of the early work of the Centre for Contemporary Cultural Studies in Birmingham, UK (Hall & Jefferson, 1976; Hebdige, 1979).

2. Thompson (1990) also has an interesting discussion on the work of Innis and McLuhhan and their contribution to analysis of space and time.

3. A *Manchester Guardian Weekly* article highlights the findings by British researcher Tony Sewell that black youth culture was to blame for lack of academic success (Hinsliff & Bright, 2000).

4. Previous to entry into the "field," I kept a field journal of events, perspectives, and other reflections. This journal proved useful in illustrating the research process and encouraged a process of self-reflexivity during the varying stages of the research. The abbreviations in the journal correspond with Laurel Richardson's (1994) categorization:

   *Observation notes* (ON): These are as concrete and detailed as I am able to make them.

   *Theoretical notes* (TN): These are hunches, hypotheses, poststructuralist connections, critiques of what I am doing/thinking/seeing.

   *Personal notes* (PN): These are feelings, statements about the research, the people I am talking to, myself doing the process, my doubts, my anxieties, my pleasures.

5. Hair that has been plaited close to the head in straight rows from front to back of the head.

6. In previous research conducted in high schools, a similar issue arose with regard to the operation of a "closed" activity in an "open" school. Refer to Kelly, 1998.

7. In an initial draft document produced by the Western Canadian Protocol committee for social studies, it was noticeable that while the document highlighted Charter groups such as Francophone and Anglophone, alongside Aboriginal students there was an erasure of

racialized/ethnic identities under "Other." No mention was made as to the complex identity formation that students experience. A May 2003 update identifies citizenship and identity as core concepts in the curriculum.

8. The pioneers came as part of attempts to settle the West with immigrants from the United States of America, United Kingdom, and Eastern Europe.

9. See *Alberta: A New History* by Howard Palmer (1990, p. 78) Edmonton: Hurtig Publishers.

10. As well as Velma Carter and Gwen Hooks's books, Bruce Shepard's *Deemed unsuitable* (1997) and the NFB video *I remember Amber Valley* provide useful information on the settlements.

11. The latter information with regard to the complex nature of immigration during the 1960s was garnered during personal correspondence with Nigel Darbasie, a writer whose parents immigrated during this period.

12. Draft Foundation Document for the Development of the Western Canadian Protocol Social Studies K-12 Common Curriculum Framework (1998) was produced by officials at Alberta Learning. In 2001 a more updated document was presented.

13. This idea of identity as performance is not new, and here I draw partially on Judith Butler's work on sexual identity, wherein she suggests that gender identity is a performance— "constituting an identity, the identity that it is purported to be" (Butler, 1990, p. 25).

## Chapter 2. Diaspora as Collectivity?

1. Stepping is a rhythmic hand clapping and foot stomping performance.

2. The question of mixed relations are discussed more fully in Kelly, 1998.

3. Slow movement of the waist while dancing.

4. Minister Faust has a radio program which plays music from Africa. The Afrika All-World News Radio, and The Phantom Pyramid. His programs broadcast on FM 88.9, the University of Alberta's radio station CJSR.

5. Stephens suggests that in 1988 when U.S. DJ Red Alert began playing dancehall music; he was "perhaps the first hip-hop radio DJ. to acknowledge stylistic links between the two genres" (Stephens, 1996, p. 270).

6. Gilroy argues that the shift in reggae towards violent lyrics can be related to the "consolidation of Seaga's regime and the consequent militarization of ghetto life" (1987/91, p. 188).

## Chapter 3. Music and Regimes of Representation

1. "'Breakin' was a set of specific dance moves done on playgrounds and club dance floors in the late 1970s and early 1980s; from twists and spins, headstands, and elaborately orchestrated footwork to the standard individual dance moves of " 'top rockin' and up-rockin.'" (Perkins, 1996, p. 15). In recent years this art form has again begun to gain prominence among youth.

2. Tricia Rose's book *Black Noise* (1994) provides a useful analysis of the emergence of hip-hop and its cultural implications. In particular, Chapter 2, "'All Aboard the Night Train'—Flow, Layering and Rupture in Postindustrial New York," gives a good political and economic analysis of the development of hip-hop.

3. Stanley Cohen in his book *Folk Devils and Moral Panics* defines a moral panic as when "a condition, episode, person or group of persons emerges to become defined as a threat to societal values and interests" (p. 9)

4. Angela McRobbie's work on dance hall culture in the U.K. is useful in analyzing the ways such locations operate as sites for social formations.

5. Puff Daddy changed his name to P. Diddy after some of the data was collected.

6. In Rick Rubin, Simmons found a partner who shared his vision of "rap as rock." Rubin "reduced" rap tracks, moving the music away from the R&B that supported Kurtis Blow and the Furious Five to a hard, stark, aural assault with the antecedents in AC/DC's "Back in Black" and Billy Squier's "The Big Beat" (*George*, 1998, pp. 65–66).

7. Larry McShane in an *Edmonton Journal* article on January 25, 2000 suggests that many anti-P. Diddy websites are prevalent. According to the article P. Diddy was the "king of rap crossing over into the mainstream" (*Edmonton Journal*, 25 January 2000, C1).

8. This alignment of hip-hop with overt symbols of capitalism is not unusual within the genre. "Hip-hop is the only art form that celebrates capitalism openly. Rap's unabashed materialism distinguishes it sharply from some of the dominant musical genres of past century." "These guys are so real, they brag about money," says Def Jam's Simmons. They don't regret getting a Coca-Cola deal. They brag about a Coca-Cola deal (Farley, Feb 8th 1999:47).

9. Rose (1994) argues that the importance of authenticity via black lived experiences to reception of rap was highlighted by Vanilla Ice's embellishment of his past to include experiences of growing up with African Americans.

## Chapter 4. Films and Regimes of Representation

1. Refer to Thompson, 1990, Chapter 4, "Cultural Transmission and Mass Communication" for a coherent discussion of the growth of the media industry as a "specific historical process that accompanied the rise of modern societies" (p. 163).

2. Queen Latifah, one of the most influential women rappers in the United States., is noted for her feminist song "Who are they calling bitch?" that urges young women to question labels such as "ho" and "bitch" as frequently used by male rappers.

3. Following the collection of data, a new drama series based on the experiences of young blacks in Toronto was aired on Canadian Broadcasting Corporation. These programs were not discussed.

4. This lack of television programs with black lead characters would seem to be correct in that when I last interviewed students in 1994 references were made to many more new series for highlighting black characters.

5. Moses Znaimer is also co-founder, president; and executive producer of Toronto's radical and popular and independent television station Citytv (1972), MusiquePlus (1986), and MusiMax (1997), Bravo Canada's NewStyleArtsChannel (1995). (In 1998 he founded MuchMore Music. (Http://www.chumcity/bios/moses.html 11/3/00).

6. Znaimer's company Chum Ltd. is also responsible for continuing this process of border crossing with the expansion of his videomusic channels into the Latin American market. (RDS data base Acc# 1830340).

7. In 1988 MTV moved across the Atlantic to form MTV Europe. In 1991 MTV Asia was formed.

## Chapter 5. Riding the P. Diddy Train: Style as Performance

1. Harvard students Jon Schecter and David Mayes along with African American Ed Young started *The Source* in 1988. Following a failed bid to buy *The Source,* Qunicy Jones and Time Warner created *Vibe.*
2. *The Source* represents East Coast; *RapPages* represents West Coast (Stephens, 1996, p. 268).
3. Since the generation of the data various brand outlets have opened in the city.
4. If one examines copies of *The Source* and *Vibe,* one can easily attest to the dominance of white designers such as Nautica and Nike.

## Chapter 7. Borrowed Identities

1. Carol Tator and Frances Henry have recently completed a study of "Racist Discourses in Canada's English Print Media." Findings include: people of color are underrepresented and largely invisible in the media; when people of color do appear in media coverage, they are often misrepresented and stereotyped; the executive corporatist nature of the media influences the kind of news that is produced and disseminated (Executive Summary, March 2000).
2. *RapCity* is a program, concentrating on the genre of rap and closely–related hybrids (rap, reggae, "hip-hop" in general. This is a relatively "political program in the content of videos broadcast" and former VeeJay Michael Williams's commentary, " the definitive look at hip-hop and rap." It documents the artists, issues, and lifestyles surrounding today's most exciting new forms of music.
3. *XtenDaMix* was a program concentrating on dance music and intersects such genres as reggae and R&B. As many as six videos were commonly played back to back, possibly in aid of the program's use as dance music practice. MuchMusic now has a program called *downLo* as well as *Vibe* the show and Vibe the channel.
4. Rascalz is a Canadian rap group that has developed a consistent following. Celine Wong (1998) indicates that *Mastermind Street Jam* is the sole hip-hop show on commercial radio. In an interview with Ms. Wong, host Paul Parhar expressed the view that "I think the reason Toronto hasn't exploded is because of the lack of radio stations." Celine Wong continues, "due to the sparse nature of commercial programming, community/university radio stations have thankfully established themselves as hip-hop institutions." This is also true in Edmonton—the location of the study.
5. Adam Matthews in a *Rap Pages* article "Northern Exposure" suggests, "hip-hop market in Canada is very narrow. The total population of Canada is approximately 25 million. A gold album in Canada means sales of 50,000 copies as compared to 50000 in the United States. Video Fact, a quasi-government organization that provides grants to artists to make videos, funds most videos. The grants are usually $12,000 to $15,000—chump change when compared to high-budget U.S. productions. Even winning the rap Juno doesn't equal success in the US" (p. 71).
6. This dominance applies to most forms of western mass-produced music.
7. Career and Life Management Skills (CALM) is a required course for all high school students. Its intention is to give students an understanding of necessary skills for survival as adults.

## Chapter 8. Stylish Solidarity

1. In 1978 Stokely Carmichael changed his name to Kwame Ture in order to honor Kwame Nkrumah and Ahmed Sekou Toure, two African socialist leaders.
2. This phrase is becoming common parlance. I noticed that a recent flyer sent to my house used this distinction to advertise its fall back-to-school sale.

## Chapter 9. Bringing It Back Home

1. The Canadian content quota was introduced on AM radio stations in 1971 and in FM radio in 1976. What constituted Canadian had to pass the MAPLE test whereby at least two of the following must apply: "M"=Music composed by a Canadian; "A"= artist (principal performer is a Canadian); "P"= performance/production in Canada; "L" =lyrics are written by a Canadian. (Shukur, 2001, p. 75)
2. Diran Adebayo in the *Observer* newspaper indicates the ways in which patois is being used beyond the confines of the Caribbean community.
3. A similar but more detailed schema is discussed in Norman Fairclough's book *Media Discourse* (1995).
4. At present there seems to be a change in the marketability and desire for the types of branded goods. The following appeared in the Dow Jones Interactive [http://ptg.djnr.com/ccroot/asp/publib/story.asp retrieved 07/10/2002].

   "Gap Inc. is still struggling and Tommy Hilfiger and Polo Ralph Lauren are losing luster among the young. It seems there is no one brand or chain that's dictating style for youth these days." "The lack of focus became more apparent for the back-to-school season, which was grim, as a sluggish economy has forced companies to rein in their creativity, analysts said." "There isn't that excitement or sense of got-to-have it in fashion this year," said Wendy Liebmann, president of marketing consultant WSL Strategic Retail in New York. "There's no one creating the fizz and bubble."

# References

Abdul-Lateef, M. (1998). Love's gonna get'cha. *Rap Pages*. July. 77–78; 80–81.

Aboud, F. (1981). Ethnic self-identity. In R. Gardner & R. Kallen (Eds.), *A Canadian social psychology of ethnic relations* (pp. 37–56). Toronto: Methuen.

Adebayo, D. (Nov 2001). Young gifted, black . . . and very confused. [Retrieved 01/08/2002 http://www.observer.co.uk/race/story/0,11255,605333,00.html].

Adorno, T. & Horkheimer, M. (1979). *Dialectic of enlightenment* (Trans. J. Cummings). London: Verso.

Adorno, T. (1991). *The culture industry*. London: Routledge.

Alberta Teachers' Association (1999). Code of Conduct. Edmonton: Alberta.

Alexis, A. (1995). Borrowed blackness. *This Magazine*, May, 28(8), 14–20.

Allen, E. (1996). Making the strong survive: The contours and contradictions of "message rap." In W. E. Perkins (Ed.), *Droppin' science: Critical essays on rap music and hip-hop culture*. Philadelphia: Temple University Press.

Althusser, L. (1971). Ideology and Ideological state apparatuses in L. Althusser, *Lenin and philosophy and other essays*. London: New Left Books.

Andermahr, S., Lovell, T. & Wolkowitz, C. (Eds.) (1997). *A glossary of feminist theory*. London: Arnold.

Ang, I. (1985). *Watching Dallas: Soap opera and the melodramatic imagination*. London: Methuen.

Appadurai, A. (1990). Disjuncture and difference in the global cultural economy. In M. Featherstone (Ed.), *Global culture: Nationalism, globalization, modernity* (pp. 295–311). London: Sage.

Aronowitz, S. (2000). Against race. [Review of the book *Against race*] *The Nation*, 11/06.271 (4) 28–31.

Aronowitz, S. & Giroux, H. (1993). *Education still under siege*. Toronto, ON: OISE.

Asante, M. (1989). (2nd printing). *Afrocentricity*. Trenton: Africa World Press Inc.

Asante, M, K. (2001). Against Race: Imagining political culture beyond the colour line. [Review of the book *Between Camps*] *Journal of Black Studies* 31(6), 84–85.

Ashcroft, B., Griffiths, G., & Tiffin, H. (1998). *Key concepts in post-colonial studies*. London: Routledge.

Baker, Jr. H. (1993). *Rap and the academy*. Chicago: University of Chicago.

Baker, Jr. H., Diawara, M., & Lindeborg, R. (Eds.). (1996). *Black British cultural studies*. Chicago: University of Chicago Press.

Banks, J. (1997). MTV and the globalization of popular culture. *Gazette* 59(1), 43–60.

Bannerji, H. (1995). (Ed.). *Under the gaze: Essays in racism, feminism and politics*. Toronto, Ontario: Sister Vision.

Bannerji, H. (2000). *The dark side of the nation: Essays on multiculturalism, nationalism and gender*. Toronto: Canadian Scholars' Press.

Barker, C. (1999). *Television, globalization and cultural identities*. Buckingham: Open University.

Barthes, R. (1977). Image-music-text. London: Routledge.

Baudrillard, J. (1983). The ecstasy of communication. In H. Foster (Ed.), *The anti-aesthetic: Essays on postmodern culture*, pp. 126–34. Seattle: Bay Press.

Bell, D. (1976). *The coming of post-industrial society: A venture in social forecasting*. New York: Harper Collins.

Bennett, T. (1986). Popular culture and the turn to Gramsci. In T. Bennett, C. Mercer, & J. Woollacott (Eds.), *Popular culture and social relations* (pp. vii–xi). Milton Keynes: Open University Press.

Bennett, T. Mercer, C., & Woollacott J.(1986). (Eds.) *Popular culture and social relations*. Milton Keynes: Open University Press.

Bennett, T., Emmison, M., & Frow, J. (Eds.) (1999). *Accounting for tastes: Australian everyday cultures*. New York: Cambridge University Press.

Bhabha, H. (1990). The third space. In J. Rutherford (Ed.), *Identity community, culture, and difference*. London: Lawrence & Wishart.

Bhabha, H. (1994). *The location of culture*. London: Routledge.

Billig, M. (1995). *Banal Nationalism*. London: Sage.

Billig, M. (1997). From codes to utterances: Cultural studies, discourse and psychology. In M. Ferguson & P. Golding. (Eds.), *Cultural studies in question* (pp. 205–226). London: Sage.

Black Women's Working Group. (2000). *Black women and economic autonomy*. Edmonton: BWWG.

Brand, D. (1997). *Land to light on*. Toronto: McClelland and Stewart.

Braxton, C. (1998 July). Soulman, *Rap Pages*, 86–90.

Britzman, D. (1991). Decentering discourses in teacher education: Or, the unleashing of popular things. *Journal of Education*, *173(3)*, 60–80.

Brown, D. & Kelly, J.(2001) Curriculum and public space. *British Journal of Sociology of Education (22)(4)*, 501–518.

Brunsdon, C. (1996). A thief in the night: Stories of feminism in the 1970s at CCCS. In D. Morley & K-H Chen (Eds.), *Stuart Hall: Critical dialogues in cultural studies* (pp. 276–286). London: Routledge.

Butler, J. (1990). *Gender trouble*. London: Routledge.

Butler, J. (1993). *Bodies that matter*. London: Routledge.

Butler-Evans, E. (1989). Beyond essentialism: Rethinking Afro-American Cultural theory. *Inscriptions* 5, 121–27.

Bynoe, Y. (July 14, 2000) The white boy shuffle, *Politically Black* [http://politically black.com/Full%20Disclose.html].

Calliste, A. (1987). Sleeping car porters in Canada: An ethnically submerged split labor market. *Canadian Ethnic Studies* 19(1), 1–20.

Calliste, A. (1993–1994). Race, gender and Canadian immigration policy: Blacks from the Caribbean, 1900–1932. *Journal of Canadian Studies, Winter* 28(4), 131–48.

Carby, H. (1994). Encoding white resentment. In C. McCarthy, & W. Crichlow (Eds.), *Race identity and representation in education* (pp. 236–47). New York: Routledge.

Carr, W., & Kemmis, S. (1983). *Becoming critical: Knowing through action research.* Victoria: Dean University.

Carmichael, S., & Hamilton, C. (1967). *Black power.* London: Penguin Books Ltd.

Carter, V., & Leffler Akili, W. (1981). *The window of our memories.* B.C.R Society of Alberta.

Centre for Contemporary Cultural Studies. (1982). *The empire strikes back.* London: Hutchinson.

Chalmers, V. (1997). White-out: Multicultural performances in a progressive school. In M. Fine, L. Weis, L. Powell, & L. Mun Wong (Eds.) *Off White: Readings on race, power, & society* (pp. 66 –78). New York: Routledge.

Chandler, D. (1998). Semiotics for beginners [wysiwyg://82/http://www.aber.ac.uk /media//Documents/S4B/semo2a.html Retrieved 15/05/00].

Chang O'Brien, K., & Chen, W. (1998). *Reggae routes: The story of Jamaican music.* Kingston, Jamaica: Ian Randle.

Chen, K. H. (1996). The formation of a diasporic intellectual: An interview with Stuart Hall by Kuan-Hsing Chen. In D. Morley & Kuan-Hsing Chen (Eds.), *Stuart Hall critical dialogues in cultural studies* (pp. 484–503). London: Routledge.

Clarke, G.E. (1996). Must all Blackness be American?: Locating Canada in Borden's "Tightrope Time," or nationalizing Gilroy's Black Atlantic. *Canadian Ethnic Studies,* 28 (3) Special Issue, 56–71.

Clarke, K., & Clarke, M. (1939). The development of consciousness of self and the emergence of racial identification in Negro pre-school children. *Journal of Social Psychology 10,* 591–99.

Cohen, S. (1973). *Folk devils and moral panics.* London: MacGibbons and Kee.

Collins, P. H. (1990). *Black feminist thought.* New York: Unwin Hyman.

Cooke, B. (1911). The Black Canadian. *Maclean's Magazine.*

Daspit, T. (1999). Rap pedagogies: "Bring(ing) the noise" of knowledge born on the microphone to radical education. In T. Daspit & J. A. Weaver (Eds.). *Popular culture and critical pedagogy: Reading, constructing, connecting* (pp. 163–81). New York: Garland.

Deleuze, G. & Guattari, F. (1987) (1980). *A thousand plateaus: Capitalism and schizophrenia.* (Trans. B. Massumi). Minneapolis: University of Minnesota Press.

Denzin, N. (1989). *Interpretive interactionism.* California: Sage Publications, Inc.

Denzin, N., & Lincoln, Y.S. (1994). Introduction: Entering the field of qualitative research. In N. Denzin & Y. Lincoln (Eds.), *Handbook of qualitative research* (pp. 1–17). California: Sage.

Diawara, M. (1996). Black British cinema: Spectatorship and identity formation. In H. A. Baker, Jr., M. Diawara, & R. Lindeborg (Eds.), Black British cultural studies. Chicago: University of Chicago Press.

Easthope, A., & McGowan, K. (Eds.) (1992). *A critical and cultural theory reader*. Toronto: University of Toronto Press.

*Edmonton Daily Bulletin.* (1911). Campaign of discouragement checks immigration of Negroes. June 5 (p. 1).

Fairclough N. (1992). *Discourse & social change*. London: Polity Press.

Fairclough, N. (1995). *Media discourse*. London: Arnold.

Fanon, F. (1967). *Black skins White masks*. New York: Grove Cross.

Ferguson, A. (1996). Can I choose who I am? And how would that empower me? Gender, race, identities and the self. In A. Garry & M. Pearsall (Eds.), pp. 108–26. *Women, knowledge and reality: Explorations in feminist philosophy*. London: Routledge.

Ferguson, M., & Golding, P. (1997) (Eds). *Cultural studies in question*. London: Sage.

Fiske, J. (1987). *Television culture*. London: Methuen.

Fiske, J. (1988). Meaningful moments. *Critical Studies in Mass Communication* (Sept.) (pp. 246–250).

Fiske, J. (1994). Audience: Cultural practice and cultural studies. In N. Denzin & Y. Lincoln (Eds.), *Handbook of qualitative research* (pp. 189–98). California: Sage.

Forman, M. (2001). "Straight outta Mogadishu": Prescribed identities and performative practices among Somali youth in North American high schools. *Topia: A Canadian Journal of Cultural Studies 5*, 1–19 [retrieved from http://www.utpjournals.com/topia/2forman.html 20/09/02].

Foucault, M. (1970). *The order of things*. London: Tavistock.

Foucault, M. (1980). *Power/Knowledge: Selected interviews and other writings, 1972–1977* (Ed. Colin Gordon). New York: Pantheon.

Foucault, M. (1984). *The history of sexuality*. Harmondsworth: Penguin.

Foucault. M. (1988). Technologies of the self. In L. Martin, H. Gutman, & P. Hutton (Eds.), *Technologies of the self, a seminar with Michel Foucault*, Amherst: University of Massachusetts Press.

Fraser, N. (1995). From redistribution to recognition? Dilemmas of justice in a "Post Socialist" age, *New Left Review 212* (July/August): 68–93.

Garry, A., & Pearsall, M. (1996). *Women, knowledge and reality: Explorations in feminist philosophy*. London: Routledge.

Gates, H. L. (1990). *New York Times*, June 19, 1990.

George, N. (1992). *Buppies, b-boys, baps, bohos: Notes on post-soul Black culture*. New York: HarperCollins.

George, N. (1998). *Hip-hop America*. New York: Penguin.

Giddens, A. (1976). *New rule of sociological method*. London: Hutchinson.

Giddens, A. (1984). *The constitution of society*. London: Polity Press.

Giddens, A. (1990). The consequences of modernity. London: Polity Press.

Gillespie, M. (1995). *Television, ethnicity and cultural change*. London: Routledge.

Gilroy, P. (1987). *There ain't no Black in the Union Jack*. London: Hutchinson.

Gilroy, P. (1992). Cultural studies and ethnic absolutism. In L. Grossberg, C. Nelson, & P. Treichler (Eds.), *Cultural studies* (pp. 187–98). New York: Routledge.

Gilroy, P. (1993). *The Black Atlantic*. Cambridge, MA: Harvard University Press.

Gilroy, P. (1995). Roots and routes: Black identity as an outernational project. In H. Harris, H. Blue, & E. Griffith (Eds.), *Racial and ethnic identity: Psychological development and creative expressions* (pp. 15–30). New York: Routledge.

Gilroy, P. (1996). British cultural studies and the pitfalls of identity. In H. Baker, Jr., M. Diawara, & R. Lindeborg (Eds.), *Black British cultural studies* (pp. 223–39). Chicago: University of Chicago Press.

Gilroy, P. (1997). Diaspora and the detours of identity. In K. Woodward (Ed.), Identity and difference (pp. 299–346). London: Sage.

Gilroy, P. (2000). *Between camps*. London: Allen Lane, Penguin Press.

Giroux, H., & Simon, R. (Eds). (1989). *Popular culture: Schooling and everyday life*. Toronto: OISE.

Giroux, H. (1993). Living dangerously: Identity politics and the new cultural racism: Towards a critical pedagogy of representation. *Cultural Studies, 7*(1), 1–27.

Giroux, H. (1996). Fugitive cultures: Race, violence & youth. New York: Routledge.

Giroux, H. (1997). *Channel surfacing: Race talk and the destruction of today's youth*. New York: St. Martin's.

Giroux, H. (2000). Public pedagogy as cultural politics: Stuart Hall and the 'crisis' of culture. *Cultural Studies 14*(2) 341–60.

Gitlin, T. (1997). The anti-political populism of cultural studies. In M. Ferguson & P. Golding (Eds.), *Cultural studies in question* (pp. 25–38). London: Sage.

Glazer, M. (1998). *The Source*. De Gal dem sugar pp. 119–20, 260.

Gordon, C. (1980). Afterword. In M. Foucault, *Power/Knowledge: Selected interviews and other writings 1972–1977* (pp. 229–59) (Ed. Colin Gordon). New York: Pantheon.

Gramsci, A. (1971). *Prison notebooks*. London: Lawrence & Wishart.

Gray, H. (1993). African-American political desire and the seductions of contemporary cultural politics. *Cultural Studies, 7*(3), 364–73.

Gray, H. (1995). *Watching race*. Minneapolis: University of Minnesota.

Grizzle, S. (1998). *My name's not George*. Toronto: Umbrella Press.

Grossberg, L. (1997). *Bringing it all black home*. Durham & London: Duke University.

Grossberg, L. (1996). On postmodernism and articulation: An interview with Stuart Hall. In D. Morley & Kuan-Hsing Chen (Eds.), *Stuart Hall critical dialogues in cultural studies* (pp. 31–150) London: Routledge.

Guba, E., & Lincoln, Y. (1981). *Effective evaluation*. San Francisco: Jossey-Bass.

Hall, S. (1980). Encoding/decoding. In S. Hall, D. Hobson, A. Lowe & P. Willis (Eds.), *Culture, media, language* (pp. 128–38). London: Hutchinson.

Hall, S. (1988). The toad in the garden: Thatcherism among the theorists. In L. Grossberg & C. Nelson (Eds.), *Marxism and the interpretation of culture* (pp. 35–57). Urbana and Chicago: University of Illinois Press.

Hall, S. (1989). New ethnicities. In K. Mercer (Ed.), *Black film, British cinema* BFI/ICA Documents 7, 27–31.

Hall, S. (1990). Cultural identity and dispora. In J. Rutherford (Ed.), *Identity, community, culture, and difference* (pp. 222–37). London: Lawrence & Wishart.

Hall, S. (1991). The local and the global: Globalization and ethnicity. In A. King (Ed.), *Culture, globalization and the world-system* (pp. 19–40). London: Macmillan.

Hall, S. (1992). The question of cultural identity. In S. Hall, D. Held, & T. McGrew (Eds.), *Modernity and its futures* (pp. 274–323). Milton Keynes: Open University.

Hall, S. (1996a). New ethnicities. In H. Baker, Jr., M. Diawara, & R. Lindeborg (Eds.), *Black British cultural studies* (pp. 163–72). Chicago: University of Chicago.

Hall, S. (1996b). Cultural studies and its theoretical legacies. In D. Morley & Kuan-Hsing Chen (Eds.), *Stuart Hall critical dialogues in cultural studies* (pp. 262–75). London: Routledge.

Hall, S. (1996c). Cultural identity and cinematic representation. In H. Baker, Jr.. M. Diawara, & R. Lindeborg (Eds.), *Black British cultural studies* (pp. 163–72). Chicago: University of Chicago.

Hall, S. (Ed.). (1997). *Representation, cultural representation and signifying practices.* London: Sage.

Hall, S., & Jefferson, T. (Eds.). (1976). *Resistance through rituals: Youth subcultures in post-war Britain.* London: Hutchinson.

Harrison, T., & Kachur, J. (Eds.). (1999). *Contested classrooms.* Edmonton: University of Alberta.

Harker, J. (2002). Rap culture has hijacked our identity. We must reclaim from the street thugs what it means to be black. *Manchester Guardian.* March 6.

Hartley, J. (1994). Culture. In T. O'Sullivan, J. Hartley, D. Saunders, M. Montgomery, & J. Fiske (Eds.), *Key concepts in communication and cultural studies* (pp. 68– 71). London: Routledge.

Hartsock, N. (1998). *The feminist standpoint revisited and other essays.* Colorado: Westview.

Harvey, D. (1989). *The condition of postmodernity.* Oxford: Blackwell Publishers Ltd.

Hayashi-Tennant, J. (1999). Musicmaster, TV Times. *Edmonton Journal.* April 23–29.

Haynes, V. D. (1999). TV "whitewash" slammed. *Edmonton Journal* C3. July 14.

Hebdige, D. (1979). *Subculture: The meaning of style.* London: Methuen & Co Ltd.

Hebdige, D. (1988). *Hiding in the light.* London: Routledge.

Henriques, J., Holloway, W., Urwin, C., Venn, C., & Walkerdine, V. (Eds.). (1984). *Changing the subject: Psychology, social regulation, and subjectivity.* London: Methuen.

Henry, F., & Tator, C. (2000). *Racist discourses in Canada's English print media.* Toronto: The Canadian Race Relations Foundation.

Hinsliff, G., & Bright, M. (2000) Black youth culture blamed as youths fail. *Guardian Weekly* Aug 24–30, p. 7.

hooks, b. (1990). Postmodern blackness. *Postmodern Culture,* 1(1), 1–14.

hooks, b. (1992). *Black looks.* Toronto, Ontario: Between the Lines.

hooks, b. (1994). *Outlaw culture: Resisting representations.* New York: Routledge.

hooks, b. (1996). *Reel to reel: Race sex and class at the movies.* New York: Routledge.

Hooks, G. (1997). *The Keystone legacy: The recollections of a black settler.* Edmonton: Brightest Pebble.

Ibrahim, A (2000). "Hey ain't I Black too?: The politics of becoming Black. In R. Walcott, (Ed.). *Rude, contemporary Black cultural criticism* (pp. 109–36). Toronto: Insomniac.

Isajiw, W. (1999). *Understanding diversity: Ethnicity and race in the Canadian context*. Toronto: Thompson Educational Publishing Inc.

Jackson. P. (1968). *Life in classrooms*. New York: Holt, Reinhart.

James, W. (1996). The making of black identities. In J. Hutchinson & A. Smith (Eds.), *Ethnicity*. Oxford: Oxford University Press.

Jameson, F. (1991). *Postmodernism, or the cultural logic of late capitalism*. Durham: Duke University Press.

Jarvis, S. (1998). *Adorno: A critical introduction*. New York: Routledge.

Jensen, K. B. (2002). (Ed.). *A handbook of media and communication research: Qualitative and quantative methodologies*. London: Routledge.

Jatz, J. (1995). *Vancouver Sun*, August 19, 7–8.

Kelley, R. (1994). *Race rebels: Culture, politics and the Black working class*. New York: Free Press.

Kellner, D. (1995). *Media culture, cultural studies, identity and politics between the modern and the postmodern*. New York: Routledge.

Kelly, J. (1998). *Under the gaze: Learning to be Black in White society*. Halifax: Fernwood Press.

Klein, N. (2000). *No Logo: Taking aim at the brand bullies*. Toronto: Vintage Canada.

Koza, J. E. (1994). Rap music: The cultural politics of official representation. *The review of education /pedagogy/cultural studies* (16) 2, 171–96.

Laclau, E., & Mouffee, C. (1985). *Hegemony and socialist strategy*. London: Verso.

Lambertson, R. (2001). The Dresden story: Racism human rights and the Jewish labour committee of Canada. *Labour/Le Travail 47*, 43–82.

Lather, P. (1991). *Getting smart: Feminist research and pedagogy with/in the postmodern*. New York: Routledge.

Layder, D. (1994). *Understanding social theory*. London: Sage.

Lemert, C. (2000). *Postmodernism is not what you think*. Massachusetts: Blackwell.

Mahiri, J. (1998). Streets to schools: African American youth culture and the classroom. *The Clearing House 71*(6) July–August, p. 335(4).

Marable, M. (1992). The life and legacy of Malcolm X—A speech by Manning Marable. Metro State College, Denver, Colorado. http://www.lbbs.org/zmag/articles/barmarable.htm Feb. 21 (1–7).

Marable, M. (1995). Beyond racial identity politics. In M. Anderson & P. Hill Collins (Eds.), *Race, class, and gender* (pp. 363–65). California: Wadsworth.

Marcuse, H. (1964). *One-dimensional man*. Boston: Beacon Press.

Mathieu, S-J. (2001). North of the colour line: Sleeping car porters and the battle against Jim Crow on Canadian Rails, 1880-1920. *Labour/Le Travail 47*, 9–41.

Matthews, A. P. (1998). Northern exposure. *Rap Pages* June. 66–72.

McBride, S. (2001). *Paradigm shift: Globalization and the Canadian state*. Halifax: Fernwood.

McCarthy, C. (1997). Nonsynchrony and social difference: An alternative to the current radical accounts of race and schooling. In A. H. Halsey, H. Lauder, P. Brown, & A.

Stuart Wells (Eds.), *Education, culture economy society* (pp. 541–56). Oxford: Oxford University Press.

McCaskell, T. (1995). Anti-racist education and practice in the public school system. In S. Richer & L. Weir (Eds.), *Beyond political correctness: Toward the inclusive university*. (pp. 253–72). Toronto: University of Toronto.

McGuigan, J. (1997). Cultural populism revisited. In M. Ferguson & P. Golding (Eds.), *Cultural studies in question* (pp. 138–54). London: Sage.

McLaren, P. (1993). Border disputes: Multicultural narrative, identity formation and critical pedagogy in postmodern America. In J. McLaughlin & B. Tierney (Eds.), *Naming silent lives: personal narratives and the process of educational change* (pp. 201–35) London: Routledge.

McLaren, P. (1994). *Life in schools: An introduction to critical pedagogy in the foundations of education*. New York: Longman Publishing Group.

McLuhan, M. (1964). *Understanding media*. London: Routledge.

McRobbie, A. (1991). New times in cultural studies. *New Formations 13*, 1–18. London: Routledge.

McRobbie, A. (1994). *Postmodernism and popular culture*. London: Routledge.

McRobbie, A. (1997). The es and the anti-es: New questions for feminism and cultural studies. In M. Ferguson & P. Golding (Eds.), *Cultural studies in question* (pp. 170–86). London: Sage.

McRobbie, A. (1999). *In the culture society: Art, fashion and popular music*. London: Routledge.

Mead, G. H. (1934). *Mind self and society*. Chicago: University of Chicago Press.

Mercer, K. (1994). *Welcome to the jungle*. London: Routledge.

Merriam, S., & Simpson, E. (1995). (2nd Ed). *A guide to research for educators and trainers of adults*. Malabar, FL: Krieger Publishing Company.

Morley, D., & Robins, K. (1995). *Spaces of identity: Global media, electronic landscapes and culture boundaries*. London: Routledge.

Morrow, R. (1991). Critical theory, Gramsci and cultural studies: From structuralism to poststructuralism. In P. Wexler (Ed.), *Critical theory now* (pp. 27–70). London: Falmer Press.

Morrow, R., & Torres, C. (1995). *Social theory and education*. Albany, NY: SUNY Press.

Mukerjee, C., & Schudson, M. (Eds.). (1991). *Rethinking popular culture*. Berkeley: University of California Press.

Murdock, G. (1997). Base notes: The conditions of cultural practice. In M. Ferguson & P. Golding (Eds.), *Cultural studies in question*. London: Sage.

National Film Board (2002). Protecting Canadian culture. In *Mediasphere*. (Retrieved from http://mediasphere.nfb.ca/E/history/content/protecting_canadian_culture.epl).

Neal, M. A. (1997). Sold out on soul: The corporate annexation of Black popular music. *Popular Music and Society, 21*, 3 Fall, p. 117.

Neal, M.A. (1999). *What the Music Said: Black popular music and Black public culture*. London: Routledge.

Negus, K. (1996). *Popular theory in music: An introduction*. Hanover, NH: Wesleyan University Press.

Nightingale, V. (1996). *Studying audiences: The shock of the real*. London: Routledge.

Nourbese Philip, M. (1992). *Frontiers, essays and writings on racism and culture*. Ontario: Mercury.

Omi, M. (1989). In living color: Race and American culture. In I. Angus & Sut Jully (Eds.), *Cultural politics in contemporary America*. New York: Routledge.

Omi, M., & Winant, H. (1993). On the theoretical concept of race. In C. McCarthy & W. Crichlow (Eds.), *Race identity and representation in education* (pp. 3–10). New York: Routledge.

O'Sullivan, T., Hartley, J., Saunders, D., Montgomery, M., & Fiske, J. (Eds.). (1994). *Key concepts in communication and cultural studies*. London: Routledge.

Palmer, H. (1990). *Alberta: A new history*. Edmonton: Hurtig.

Perkins, W. (1996). (Ed.), *Droppin' science: Critical essays on rap music and hip-hop culture*. Philadelphia: Temple University Press.

Peshkin, A. (1988). In search of subjectivity—One's own. *Educational Researcher* 17(7), 7–22.

Pieterse, J. (1992). *White on black: Images of Africa and blacks in western popular culture*. New Haven: Yale University Press.

Pieterse, J. (1995). Globalisation as hybridization. In M. Feathersone, S. Lash & R. Robertson (Eds.), *Global modernities*. London: Sage.

Purvis, T., & Hunt, A. (1993). Discourse ideology. *British Journal of Sociology* 44(3), 473–99.

Razack, S. (2002). (Ed.), *Race space and the law: Unmapping a White settler society*. Toronto: Between the Lines.

Richardson, L. (1994). Writing: A method of inquiry. In N. Denzin & Y. Lincoln (Eds.), *Handbook of qualitative research* (pp. 516–29). California: Sage.

Rose, T. (1994). *Black noise*. Hanover: University Press of New England.

Scannel, P. (1990). Public service broadcasting: The history of a concept. In A. Goodwin & G. Whannel (Eds), *Understanding television*. London: Routledge.

Schick, C. (1995). Racial formation in the reporting of Canadian immigration figures. *36th Annual Adult Education Research Conference*. Edmonton: University of Alberta.

Schroder, K. C. (2000). Making sense of audience discourses. Towards a multidimensional model of mass media reception. *European Journal of Cultural Studies* 3(2), 233–58.

Schick, C. (1995). Racial formation in the reporting of Canadian immigration figures. *36th Annual Adult Education Research Conference*. Edmonton: University of Alberta.

Schutz, A. (1972). *The phenomenology of the social world*. London: Heinemann.

Schwandt, T. (1984). Constructivist, interpretivist approaches to human inquiry. In N. Denzin & Y. Lincoln (Eds.), *Handbook of qualitative research* (pp. 118–37). California: Sage.

Shepard, B. (1976). Black migration as a response to repression: The background factors and migration of Oklahoma blacks to western Canada 1905–1912 as a case study. Master's thesis. Saskatoon: University of Saskatchewan.

Shepard, B. (1997). *Deemed unsuitable*. Toronto: Umbrella.

Shuker, R. (1998). *Key concepts in popular music*. New York: Routledge.

Shuker, R. (2001, 2nd ed). *Understanding popular music*. London: Routledge.

Sim, S. (Ed.) (1998). *The icon critical dictionary of postmodern thought*. London: Routledge.

Smith, P. (1988). *Discerning the subject*. Minneapolis: University of Minnesota Press.

Smith, P. (1999). Tommy Hilfiger in the age of customization. http://mason.gmu.edu/~psmith5/hilfigertext.html.

Solomon, P. (1992). *Black resistance in high school: Forging a separatist culture*. Albany, NY: SUNY Press.

Spiegler, M. (1996). Marketing street culture; bringing hip-hop style to the mainstream. *American Demographics 18* (11) p. 28.

Springer, J., & Morton, L. (1998). *Ringmaster!* New York: St. Martins.

Statistics Canada (1996). 1996 Census: ethnic origin, visible minorities. *The Daily Statistics Canada*.

Stern. L. (2000, March 12). Urban legends: The irresistible bait of a great tale. *Edmonton Journal*, E8.

Stephens, M. (1998). Babylon's 'natural mystic': The North American music industry, the legend of Bob Marley, and the incorporation of transnationalism. *Cultural Studies 12*(2) pp. 139–67.

Stephens, R.J. (1996). Keepin' it real: An Afrocentric aesthetic analysis of rap music and hip-hop subculture. Ph.D. Dissertation, Temple University.

Storey, J. (1996). *Cultural studies & the study of popular culture*. Athens: University of Georgia Press.

Stratton. J., & Ang, I. (1996). On the impossibility of a global cultural studies. In D. Morley & K-H Chen (Eds.), *Stuart Hall: Critical dialogues in cultural studies* (pp. 361–91). London: Routledge.

Strinati, D. (1995). *An introduction to theories of popular culture*. London: Routledge.

Taylor, C. (1987). Overcoming epistemology. In K. Baynes, J. Bohan, & T. McCarthy (Eds.), *After philosophy: End or transformation?* (pp. 464–88). Cambridge: MIT Press.

Thakur, A. (1988). *The impact of schooling on visible minorities: A case study of black students in Alberta secondary school*. Nanimo, BC: Malaspino College.

Thompson, J. (1990). *Ideology and modern culture*. Stanford, California: Stanford University Press.

Thwaites, T., Davis, L., & Mules, W. (Eds.). (1994). *Tools for cultural studies: An introduction*. South Melbourne: Macmillan.

Torczyner, J. (1997). *Diversity, mobility, and change: The dynamics of Black communities in Canada*. Quebec: University of McGill: McGill Consortium for Ethnicity and Strategic Social Planning.

Turner, G. (1992). *British cultural studies*. London: Routledge.

Walcott, R. (1995). Performing the postmodern: Black Atlantic rap & identity in North America. Unpublished Doctoral Thesis, University of Toronto.

Walcott, R. (1997). *Black like who?* Toronto: Insomniac Press.

Walcott, R. (2000). *Rude*. Toronto: Insomniac Press.

Weedon, C. (1987). *Feminist practice and poststructuralist theory*. Oxford: Basil.

West, C. & hooks, b. (1991). *Breaking bread*. Toronto: Between the Lines.

Wesband, E. (1995). *SPIN Alternative Record Guide*. New York: Vintage/Random House.

White, A. (1995). *The resistance: Ten years of pop culture that shook the world*. New York: Overlook.

Williams, R. (1958/1993). Culture is ordinary. In J. McIlroy & S. Westwood (Eds.), *Border country* (pp. 89–102). Leicester: National Institute of Continuing Adult Education.

Williamson, J. (1996). Two kinds of otherness: Black film and the Avant-garde. In H. A. Baker, Jr., M. Diawara, & R. Lindeborg (Eds.) *Black British cultural studies.* (pp. 173–82). Chicago: University of Chicago Press.

Willinsky, J. (1999). Curriculum, after culture, race, nation. *Discourse: Studies in the Cultural Politics of Education* 20(1), 89–112.

Willis, P. (1977). *Learning to labour*. Farnborough: Saxon House.

Willis, P. (1990). *Common culture*. Milton Keynes: Open University Press.

Wiltz, T. (2002). Washington Post Staff Writer, Tuesday June 25th, page CO1.

Winks, R. (1971). *The Blacks in Canada*. New Haven: Yale University Press.

Wong, C. (1998). Airwaves from the underground. *Rap Pages*. July, 69.

Wong, C. (1998). Avengers assemble *Rap Pages*. July, 72.

Woodward, K. (1997). (Ed.). *Identity and difference: Culture media and difference*. Milton Keynes: Open University/Sage.

# Index

# Intersections in Communications and Culture

Global Approaches and Transdisciplinary Perspectives

**General Editors: Cameron McCarthy & Angharad N. Valdivia**

*An Institute of Communications Research, University of Illinois Commemorative Series*

This series aims to publish a range of new critical scholarship that seeks to engage and transcend the disciplinary isolationism and genre confinement that now characterizes so much of contemporary research in communication studies and related fields. The editors are particularly interested in manuscripts that address the broad intersections, movement, and hybrid trajectories that currently define the encounters between human groups in modern institutions and societies and the way these dynamic intersections are coded and represented in contemporary popular cultural forms and in the organization of knowledge. Works that emphasize methodological nuance, texture and dialogue across traditions and disciplines (communications, feminist studies, area and ethnic studies, arts, humanities, sciences, education, philosophy, etc.) and that engage the dynamics of variation, diversity and discontinuity in the local and international settings are strongly encouraged.

## LIST OF TOPICS

- Multidisciplinary Media Studies
- Cultural Studies
- Gender, Race, & Class
- Postcolonialism
- Globalization
- Diaspora Studies
- Border Studies
- Popular Culture
- Art & Representation
- Body Politics
- Governing Practices
- Histories of the Present
- Health (Policy) Studies
- Space and Identity
- (Im)migration
- Global Ethnographies
- Public Intellectuals
- World Music
- Virtual Identity Studies
- Queer Theory
- Critical Multiculturalism

Manuscripts should be sent to:

**Cameron McCarthy OR Angharad N. Valdivia**
Institute of Communications Research
University of Illinois at Urbana-Champaign
222B Armory Bldg., 555 E. Armory Avenue
Champaign, IL 61820

To order other books in this series, please contact our Customer Service Department:

(800) 770-LANG (within the U.S.)
(212) 647-7706 (outside the U.S.)
(212) 647-7707 FAX

Or browse online by series:

www.peterlangusa.com